Copyright @2022 by (Kevin Fodor)

All rights reserved. No part of this book may be reproduced in any form or by any electronic or mechanical means, including information storage and retrieval systems, without permission in writing from the publisher, except by reviewers, who may quote brief passages in a review.

This publication contains the opinions and ideas of its author. It is intended to provide helpful and informative material on the subjects addressed in the publication. The author and publisher specifically disclaim all responsibility for any liability, loss or risk, personal or otherwise, which is incurred as a consequence, directly or indirectly, of the use and application of any of the contents of this book.

WORKBOOK PRESS LLC
187 E Warm Springs Rd,
Suite B285, Las Vegas, NV 89119, USA

Website:	https://workbookpress.com/
Hotline:	1-888-818-4856
Email:	admin@workbookpress.com

Ordering Information:
Quantity sales. Special discounts are available on quantity purchases by corporations, associations, and others. For details, contact the publisher at the address above.

Library of Congress Control Number:
ISBN-13:   000-0-00000-000-0 (Paperback Version)
             000-0-00000-000-0 (Digital Version)

REV. DATE: 09/23/2022

TURN IT UP! CONFESSIONS OF A RADIO JUNKIE

KEVIN FODOR

Turn It Up!   Confessions Of A Radio Junkie

© 2022

By Kevin M. Fodor

(Aka: Jason Michaels/Jason Roberts AND "Rowdy J")

5570 Penn Avenue

Dayton, Ohio 45432

All Rights Reserved.

FOREWARD

It was the summer of 1964. Beatlemania had been in force for about 6 or 7 months. Me? I was all of 7 years old visiting my 5 cousins for a few days before summer ended and it was time for all of us to go back to school.

My older cousin, Suzanne was an absolute Beatles freak. Posters of the Fab Four on her walls at the time…you get the picture. One night, Suzanne came up to me and said…"Hey, Kevin…get this…I'm going to call the radio station, ask them to play a song, and they'll play it on the air!"

So, I followed Suzanne to the telephone, she called our local top 40 powerhouse, WING-AM in Dayton, made the request and, sure enough, about 15 or 20 minutes later, the DJ played a song and said, "here's a song for the gang on Robertanne Drive".

I thought it was cool. But then, a light bulb went off in my head. I started thinking, "Wow! This guy plays rock and roll records… and gets paid for it! What a way to make a living". I think that was the moment I was bitten by "The Bug".

Unfortunately, "The Bug" is the most virulent viral strain ever created. Once it's in your blood, you're hooked. And, there's no cure. You can walk away from the business, but The Bug never…ever…leaves your body.

It's the Radio Bug…It's been over 47 years since I was bitten. But it's been one hell of a ride.

I wish I could tell you I was as rich as Howard Stern, Ryan Seacrest or Rush Limbaugh, but I'm not. Those guys? They're the tip of the iceberg. Me? I make a decent living out of it…but to me, the more intoxicating part of it is: I'm able to make a difference.

There are thousands of DJ's, Radio news people and programmers all over the country. The Sterns and Seacrests of the world are the tip of the iceberg. The rest of us do OK, some do better than OK, but we get great personal satisfaction from what we do. And that, sometimes anyway, makes up for the fact that most of us aren't super rich.

Now, I do not suggest that all of the experiences you'll read about in this book are exclusively mine. Everybody who has been in radio, if they have been around long enough, has been fired at least once. Everybody in radio has most likely met famous and infamous people. Everybody probably knows someone who "knew a thing or two" about payola…even if they didn't take it. Or, the drugs which were once handed out by record reps. (No, I was never offered any, but I know it happened.) But, these types of things were all experienced by me.

I offer them in the sincere hope that they may entertain you, may make you chuckle, smile, maybe laugh, or even make you sad. But, at the end of the day, I hope they make you realize that radio is still today, one of the most resilient businesses ever invented. It is an honorable profession…and if you have a child or grandson or granddaughter who wants to get in it, don't discourage them from doing it if that is their passion. It has sustained me now for 46 years and counting.

This book is dedicated to the people who toil away day after day in radio studios attempting to be entertaining and informative in a day and age when it would be far easier, and cheaper, to let the computers do it all. And this book is dedicated to the young people who still think, despite what some of radio's detractors would like you to think, that being on the radio would be "cool". God bless them. They're the future of our business.

You see, the real survivors are not just those who think of themselves as being "DJ's", we are "Broadcasters". There's a big difference between the two…and I hope you'll get a sense for it as you read this book.

Chapter 1 – Nurturing The Passion

I suppose I grew up as any normal boy would have. But, my earliest memories are from my family's small home on Hearthstone Drive in Dayton, Ohio. (We called it "HERTH-stone" back then...today, they refer to it as "HARTH-stone". Oh well.) It was in what is known as the Belmont District. And, both the district and the house are still there. In fact, I drive past it going home from work almost every day. I keep hoping to see whoever it is that lives there outside working in the yard, so I can stop and say hello. But, I almost never see them...I only see their car sitting in the driveway.

One of those memories was getting my tonsils removed. I must have been, maybe three years old. Don't remember the actual operation, of course. I just remember my parents telling me that, if I was a good boy, I'd get lots of ice cream after it was all over and my Grandfather would get me a special present.

I remember coming home from St. Elizabeth's hospital to a big dish of vanilla ice cream and my grandfather bringing me an album by David Seville and the Chipmonks. You know, the one that had "Witch Doctor" and "The Chipmonk Song (Christmas Don't Be Late" on it? Oh yes, and a record player to play it on. I think I had that album worn out in record time.

The 1960's was a great time to grow up in Dayton, Ohio, and even in the Midwest. Dayton then was a city of industry with a vibrant downtown area and a population of close to a quarter million people. It's not that way now. For too long, Dayton hung on to the notion of being a big manufacturing town...and, ultimately, most of the manufacturers packed up and moved to other areas. Dayton is in the midst of trying to stage a comeback now.

But, in the 60's...it was a whole different story. And broadcasters in that area back then were on the leading edge of the business's growth.

Dayton's TV stations, for the most part, were innovators of the time. WLW-D, Channel 2 was part of the Midwestern network of stations owned by the Aviation Corporation, or AVCO Broadcasting. Many daily, live programs were beamed to the stations in Dayton, Columbus and Indianapolis from AVCO's home base in Cincinnati.

My first exposure to this type of entertainment came from my mother's rule that every day at noon, the TV had to be turned on to Channel 2 for hostess Ruth Lyons and her "50/50 Club". The program featured live music from the Cliff Lash Orchestra, a cast of singers who varied over the years while Ms. Lyons provided commentary and interviews with big name (and little name) stars of the day. Word was, if you wanted to advertise on the program, Ruth had to approve the product, and you had to wait for 6 months to a year because advertising demand was that backlogged. But, when Ruth plugged a product…it sold like hotcakes. I would hold the cord of the coffee pot like a microphone and sing along with Miss Lyons, when she'd come on the set singing "Let Me Entertain You". She became as big of a star for her day as Oprah was and as Ellen DeGeneres is today. There are books and even a video out about her life that are worth reading and/or watching if you are so inclined. Particularly if you are concerned about such a thing as a "glass ceiling" for women in the workplace. Ruth story shows you how to smash through it…because she did. She was offered her own network television show with NBC once at a salary of $100,000 a year in the 1950's. She declined. Why? She was already making more than that.

Earlier in the morning, the network aired a similar, yet different program from a former radio DJ named Paul Dixon. While Ruth Lyons' show was more about interviews and stars, Dixon's show was more about improvisational comedy and the people in the audience. Paul Dixon was a master at playing his audience, calling the front row where young housewives would sit in miniskirts, "Kneesville" (of which he was the Mayor). He did the many of the same bits day after day ("How many of you girls took a bath this morning?", Feigning a look of disgust, Dixon would grab a spray bottle and sprayed the audience, telling them, "That's weed killer…it'll kill anything".), and the audience, both in-studio and at home, ate it up.

In 1969, two rubber chickens who were props for live commercials on the show for the Kroger grocery chain were "married" by Dixon on-air. (Remember he was the "Mayor" of "Kneesville", so technically he could perform a wedding ceremony!) That day's show brought the biggest ratings ever. Kids stayed home from school (with Mom and Dad's permission) to watch this farce! But it was sure funny, especially when they got to the "I Do's"…Dixon asked "Harry" for his approval and, on cue, came the sound effect of a rooster crow! But, when it came to "Henrietta"…nothing! Until the control room informed Dixon they forgot to rewind the tape!

Turns out, I wasn't the only kid watching and dreaming of a future as a broadcaster. Over in Indianapolis, a young kid inspired by all this would try his hand as a radio talk show host and later a TV weatherman, before moving to the West Coast to try standup comedy. David Letterman has done a whole lot better than I have, but I'll bet he'd agree that the passion shows such as Dixon's inspired in the both of us was the same.

It was around that time that I would be introduced to a radio station's request line. In 1964, the neighborhood where my cousins lived would build a float for an annual "Holiday At Home" parade. Since it was still summertime and I had about a week before I had to start school, my parents let me spend a few days at their house so I could help with building the float. The float was of "Puff, The Magic Dragon" (from the 1963 hit by Peter, Paul and Mary).

So, one evening, my cousin, Suzanne Williams (now

Suzanne Moore under her married name) comes to me and says, "Hey Kevin…come here in the kitchen. I want to show you something. I'm going to call the radio station and request a song…and they'll play it on the radio and dedicate it to US!" Remember that 1964 WAS the beginning of "Beatlemania" and Suzanne was crazy about Paul McCartney! So, she called the big local AM Top 40 station, requested a Beatles song and, sure enough, 15 minutes later, it was played on the radio! (I'm sure it wasn't "really" a request. It was probably coming up in the record rotation…which, for a new Beatles single was about every 45 minutes or so!).

But then…a light bulb lit up over my head. "Wow! You mean to tell me that a guy gets to sit in a room, do nothing but play rock and roll records and talk on the radio…and gets paid to do it? I WANT TO DO THAT FOR A LIVING!!!$$$##!!". That's when it all started.

There was live TV on every station in Dayton then. WHIO-TV, then and today the market's news leader had their live news broadcasts and afternoon kids shows, which included the late Joe Rockhold as "Uncle Orrie" and Ken Hardin as "Ferdy Fussbudget". Later, WKEF, Channel 22 produced "Clubhouse 22" with various hosts and a local ghoul known as Dr. Creep. The good doctor would show up on the weekends as the host of the local horror movie show, "Shock Theater"…and it was improv at its best.

On radio, there were three main stations, originally… with more that came along. The big gun for the kids was 1410/WING…broadcasting from what was called a "showcase" studio in downtown Dayton. You could walk past the window 24 hours a day and watch the DJ's in action. The station even had an intercom hooked up where you could talk to the DJ.

One of WING's original morning hosts was comedian Jonathan Winters. One of its' most memorable DJ's was beloved for over 40 years before his untimely death in 2001…his name was Gene "By Golly" Barry. If you talk with people over 50 in Dayton about radio today, chances are his name will come up. WING's most memorable morning host is a former Cincinnati DJ who joined the WING staff on Labor Day, 1967. His God-given name is Steven Kirkpatrick. On the air, he was "Steve Kirk" (also known as "Kirkie"). He would do the morning show on WING until his retirement in 1992.

When Kirkie was in Cincinnati, he had the opportunity to be part of an investor group to bring The Beatles to Crosley Field. They came on a beautiful summer day in 1966. The promoter thought the weather was SO good, they took the cover off the stage. Bad move. A late afternoon thunderstorm came up and drenched the stage, prompting Beatles management to threaten not to perform because their contract requiring a cover over the stage had been violated.

As Kirkie would tell you, the two sides argued back and forth until, finally, John Lennon spoke up. "So, where are we playing tomorrow night?", John asked. He was told, "St. Louis". Lennon asked how long it took to get from Cincinnati to St. Louis by plane. He was told, "about 90 minutes".

John Lennon said, "OK, it's settled. Go out there and tell the people to come back with their ticket stubs tomorrow afternoon at 1. We'll play the concert and then leave for St. Louis."

Unfortunately, the extra security needed to keep the Beatles in Cincinnati that night broke the budget, and Kirkie's investor group lost money. He's probably the only promoter who ever lost money booking the Beatles. (Well truthfully, he wasn't the only one…but still…) How did I know all this? Steve Kirk told it to me personally years later. And I have kidded him mercilessly about it for years. The truth is, Steve still has, in his possession, a dollar bill he had signed by all four Beatles. I have seen it. In fact, he actually let me hold it…once…for about 30 seconds (at an appearance he made about ten or so years ago at a Casino near Cincinnati). And by, God! The signatures of John Lennon, Paul McCartney, George Harrison and Ringo Starr are on it!

In the summertime, when school wasn't in session, I would go downtown with my father some mornings when he needed to go into his insurance office and do paperwork. Me? I'd go over to WING and watch the DJ's work. One morning, Steve Kirk came out of the studio to offer me a doughnut. I never forgot his kindness for reasons I'll tell you later.

One day just before my tenth birthday in 1967, my Dad happened to run into Jim Bennett, then the General Manager of WING at a downtown coffee shop. He explained my interest in radio to Mr. Bennett, told him of my impending birthday and asked if there was any way to take me on a tour of the station. Mr. Bennett said they usually only did tours for organized groups such as the Boy Scouts/Girl Scouts, etc. But, then he told my Dad he had to come in the next Saturday (my birthday) to do some paperwork and said if my Mom and Dad would bring me down, he…Mr. Bennett would show us around.

So, there I was…on my tenth birthday, in the WING studio…in the window being shown how it was done by a DJ who also told me it was HIS birthday that day, too. Jim Quinn has been a very successful talk show host in Pittsburgh for decades and, after leaving WING, continued his DJ and later, talk host career at 1410/KQV Radio.

For the adults, the big gun was 1290/WHIO Radio. WHIO was the opposite of WING. Staid, adult music…never too harsh and for a while back then, never very hip, in fact, the station's idea of "hip" was playing "Supercalifragialisticexpialidiocious" (or however it's spelled…from the movie "Mary Poppins".) Their morning host was a gentleman who had worked at the station since 1941. His name was Lou Emm. He would be on the air in Dayton for 50 years. People said Dayton was special, because it had 3 kinds of radio…AM…FM…and Lou Emm. And when

Lou died, every Dayton station did something it had never done before...or since. On the day of Lou's funeral, all of Dayton's radio stations stopped...for a moment of silence.

My parents...and my grandparents listened to WHIO. As a young child at night, my grandmother would put me to sleep in a big bedroom when I visited her home and would put an AM/FM transistor radio under my pillow always...tuned to Lou Emm. (Lou recorded what today are considered "voice tracks" for an evening show on WHIO's FM station, called "Concepts In Music", which was elevator music. In fact, until 1989 the whole station was elevator music!)

Years after my grandmother died, I was shown one of her diaries. In it, I read my grandmother say, it was always her dream that one of her grandchildren would be an entertainer. In it one night, she had written, "I can't help but get the feeling that someday, some way, Kevin will make it into show business." Well, this might not have been the type of "show business" my grandmother hoped I would have gotten into, but it was close enough.

I started "pretending" to "be a DJ" at home. My grandfather "built" me my first "control board"...actually it was kind of a kid's "busy box" with toggle switches and dials underneath them. By then, I had acquired 2 record players and I put them side by side on an organ bench to my left in front of the storm door in the living room. (My "showcase" window.) Had a microphone hooked up to a mike stand with a gooseneck on it. And, volia! Instant "pretend" radio control room. I even had an old pair of headphones which I put on as I "cued" the songs and played them back to back.

"Cueing" records? What the heck was that? Most turntables come up to speed in about a quarter turn. The notion behind "cueing" was to place a felt pad on the turntable platter (in radio, they glued the felt to the platter), put a 45 or album on it, place the tone arm on the record and "spin" the record with your hand until you heard the start of the song...then, bring it back about a quarter of a turn. When you started the motor of the turntable, the song would start in about a half a second. Get the timing down right, and you make a perfect mix. You can even do it on laptop computer today.

Add to all this, another Top 40 station was on the air in Dayton. Though WONE gave up the ghost around the time Kirkie arrived. They would later become a country music powerhouse. Still and yet, there were a LOT of WONE veterans out there. "Tall" Tom Campbell was one of them. He had something unheard of in the 1960's...a "car phone". I had the number and called him about once a week, until he moved to L.A. (Interestingly enough, someone just posted on Facebook, and I saw it the other day, an ad some station where Tom once worked, who had posted his home telephone number, his car phone number and his work number on it with instructions to the listeners to "call him anytime". (Tom must have been a glutton for punishment. Today, home and cell phone numbers of radio people are kept almost as secret as the President's nuclear codes!) Dave Hull was another WONE vet. He also went to the west coast as "The Hullabalooer" on KRLA-AM in Los Angeles. The station's "Johnny Midnight" (aka Don Williams) is a good friend of mine today.

In 1964...a new station came on the air on FM in Dayton. WDAO Radio was the first FM station to offer soul and R & B music 24 hours a day. Back then, it meant live DJ's around the clock playing Motown and Soul. By 1969, it was not only a player in town, it was becoming a rating's monster...way exceeding the ratings of its sister AM, and closely challenging the dominance of WING and WHIO. It would lead the charge for young Dayton to eventually switch to FM. Interestingly enough, just as a hip hop station today gets an audience of roughly 40% white teenagers, so too, did WDAO-FM back then. The music may have changed over the years, but those stats don't.

And because WONE was successful as a country station,

Group One Broadcasting, their owners began to look at the automated FM station they had on 104.7. It was a hodgepodge of gospel music in the morning and country at night. So, they decided to begin running Top 40 music on the automation at night, telling the Program Director at the time to "cut into WING's teen audience, but don't do too good a job to where the FM overtakes the AM" as WDAO did. (WDAO's sister station was WAVI-AM…a tiny tea kettle 250 watt daytime only station…over the years it had been everything…from Dixieland to Jazz to chicken rock and finally made it as a talk station.)

Group One's gamble began to pay off. They hired a guy who was the brother-in-law of the manager of WHIO to be "Program Director" of WONE-FM. And slowly, but surely as the Top 40 music began to attract an audience, one by one, the station began to hire disc jockeys. And in 1971, the call letters were changed to WTUE-FM (W-1 and W-2, so to speak). WTUE would survive as a Top 40 station and DID take WING's teens with PD Bill Struck, and DJ's Greg Mason (aka Terry Dorsey), Sean McKay (Dan Danes, Dave Michaels (Ingersol) and overnight guys Bwana Johnny (Don Everhart) and Jason Roberts (aka Mark Elliott). Others would follow, too including Al "bum" Morgan who would leave and go to KHJ/Los Angeles and still works doing radio voiceovers today.

I began playing guitar at age 9, primarily because of the inspiration I had gotten from watching Mike Nesmith on "The Monkees" TV show. Interestingly enough, I "discovered" that, though yes, the music on the show was "pantomimed", Nesmith always "pretended" to play the right chords. I watched his hands on the fretboard, then went back to my bedroom and picked up the guitar and tried to play the song. Son-of-a-gun…those chords were the right ones! And from that, I guess I developed an "ear" for music…one that was noticed by a music teacher my parents took me to see one evening.

"Your son is very gifted", he told Mom and Dad. "He's able

to hear the song in his head and can pick the chords from the songs just by the way they sound. If I were you, don't waste your time getting him guitar lessons…just buy him a book of songs with the guitar chords in them. He'll pick them up soon enough."

So, I got into a neighborhood rock band. And we practiced in my drummer-friend, Dan Patrick's garage with various lineups of neighborhood kids and various musicians.

I remember playing an end of school year party at an elementary school. The little girls reacted like were the Beatles or something. I had never dealt with an audience that was screaming for me before. Nor, was I ready for them chasing me and my band mates through the school after the show. We dashed into a car and were driven off before the screaming little girls could tear us to shreds. After all, we had just gotten custom band shirts made!

Now, I DID have interests other than being a performer. And you can blame my grandmother for that, too.

In 1968, and the insurance salespeople for the company for which my Dad worked went on strike. As a family, we never had that much money…Dad kept a roof over our heads and we were able to keep food on the table, but we weren't rich. So, Grandma Williams came to the rescue again.

So, in late spring, the phone rings…and, it's Grandma on the line calling from the home she and Grandpa bought after he retired in Clearwater, Florida. She knows that, with Dad on strike, things were going to get very dicey financially for us and Dad surely didn't need me around…I was, at that point, just one more mouth to feed.

Mom hangs up the phone and says to me, "Kevin… how would you like to spend the summer in Florida with your Grandparents? Grandma says if you want, she'll send you a plane ticket…you can go down there with your Uncle Walter and you won't have to come back until it gets time for you to go back to school."

Now, you're a kid living in Ohio where you deal with nice weather for about 6 months out of the year. And your Grandmother has just offered to let you spend three months in a tropical paradise. I knew Grandpa had a speed boat…and a fishing dock…and a pool table in a "Florida Room" and a house that "seemed" like almost a mansion. What would YOU say to an offer like that?

So, early one morning as soon as school let out for the summer, I was at Dayton International Airport with my Uncle. We left on a Delta Airlines DC-8 heading first, for Atlanta, where we had a short layover and would grab another Delta jet from there for a quick hour or so flight to Tampa. It was my first time on a plane.

WOW! The acceleration on the runway, and getting pushed back into my seat from it made me think for a second that we were about to head for the Moon. (After all, this was 1968…and we hadn't done that yet, but there was every expectation that NASA would be headed there soon.)

We arrived in Atlanta…and, for a few minutes, Uncle Walter and I got separated. But, I managed to find him just in time for us to catch our connecting flight. (There would surely have been hell to pay from Grandma had I got left in Atlanta.) And, a short time later, we were up in the air, again. After about an hour and a half, we were touching down in Tampa…and I was seeing palm trees out the plane's window for the first time in my life.

It's a sight I love to see now…because I know what it's going to feel like when the plane's door opens. There, it can be 80 degrees in February. You're lucky to get 40 here in Ohio most of the time then. And Grandma and Grandpa were there waiting for me, I said goodbye to my Uncle, and my grandparents and I took off for the 30 minute drive to their home, which was on what is known as a "finger island". You had to take a causeway across

Clearwater Bay to get there. Put me on that causeway today, and I can still drive to that house.

We fished…on the dock and off the side of my Grandpa's boat. We went to Clearwater Beach and I swam in the Gulf of Mexico. Grandpa even got us stuck on a sandbar while we were out in the Bay one day. It took about an hour before the Coast Guard arrived to get us off the sandbar. And, Gramps caught the wrath of Grandma for it when we got back.

One morning, we headed across state to Titusville, where my grandparents took me on the tour at Kennedy Space Center. I was captivated by seeing the old Mercury Control Center where Alan Shepard and John Glenn's flights were monitored and controlled. And we saw pad 34, where, just about a year earlier, we had lost Gus Grissom, Ed White and Roger Chaffee in a fire in the Apollo capsule during a routine test. And, yes…we did see the giant Vehicle Assembly Building and launch pad 39-A, from where the moon flights would soon depart. We took a ride on a glass bottom boat at Cyprus Gardens and went to a great restaurant called the Kapok Tree Inn. It is no longer there, but the food was out of this world. (I loved the Hush Puppies which were served warm with maple syrup that you poured on them!)

And, of course, we went to the just-recently-opened, Walt Disney World where I hung out with Mickey and Minnie and Donald, Goofy, Pluto and the gang. I think back then you could get in for around 20 bucks…a price that might get you a small soda there today.

It was a summer to remember…but, it came to an abrupt end. One Saturday morning, I am watching the cartoons on the color TV when the words "Hurricane Warning" come on the screen. My grandparents and I learned that a big storm called "Camille" was heading our way. So, grandma and grandpa decide the house wasn't a good place to ride out such a storm and, within about 90 minutes, we were packed, in the car and heading up

I-75 on our way back to Ohio.

That's where I learned highway navigation via a "Triptik" from Triple-A. We had one for the entire trip back and my grandparents relied on me to tell them where to go. Today, of course, you'd just turn on the GPS…but only NASA had something like it at the time.

Hurricane Camille chased us the whole way back to Ohio and we were about 12 hours ahead of it the whole time. Fortunately, my grandparent's home came out OK. And, after about a day and a half drive, I was back with Mom and Dad. Grandpa and Grandma stayed for a week or so before they headed back to Florida, because a good part of the state had been devastated by the storm.

But, one thing I DID get from that vacation that stuck with me was…I LOVED flying. I had saved a few hundred dollars from our band's performances. And, one day, Dad (who was back at work now), agreed to pay for a 30 minute test ride with a flight instructor in a Cessna twin seat, single engine plane. Of course, the instructor had ME fly in the Pilot's seat. I was hooked and began taking flying lessons out at what is, today, known as Wright Brothers Airport which is south of the Dayton Mall.

I loved it. Took a "check ride" with another instructor who, I was told, had been a fighter pilot in Vietnam. He noticed that I was being somewhat "careful" with the plane and asked me why. I told him I didn't want to crash. It was an honest statement, but not the thing I should have said. His reply? "You can't crash this plane. Watch this…"

Next thing I know, we're doing aerobatics in a Cessna 150. The ground was above me, aside me, below me, seemingly all at once. He puts us in a "parabolic curve"…that's how astronauts practice being weightless. You dive down…pull up (doing about 2 or 3 G's in the process) and just when you come over the top of that curve, your seat belt and harness straps are coming up and, for a few seconds, you are weightless.

It wasn't too long after that, when, during an instruction flight upon landing, the instructor told me I was ready to solo. Told me to go back up by myself, do three "touch and go's" and then, taxi back to the flight line.

Next thing I know, I'm 2000 feet in the air and I am at the controls with no instructor in the plane and nobody to save my little pink butt, but me. And I didn't even have my driver's license yet. (Somebody told me that was the case with Neil Armstrong, too. That is probably the ONLY thing I can say that was similar about the two of us, but…)

I made three perfect landings that day…didn't even bounce once…and made one landing so smoothly that I wasn't even sure I was on the ground till I hit the brakes.

I wish I could say I got my pilot's license, but…I ran out of money before I could finish. But, I still have my log book…and my training books and instruments. Recently, I WAS able to start flight training again. I'm still looking for my old log book (Damn it!), but I'm back in the air…not bad for a guy now in his 60's.

But, now, it was onto high school. My parents gave me a choice. I had gone to two Catholic grade schools, but Mom and Dad told me I could go to the public high school if I wanted. And, having been tired of not being in school with most of my friends from the neighborhood, I chose Miamisburg High School for my secondary education.

And, truth be told, that was where I was bit by the acting bug. I was in a drama class taught by the man who would also be my journalism teacher. He suggested I try out for a part in the school's fall musical, "Babes In Toyland". Yes, it was a minor role, but it was a first for me. And I had to learn about makeup, projecting for microphones placed around the stage, memorizing lines and yes, even learning choreography and dance moves for the shows. (Want to lose weight fast? Join a dance class. I guarantee you that you can lose 20 pounds in a month, easily!)

I acted in about 15 plays and/or musicals during my days at Miamisburg. My 2 most memorable roles in high school were as "Marryin' Sam" in "Lil' Abner" and the role which I will never live down and am grateful forever to my drama coach. "Snoopy", in the musical "You're A Good Man, Charlie Brown".

Truth is, I never thought I was the Snoopy type. You see, I suffered from an extreme lack of self-confidence in high school. I thought, and tried out for, the part of Charlie Brown…you know…the lovable loser at everything. Thought I was a cinch for it, because, well, I thought it would be type casting.

The drama teacher thought otherwise. He decided Snoopy was just the part I needed to break me out of my shell. He was right. When the cast was announced, my first thought was shock. Snoopy? "Chief…"(that's what we called the drama coach, Richard Arrowood), "You have got to be kidding!" But, you never declined a part…you might not get one again. So, I had the album from the off Broadway cast (and still do). The original "Charlie Brown" was a guy by the name of Gary Burghoff…who is known today as "Radar O'Reilly" from the TV show "M*A*S*H" and I began learning the show's songs.

I worked my ass off getting ready for that show. Practiced the dance moves until my legs throbbed with pain. Memorized my lines. And realized…hey wait a minute! I think I CAN do this character. And so, I threw myself into it like I had never thrown myself into a part. Maybe I'm not much of an athlete…so what? You have to be in shape to dance like Snoopy. Because you have to sing while you're dancing. Try it sometime.

Opening night, I hit that stage and played that part to the hilt. I got on top of my "doghouse" with aviator goggles and scarf and, by God…I WAS the daring World War One flying ace, scouring the skies searching for the infamous Red Baron.

Everything I did got laughs...big laughs...from the audience. And when I got to the next to last scene...when Snoopy does his "Suppertime" routine, I stopped the show! Swinging "Charlie Brown" around and around and letting him go to the point where he did a somersault over a set piece, while screaming, "NOW, CUT THAT...(dropping to the ground and staring at me)..."OUT!"

He looked at me...and I stared right back. Said, Charlie Brown, "Why can't you eat your meal quietly and calmly...LIKE ANY OTHER NORMAL DOG?"

I just shrugged, looked at the audience and said, "So, what's wrong with making mealtime...a joyous occasion?" And, finished the song, striking a pose on the last note.

The audience erupted again. Standing ovation number 1. I went in the doghouse.

Next thing I know, everybody in the wings is signaling me to come out again and take another bow. The crowd wouldn't stop cheering. So, I did. Standing ovation number 2, Acknowledging the crowd and back into the doghouse.

But, I wasn't prepared for curtain call. When it came and it came time for me to come back out again...standing ovation number 3. I was astounded. The shy kid who didn't think he was worth a damn was a big fricking hit!

I am so grateful to my drama teacher and director, Dick Arrowood for casting me as Snoopy. I won "Best Actor" that year as well.

And, the "shell" was shattered...never for me to return.

I did more musical theater work as well. I did a part in the show about our Founding Fathers, "1776" when I was in my first radio job. It was for Wilmington College in Wilmington, Ohio. The director for it also directed a then, young eventual college graduate with a theater major there named Gary Sandy. He would go on to the role of Andy Travis in the hit TV show, "WKRP in Cincinnati".

A couple of years later, I did community theater work for Dayton Community Theater, starring in their 25th anniversary production of "Damn Yankees", playing the role of "young" Joe Hardy, who sells his soul to the Devil to play major league baseball. And ends up in a battle with the Devil for his soul which he eventually gets back.

I have even starred in a movie, though you'll probably have to go to You Tube to see it. It's a B-grade horror movie called "The Killer Hornets" which got tied up in some sort of distribution lawsuit with the guy I worked with who did the screenplay. Hopefully, it WILL get posted online before long. But, I did get International Movie Data Base credit for the movie. So, if you look "Kevin Fodor" up in the movie database, I do come up as "Frank, the station owner". I played the owner of a failing radio station who comes upon an electronic box that apparently produced a frequency that brought giant killer hornets to the Earth like a plague. I took a week off from my work at WHIO to film the movie. (You should have seen my boss's reply to my request for time off..."I wanted to share this vacation request with you", he said, "If this isn't a reason to request time off, I don't know a better one".)

I loved acting. But, I realized early on in life what a scary business it is. You need a good manager, and you never have one when you start out. So, most actors and actresses are waiting tables and washing dishes in L.A. hoping for a chance to get in the business.

I decided if I was going to be poor, being 3,000 miles from home was NOT the place to be. So, radio beckoned.

Remember, Dayton was also close to Cincinnati...it was just 45 miles down the road...with great stations like WLW-AM, WSAI-AM, WKRC-AM, WKRQ-FM and others. So, if Dayton radio was boring me one day, I tuned to Cincinnati, and often did.

I remember one Saturday afternoon. I was in the swimming pool at my grandparent's house (you see, my maternal grandfather was a Master Tool Maker for General Motors, who retired in his 60's and was, apparently a very wealthy man. Maybe not a millionaire, but my grandparents always had a beautiful home with 4 or 5 bedrooms, the pool, color televisions back when everyone else had black and white.) I was playing WSAI that day because I had heard the Monkees were going to visit. About 4 that afternoon, they were there…pretending to "take over" the station, a routine they did in just about every city they did a concert in. Take over it, they did and not always to the pleasure of the station management. (I am aware of at least one big Chicago station where the DJ told their management to "get these stupid f---s out of here!")

So, as I said…Dayton and the Midwest, was pretty fertile ground for radio and television entertainers. By the time I was around 12…there was no question in my mind that I wanted to join them.

Chapter 2 – Learning From The Best...And By Myself

The early 1970's was the beginning of "Mall-itis" in America. As malls sprang up far and wide offering a new kind of shopping experience.

When my family moved to Miamisburg, Ohio in 1963, it was just some plat homes in a fairly rural area. My school bus driver lived on a farm across the street from our neighborhood. Six years later, all of the farms were gone and all of that land was bought up for something that became known as The Dayton Mall. (which later caused more nearby land to be bought for more shopping areas. Today, there's so many shopping areas there the week before Christmas it becomes a place most people won't go because traffic is too much of a nightmare).

But in 1970, the mall was "cool". And, young teenager I was, I was there a lot. One day, I heard a little more than an unusual amount of commotion coming from the center of the mall. Turned out, it was a live broadcast on WAVI-AM/1210. I mustered the courage to introduce myself to the DJ, who was Jaye Albright. I went up to see Jaye's broadcast several times.

Then, one day, the station went into a newsbreak. Jaye turned and said to me, "Hey, Kev...you wanna help me with something here? See this switch?" (pointing to the toggle switch on the console that turned a turntable on and off). I nodded. "I've got to go get something, but I'll be back before that record runs out. Listen to the radio here...when the news ends, they'll play a station jingle. Just as that jingle is about to run out, you flip that switch and the record will start. Can you do that for me?"

I was stunned. I was 13 years old and Jaye trusted me to get the program back on the air out of the news...and I had only known Jaye for a week or so! I wasn't gonna mess this up...

no way. I listened intently to that newscast. The news anchor wrapped it up...I heard the jingle and as it ended, (the singers sang..."a—and the beat (three note musical stab)...goes on!",) I flipped the switch. Sure enough the record started right at the end of the jingle...perfectly!

Jaye came back about 30 seconds later, heard the song was playing and said, "Good job! See...you're now a DJ!" It was cool. We were on the air and, for a few seconds anyway, I was in charge!

I stood there and watched Jaye do the show, and, about 30 minutes later, it was time for sign off. (WAVI was a "daytimer" licensed only to operate between sunrise and sunset.)

The song ended, the station went back to news, and Jaye turned the turntable console off, asking me to help pack up the gear, which I gladly did.

Not long afterwards, WAVI did a Saturday afternoon live broadcast with another Dayton legend hosting...his real name was Selwyn Atchison. But, everyone in Dayton knew him as Gene "By Golly" Barry. He started at WING in the 1940's with a show called "Swing With WING"...and when Rock and Roll started, he quickly became Dayton's version of Alan Freed. Mixing R & B with Rockabilly music...and became an instant success. His nighttime ratings, I'm told were somewhere around a 60 share (meaning 6 in 10 people listening to the radio at night were listening to him.)

So, I introduced myself to him and I did, basically what I did with Jaye. Stood around watching and making mental notes of what he did. The broadcast ended and as we both walked out to a room where they kept their studio equipment at the Mall, he asked me what I was doing the following Saturday. I didn't have anything going on that day, and told him so. Gene replied, "well, I've got some work I have to do in the office Saturday, but if you can get your folks to drop you off at, let's say noon...I'll take you into one of our production rooms and show you how to run the equipment and let you make a tape." I said, "Sure!"

Mom and Dad agreed to take me to the station the next Saturday, and Gene was good to his word. He showed me around the station, then took me into a studio where there was a radio mixing board, microphone, two turntables, two machines which I learned were "cart" machines (which played plastic cartridges that had recording tape inside, the length of which was timed to different lengths), and, of course, two reel to reel tape recorders in rack cabinets off to the side.

He showed me how to work the board…how to "cue" a record (preparing it for air), how to start and stop the tape decks by remote control. Then, he handed me a few records, a couple of commercials and station jingles recorded on those "carts", and said, "I'll come back in about 20 minutes and see how you're doing", and turned me loose.

It actually took me about 40 minutes to get a tape recorded. But, I did it. At 13, I'm sure it sounded fairly terrible, but Gene thought it was pretty good. He gave me a copy on a small reel, I called my folks and they picked me up. I had a reel to reel at home, so I was able to play the tape for Mom and Dad. (I wish I still had the tape…but it's long gone. Sadly, so are tape recorders for the most part. If you want a good one, be ready to pay about two grand for it.)

Before we left, though, Gene told my parents he thought I had potential for the radio business. And he suggested they have me contact the person at the station who was in charge of its' Junior Achievement company. At 13, I was able to join, and my parents agreed. And for the next couple of months, I was at the WAVI/WDAO studios a couple times a week, preparing a 30 minute show that the Junior Achievement company sold to local advertisers, and that I and some others in the program recorded which aired twice a month. I was "on the air", and my parents thought I sounded pretty good.

About that time, as I mentioned, I had started high school. One night at practice for one of the musicals, I was talking with the stage manager. His name was Tim. He told me he, too was interested in being a DJ, and told me something I didn't know... that our rival school about 5 miles away had a real FM radio station that was on the air!

So, I said to Tim, "Why can't we have a radio station here?" Tim said, "I don't know. Hey...maybe you and I ought to go and ask the principal." I figured it couldn't hurt to ask, so I said, "OK...let's go talk with him". (By the way, that conversation began a lifelong friendship with Tim Fox, who spent many years programming 100,000 watt oldies station KIOA-FM in Des Moines, Iowa, after programming many other successful radio stations in places like Denver and Milwaukee just to name a few.)

We laid out our idea and questions to Miamisburg High School Principal Tom Robinson. Mr. Robinson told us they'd thought about starting a radio station at the school, but didn't really have the room in our cramped 3 building campus. However, T.R. (as we all called him), said that we would be moving to a new high school building in about a year and there would be room there for a station. He told us to come back as soon as we made the move, and he would discuss it more.

The new school opened in September of 1973. And even though we had a new principal in John Waddell, we went back to T.R. (now Director of Secondary Education) and asked about the radio station. Mr. Robinson challenged us. He told us to "do our homework" and come back to him in 30 days with a proposal. If he thought it was strong enough, he said he'd allow us to take it to the school board for approval.

Our now group of students and our school audio-video director, who was interested in obtaining a First Class FCC engineer's license and agreed to be our Chief Engineer, set to work. We went and talked with people at any local radio station who would give us the time of day. The local Christian station gave us advice and offered us some old equipment they had out in their garage. DJ's and programming people at a couple of the local Top 40 and Album Rock stations encouraged us and told us what we needed to do to get our Third Class FCC Operator Licenses.

So, how did we "research it"? We became pests to about every station in town. We went to WONE/WTUE and, ironically, many of those DJ's are still friends of mine...at least the ones who are still around.

I had dinner in Columbus one night a few years back with a good friend, John Anderson (who was "Billy Daniels" on WTUE back then). While we were eating, John asked if I remembered something he had told me back in high school. It didn't ring a bell with me.

He said, "I told you not only did I think you'd get into radio, but you'd make it a career and then, you'd "give back to the business" by training young people to work on the air." That stunned me. Because, he was right. I've spent over a dozen years teaching both as an instructor and a sub at the International College Of Broadcasting in Dayton. I never realized the impression I was leaving on these guys. And, that some of them think so much of me today just blows my mind.

Tim and I went over to the campus of the University Of Dayton which, at the time, owned a 50,000 watt commercial radio station of its own. WVUD-FM (99.9) was an AOR (Album Oriented Rock) station. At the time, the evening jock's name was Kevin Carroll. We'd go over on Friday night and sit in the studio with Kevin while he did his show. He taught us proper techniques of "mixing" music on air. And also, taught us how to get the major record labels to "service" our lowly 10 watt radio station with free records for airplay.

I followed his advice. And before long, I had a three or four major labels sending us records. The first was Warner/Elektra/Atlantic. The second was Columbia. And, if I recall, I also got us service from a couple of distributors in Cincinnati.

If you wanted to be "Big Man On Campus" in high school in the 70's, be the Music Director of your school radio station and get the record companies to send you the new albums by the Rolling Stones, Led Zeppelin, Brownsville Station, Billy Joel and others. My senior year was filled with messages from the front office to "come up and get your record packages...there's a bunch of them up here"! And, so I'd walk through the cafeteria with "Physical Graffitti" and others under my arm. Yes, it happened. "Hey, you guys want to listen to the new "Stones" album?" They'd say, "It doesn't come out till Friday." I'd reply, "I have it right here".

But, first, there was a station to build. Sure enough, 30 days later, the proposal was on paper. We proposed licensing, constructing and operating a 10 watt Class D non-commercial, educational FM radio station at the school on 89.7 mhz at a cost (not counting building remodeling and construction, per the school's request) of between $5,000 to $7,000. The transmitter, antenna and turntables would be purchased new. Our audio control board and the cartridge tape machines we needed would be purchased used and would be refurbished and rebuilt by the students and our AV Engineer.

At the next school board meeting, we laid it all out. The board tabled the proposal wanting to take a month to look at it. But, they told us to come back at their next meeting.

Our second meeting with the school board was short and sweet. It was obvious the board members had read our proposal. The president of the school board said, "Well...what do you think? Do we give these guys a radio station? "The secretary said, "Are you making a motion here?" The president replied, "Yes, I'm making a motion...I move we approve the proposal to build a radio station at the high school". The motion was seconded and passed unanimously. It was all over in about 60 seconds. We had the board's permission to move ahead.

I've never forgotten T.R.'s comments to us that night outside the board meeting…"See what doing your homework did? Good job, guys. Now, go build us a radio station!"

We were all on cloud nine.

Chapter 3 – Forgiveness Vs. Permission

So, now we had the school board's permission to build a real FM radio station at the high school. But first, we had to license it through the FCC. Our A/V advisor, Bob Shattuck, by then had passed the test for his First Class Radio Operator's license...and my friends and I got our Third Class license with what was called a "broadcast endorsement". Our license basically meant we could operate any radio station. Our A/V advisor's license meant he could do everything we could do, but he could fix, and tinker with the transmitter and antenna as needed.

Bob finished filling out the application for our new station's construction permit. (Which, for a measly 10 watt Class D FM non-commercial station was about an inch and a half thick...just think what a 50.000 watt commercial station's application looks like! And you wonder why station owners craved for "deregulation"!) We mailed it in and, at that point we were at the point of ordering some studio equipment but, for the most part it was "hurry up and wait". We expected to hear something from the FCC in about 6 months.

We learned shortly thereafter the FCC had accepted our application, which meant they, at least agreed in principle that the paperwork looked ok.

Finally, in October of 1973, I got a phone call late in the afternoon from my friend, Tim. Tim had just happened to be in the school office when a telegram arrived. It said, "Commission in October 3, 1973 Granted application BPED-1662. Construction permit for a new Class D Non Commercial Educational FM Broadcast Station. Permit expires October 3, 1974. Report promptly any difficulties in beginning construction. If specific call sign desired, submit within 15 days list of 5 calls in order of preference and evidence compliance with section 1.550 Commission Rules. Wallace E. Johnson Chief, Broadcast Bureau

Federal Communications Commission" We really, really did it!

But, that's when we started learning lessons about something else...bureaucracy! The builders were in building our radio/television studios and facilities, but the school board was dragging its feet over where to put the antenna. (You see, the obvious place was on the roof of the school, but some people on the board weren't sure that could be done safely and wanted "more study" of whether to do that or find a way to build a tower on the school premises.)

Before too long, the studios were done, the transmitter was mounted on the studio wall...but the antenna question remained. And, we were getting close to the FCC's deadline for finishing station construction. If the board dragged this out too much farther, we were in danger of losing our license approval.

One day our Engineer called us all into his small office in the school library. He outlined the problem, then said..."Well, I guess it's time you guys learned a lesson about "forgiveness vs. permission". Meet me back here at the school at 4 pm after the principal has gone home."

We came back at 4 pm...where about ten of us went with the engineer to the school metal shop inside which was the resting place for a 32 foot tall galvanized steel pole. We went up the roof and threw ropes down to the ground and attached them to the pole, and proceeded to begin hauling it, by rope, up the side of the school building to the roof. We managed to do that safely, and attached a two bay FM antenna, and co-axial cable to the pole.

By then, it had started to snow (this was, I think...in early February, 1974). But together, we muscled the antenna to a standing position, strapped it to an air conditioner and grounded it (gotta think about lightning protection, you know!), then extended three guy wires to contact points on the sight screen mounted around the roof, and tightened them down good and tight.

I suppose you could never do this at a high school today (too much insurance liability), but nonetheless, we, the merry band of radio station builders had our antenna up in the air, and ran the coaxial cable to our transmitter one floor below.

Fortunately it was first period the next day before the excrement hit the rotating device! Tim and I were in our first class of the day when the principal came on the school P.A... "TIM! KEVIN! BOB! IN MY OFFICE, NOW!" I smiled, looked at Tim and said, "Gee, do you think he's looked up at the roof yet?" Tim said, "Probably". So, we, together with Bob (our engineer) and went to the woodshed, er...the principal's office. (The only time I had ever been called there in my entire high school career!)

The principal ranted and raved for about, maybe five minutes about how we disobeyed his orders, etc, etc, etc. When he finally paused to take a breath, our engineer explained the time pressure we were under to finish the station's construction and said we would lose the station if we hadn't have done this. The principal thought about what the engineer told him for a minute or two, calmed down and said, "Alright, alright...I understand why you did it. I'll tell you what I'll do. I'll call the architect out here this afternoon. If he approves what you've done, we'll let it go."

The architect was only on the roof about 10 minutes before he came downstairs and said "Hey, it looks good to me...the only thing you'll need to do about every two years is send someone up there to tighten the guy wires. Otherwise, the construction is sound". The principal finally told us..."Okay, good job, you guys."

We applied to the FCC for what's called "program test authorization". You can't actually run normal programming at that time, but you can fire up the transmitter, identify your station by the construction permit number, play a few songs to test the fidelity and distortion and other engineering stuff. After determining all was up to snuff, it was time to apply for our actual license and our call letters. We knew we couldn't get call letters that had a school relationship (we'd already checked on those), so we just told the FCC to give us a call sign. They notified us by telegram we would be known as WRSF-FM and gave us the go ahead to sign on.

The next day at 2 pm, WRSF-FM/Miamisburg signed on the air. The school board, of course, never would give us an actual station phone line, so we...er...hijacked the pay phone downstairs...callers could call the pay phone and it would ring up to a receiver in the radio studio. As I recall, the telephone number was 866-9278...which spells "wart" on the phone, so it became known as "the wart line". (I'm assuming the statute of limitations is long over on that.) And yes, the hijacked pay phone did ring... several people called to tell us the station could be heard over the city loud and clear! Tim was the first DJ on the station, and I took over at 4 pm. One of our other school buddies took over at 6... and our first day on the air was over at 8.

We loved working on the air at a station we built. At the same time, I had been appointed Editor-In-Chief of the school newspaper. I'd write stories, do interviews, send it all to the Miamisburg News office downtown...then, go down there to do the paste-ups of the actual newspaper (which was a page in that weekly publication). Good thing for me I had already collected sufficient credit to graduate after the first 9 weeks of my Senior year.

Because of that, and because I needed to go downtown frequently for my work with the paper, I was given a special privilege...an "addition" to my student ID that was a permanent "get out of school free" pass. I could leave ANYTIME I WANTED!

Now, not only was I popular with the students (you see, I could go get lunch at Burger Shef and come back and we all didn't have to eat the soybean burgers in the cafeteria), but having that pass also made me popular with my teachers.

"Hey, Kevin...on your way back from the newspaper office, can you go to (store) and get us some coffee? Here's a ten for it…keep the change!"

Yes, I fetched coffee, sandwiches, donuts for the teachers. And a few sandwiches and Cokes for my classmates.

But then, came a dark, dark day. April 3rd, 1974. I had left school around 2:30, got some records I wanted to play on the station from home and got back about 3:45 pm. Walking up to the office door, I looked off to the south and saw a real ugly black cloud heading our way.

This cloud wasn't just black. It was black, green, pink, purple…and probably was heading toward plaid.

"Wow!", I thought, "Somebody's about to have a big thunderstorm."

That was the least of it…as I would learn about 45 minutes later.

I was doing my radio show when our phone rang at about 4:20 pm. It was the operator on duty at WFCJ-FM, a 50,000 watt religious radio station in Miamisburg who had donated some second hand equipment to the station. Since we didn't have the money for an Associated Press teletype and they did, they had promised if something major happened in the area that was newsworthy, they'd call and let us know what was going on.

"There's a tornado warning in effect now for southern Montgomery County (that was us) and Greene County until 5 pm". I thanked the gentleman and put the information on our air. A short time later, all hell broke loose. WFCJ's board operator called back.

"You know Xenia, Ohio, right?" I replied I did. He said, "Half of it is gone. Destroyed by a giant tornado 15 minutes ago". I was stunned. We put the information on the air.

Suddenly classmates of mine who were volunteer

ambulance drivers were sent into Xenia. They located a working pay phone and called us at the station painting word pictures of a town laying in ruins. We put it all on the air.

33 people died that day in Xenia, another 1,150 were injured. WRSF stayed on the air late that night, till 11 pm.

Not long before that day, I had done a project in my high school television class interviewing the Chief Weathercaster for WHIO-TV at the time. Gil Whitney was a very popular weatherman whose forecasts were designed by the meteorological instruments of the day, including the station's "Instant Weather Radar". Gil gave about 20 minutes warning of the approach of that storm and likely saved hundreds of lives. I knew he had to be very busy that day, but I placed a call to the station and asked to leave him a message if he had a spare minute. The lady on the switchboard promised to give him the message.

Our studio phone rang a little after 7 pm. It was Gil on the phone. He gave us a brief description of what he knew at the time about what had happened. I thanked him for calling and I have always respected the man for that. He actually took the time out of what had to be a nightmarish day in his business to call a kid who had interviewed him at his high school radio station and give him three or four minutes of actual information.

That's the kind of guy Gil Whitney was. As I recall, he died in the early 1980's. But I can tell you, he is still remembered and missed by everyone who knew him and are still working at WHIO-TV today. And just about every visitor to the station old enough to remember will ask about Gil. Every one of our meteorologists knows who Gil was…and everyone respects what he did that day. There's a great You Tube video about it if you'd ever like to check it out.

So, we signed off WRSF that night at 11 pm. But, the storms were still coming. I went to bed knowing I had to get up and go to school the next day. Out of sense of wanting to know what was going on, I put my transistor radio in my bedroom on WHIO radio and listened to overnight guy Bob Sweeney.

About 2:45 AM, Bob comes on the air, interrupting a record and says, "If you live in Miamisburg and you're listening to this broadcast, take cover immediately. Our instant weather radar is showing a possible tornado heading your way now!"

OK, now I'm scared. I leaped out of bed and ran into my parent's bedroom telling them the radio said we needed to take cover and that a tornado was coming.

"Kevin…go back to bed!" was their reply. I did, but wasn't too happy about it as I heard the wind and rain kick up outside.

Whatever it was, though, never hit. Though, I don't think I slept another minute that night and dragged my butt into school pretty tired the next morning. It wouldn't be the last time that would happen.

Despite all of the work, hassle, and B.S. we had to go through, I will always be grateful to Miamisburg High School, then-principal John Waddell and the then-Director of Secondary Education, Tom Robinson, for challenging us all to do the work ourselves. It was a great lesson for a group of high school students. More than a few students who took to the air on WRSF got into the radio business professionally. We're all over the country, me in Dayton…Tim in Des Moines, Iowa…and another student who came after I did, but told me once I was the reason he got into radio and how much he admired my work then. He's programming, at last word, WLTW-FM, the light rock station in New York City…the #1 station in radio market #1. (If he reads this I have to admit, Chris Conley, I almost cried when I read the e-mail you sent me, but thanks so much!) Not bad. Not bad at all. My friend, Jeff Shade worked for WHIO and went on to get radio and life lessons from a guy whose show he produced in New York City…Don Imus.

You see, you never know who's listening to you when you work on radio. Even if it's your 10 watt high school radio station. Who you may be influencing. And what may happen to them sometime. I influenced the guy who programs the #1 station in the #1 market in America to go into broadcasting. Little old me.

This was still the day and age of AM Top 40 radio, despite FM's rise. At night, I'd listen to Musicradio 89, WLS and DJ's like Larry Lujack, Jeff Davis, John "Records" Landecker and AM 1000, "Super" CFL (WCFL) with Big Ron O'Brien on "The Voice Of Labor"! In Detroit, there was an AM flamethrowing behemoth... the Big 8, CKLW in Detroit/Windsor. CKLW had, bar none, the biggest damn AM radio signal in North America. I heard it at night, in Dayton, as strongly as a local station. A radio station that was SO BIG, the stars came to do radio shows of their own on it. Elton John was a guest DJ there, Cheech and Chong visited on air and others. God! How I wanted to work for a station like that.

It was never to be, though. And CKLW was sentenced to death at the drop of a pen. The Canadian government killed CKLW because in Canada, the government has to approve the kind of music you play. CKLW felt the influence of FM and wanted to flip the Top 40 format onto their FM station just like many stations across America were doing at the time.

It would have worked. But, Canada's governing radio body, the CRTC said, "No. The rock music stays on the AM. And the beautiful music stays on the FM." They couldn't change when they needed to, so the Big 8 died. Dammit! One of the best damn Top 40 radio stations EVER...killed by politicians. I would have loved to worked for it. Some people I've worked with DID.

Bob Moody was my "boss" as corporate the head of Country Programming for Nationwide Communications when I worked for WCOL-FM in Columbus. He was "Cosmic Bob Moody" at the Big 8. When I found out he worked there, I was astounded.

Years later, I went to a reunion that was held in Detroit of the CKLW staff. And I'm good acquaintances with people like Charlie O'Brien, Jo-Jo Shutty McGregor (wife of veteran CKLW News Director Byron McGregor…a man with the "voice of God" who passed away quite a while ago). I can't believe I actually took news copy I had written for WHIO and showed it to her. She said, "Yep. Byron would have hired you." I can only imagine what THAT job would have been like…being a member of the infamous CKLW "20/20 News" staff. I also met "Brother Bill" Gable that day. Now, "Brother Bill" is gone, too. I had heard him on WLW/Cincinnati.

I still think CKLW could be resurrected as an oldies station and sold in combo with an FM Classic Hits station. But, Charlie O'Brien insists it would never happen. I have to take him at his word. They are, of course now, a very successful local talk radio station…but their sister, AM-540, CKWW is a tribute station of sorts to their far more powerful sister, and you can listen online today. Still…if only…

I can dream, can't I?

Chapter 4 – Public Interest, Convenience and Necessity

A couple of things about the way I feel about the "public interest" comments I made earlier. I have never considered myself a "disc jockey". There was a day when "DJ" was just one job at a station. You rarely heard a "DJ" do the news. You never heard a newscaster read a commercial. It was a day and age of vicious specialization in the radio business.

That was why it took me so long to forge a career in the business. You see, I liked being a DJ. I liked gathering, writing and delivering news. And I believe in that thing called "public interest, convenience and necessity". When the public needs me, you can bet damn sure I'm there.

Instead, I've always considered myself a "broadcaster", and that's a big difference. Not to brag, but I've been a DJ, an award winning news reporter and anchor (Winning "Best Spot News Coverage" from the Associated Press Media Editors and the Society of Professional Journalists). Over the years, I've also been an award winning Production Director, a radio News Director, an Assistant Program Director, Music Director and yes, a Program Director. And, the country station for which I work, WHKO (K-99.1 FM) won the National Association of Broadcaster's prestigious "Marconi" award in 2016, and I have my "mini-Marconi" statue (which the station gave me as a gift) in my office at home. Back then, being able to do multiple jobs wasn't valued. Ironically today, it's the reason most people hire me, and never want me to leave. Because I can do all of those jobs, and I guess, based upon ratings and such, I must do it well.

Today, though, many stations don't give a rat's poo-poo about this. And they sure as hell don't care about the "heritage" of their radio stations. Some companies will put losing formats on a heritage station simply because they don't understand the "heritage" card is one of the most valuable cards you can play in the deck of radio. And I have worked for a number of such stations.

Example: I worked for WING-AM in Dayton. WING was Dayton's first radio station. It pre-dated Powel Crosley's WLW on the air by 6 months and was licensed by the Federal Radio Commission in 1921. It simply didn't get the "WING" call sign until later. It was the 13th licensed radio station in the United States! I work today for WHIO-AM/FM in Dayton, which came on the air in February of 1935 and, up until recently, was a "1 owner station". It was put on the air by the late Governor James M. Cox and was his "first" radio station (Sorry, fans of WSB in Atlanta...). WHIO was the start of the "Cox Broadcasting" empire which has included radio and television stations and a bunch of newspapers.

According to the Cox Enterprises website, the Governor said, in christening WHIO radio, "May I express this christening sentiment – that the voice of this Miami Valley empire will always be an instrument of dignity, culture and practical service".

Today, the majority stake of the Cox media holdings (Radio and television stations) with the sole exception of the Atlanta Journal Constitution and the Dayton Daily News newspaper, are held and run by affiliates of Apollo Global Management who purchased a majority stake in "Cox Media Group" and now run those operations under that name. Some of the original senior management of "the old" CMG is still running the show, so, in a sense the day the sale was concluded was kind of a "meet the new boss, same as the old boss" type of thing for those of us who work inside the station.

Which leads me to some thoughts about the buying and selling of radio stations. Cox Media Group is very unusual in the fact that we have had but 2 owners since WHIO came on the air in 1935. (But, only in a sense...because the original CMG still holds a stake in the stations.) I can't say the same thing for the other stations in town. Other stations in town for which I've worked over the years, have been bought and sold multiple times. A few of them have had at least 3 or 4 owners since 1996, perhaps more (I've lost count). And it seems, to me anyway, the more you get sold, the more "watered down" your "heritage" gets with whomever the new owner is.

I would never waste a heritage Top 40 station playing syndicated "Sports Talk" unless you could prove to me you can make more money with it than you could playing music. Today in Dayton, we have 2 sports talk stations. Neither even gets a one share. And yet, they survive with the puny audiences they have simply because Budweiser will buy commercials on them.

And radio stations NEED air personalities. Okay today, maybe they don't ALL have to be live DJ's 24/7/365. But when you're a local DJ, you have the chance to "bond" with the people who listen to you. I am simply amazed when I go on stage to introduce a musical act at the people who applaud and cheer ME when I introduce myself. ME! The DJ. I get recognized in the grocery store and the hardware store and at the Credit Union or in bars. And it's humbling.

People depend on us to tell them what's happening. To be their friend when something goes bump in the middle of the night. To comfort them in sad times. To cheer and laugh with them in good times. And to warn them of impending danger.

Today, we have what is called "The Emergency Alert System". This rat trap of a governmental mess came out of the Cold War Era first as a system called "Conelrad". Conelrad was designed to thwart a possible nuclear attack by bomber aircraft by having the radio station switch frequencies constantly. Since in the 1950's, bombers would "ride radio waves" to reach a destination to drop bombs, it would throw them off if the stations were constantly switching frequencies.

From there, came "Conelrad 2.0". It was called "The

Emergency Broadcast System". The idea was to use code words to authenticate emergencies from Washington and have an electronic box that could take over the station from whence an authority, such as the President could give the public emergency information within seconds.

It was February 20th, 1971 on a Saturday morning that EBS proved just how ineffective this could be.

Inside Cheyenne Mountain in Colorado, someone was sending what he or she "thought" was the weekly "test" of the Emergency Broadcast System to stations across the country. You know this test by the words, "For the next 60 seconds this station is conducting a test of the Emergency Broadcast System, blah, blah, blah". (The "blahs" are mine, because this thing is the worst tune out for listening, next to too many commercials, that has EVER been devised by the federal government!)

Unfortunately for this airman, he grabbed the WRONG tape and instead, sent a message that sent every radio and television station in the country a message

"Hatefulness. Hatefulness. This is an Emergency Action Notification (EAN) directed by the President. Normal broadcasting will cease immediately. All stations will broadcast EAN Message One preceded by the attention signal, per FCC rules. Only stations holding NDEA (the authorization to stay on air) may stay on the air in accordance with their state EBS Plan. "

Now, remember, this happened on a Saturday morning. You know who works in radio stations on Saturday mornings? Usually, it's the 17 year old kid who's the son of the General Manager who knows little or nothing about these sorts of things.

And that mention of the "NDEA"? If you didn't have that authorization, you were supposed to sign off so that people could tune to stations which were broadcasting the "official news and information" that was supposed to come.

The engineers at WHIO radio told me the story of what went on inside our station on that day. We DID have news people on duty and, because we were the middle of the road "adult" radio station, our people were a touch more experienced than in some stations in town.

The news guy read the wire, more than likely felt ill immediately and rushed to the studio. You see, WE held the NDEA in town. But, yet, this message didn't seem to have the "feel" of authenticity to it. If this was "the big one", there was nothing going on in the world, no tensions that would have set the stage for a nuclear attack on the U.S. I'm not even sure that Watergate had yet happened.

So our newsperson thought, "This can't be right". Fortunately, the Cox organization has always had a Washington News Bureau, so the newsperson calls D.C. and asks what the heck is going on up there? Their answer? "I think I'd better call the White House. I'll let you know". So, he did. The White House Press Office's answer? "Uh...we'd better call the President. I'll let you know."

It is unknown just what President Richard Nixon said when getting that word. But, I would suggest it contained more than a few "expletive deleteds".

And a few minutes later, the whole emergency was over and later, the "Mr. Eberhart", said to be a 15 year employee in Cheyenne Mountain fessed up to having accidentally sent the wrong message.

At WING in Dayton, they got the message via teletype, too. And the confused young part timer reportedly called General Manager Jim Bennett to ask what to do and should he sign the station off the air.

Bennett's reported reply? "Sign off? Hell, no...we're sold out! Keep playing those commercials!" (Could this have led to a funny commercial open once suggested by a Facebook friend of mine?..."The end of the world is brought to you by Steve Tatone Buick...drive a little and save a lot!") Maybe daytimer WAVI signed off that day, but that was about it.

Go to You Tube and look this incident up and you'll find a hilarious recording of nearby station WOWO-AM in Fort Wayne, Indiana. Their morning man, Bob Sievers was on the air playing the Partridge Family's "Doesn't Somebody Want To Be Wanted" when he was given the teletype copy. Sievers is heard "trying" to follow the instructions in the message (and was actually doing a pretty decent job of it)...but you also know when he could put a record on to "gather" information, he wasn't getting much.

Why? The phones were ringing off the hook. Listeners wanted to know what was the matter?

So, Sievers takes to the air saying, "Please don't call the station asking what the matter is. We don't KNOW what the matter is...we don't know what is causing this message to come to us. All we know is what we're telling you".

Then, Sievers (who, at that point was sounding a little bit like the movie character Ron Burgundy in "Anchorman") asks for members of the WOWO News Staff to "come to the station immediately to help us figure out what's going on here". (I honestly thought when I heard this tape, he was about to yell, "Newsteam...Assemble!!!!") Sievers later called it "the longest five minutes in radio".

And for them, a few minutes later, it was over.

The problem with EBS was simple. All the BIG stations in the town were the "activating" stations, and no one in Washington ever considered where the station was located, or what was nearby.

For example, WHKO-FM is the "activating" station in

Dayton. Its' 1,000 foot tower sits on a hill within a few air miles of Wright Patterson Air Force Base in Fairborn. I can guaran-damn-tee-you that if a nuclear bomb is ever detonated over Wright Patt, WHKO is going up in the fireball.

In Cincinnati, the "activating" station is WLW-AM. Its' tower sits right next door to what once was the "Voice Of America" shortwave station...and that tower is just a handful of miles from General Electric's plant, Ford and others in northern Cincy. Guess who's going up in that fireball?

To my way of thinking...if you're going to really try and protect a community from something like nuclear holocaust, you should find a station that's away from the immediate area of first strike targets and give it special temporary authorization to radically increase its power in an emergency and keep quiet about it. Don't do these "tests" that tells you what station is going to send the alarm. Wasn't the watchword in World War II, "Loose Lips Sink Ships"? Why should it be a badge of honor for a radio station to be the "activating" station?

Today, the new system is called "EAS" for "Emergency Alert System". It's now done automatically. Has to be...too damn many stations are running without operators on consoles. So, now the National Weather Service can take control of your station and run a warning. Local cops can do it for Amber Alerts. Assuming that is, that local law enforcement has trained its people how to do issue the alarms.

A number of years back, there was this train derailment in Minot, North Dakota where a gas car ruptured and toxic gas was released...a very serious situation indeed.

The local radio station had staff on duty. But, the news director went out to the scene to cover the news. No one else was in the radio station. The local cops had access to the station via E.A.S., and could have sent an emergency message, but no one had taken the time to learn how to use it. They couldn't even find the telephone number for the station's General Manager when they needed to.

Clear Channel Communications, now known as "iHeart Media" owned the station at that time and has taken massive heat over the incident over the years. But, in reality, in my opinion, it wasn't totally their fault. The fault, dear Brutus, lies with the cops who didn't take the time to learn how to operate the system and send the emergency message when they needed to.

We've dealt with a similar situation in our state with Amber Alerts. We've learned way too late about some of these being issued and largely because the cops don't know how to send these messages. While I can appreciate that some in law enforcement would like to tell broadcast station reporters to take a hike now and then, it also behooves both of us to work together when we can. When lives are at stake, you sure don't need to be quibbling over details about getting the info out. That's why we have a microphone…to transmit life-saving information, so they're not out having to give tragic news to someone's family.

Today, it is not only important for a fledgling broadcaster to learn every aspect of the business, but it actually makes you more employable. If you know all the FCC rules and regulations, it takes a station less time to train you. The Society of Broadcast Engineers has an "Operator Certification Course". This course is, in many ways, similar to the old FCC Third Class License test I had to take and pass in 1973 in order to have the proper license to "operate" and AM or FM radio station. It can be a challenge, but if you're interested, get the book and get that certification.

You see, I hate to tell you this. But, if you have the talent, and the verbal and writing skills, you don't "need" a college education to go to work in broadcasting. Now, I would never advise a young person not to go to college…it certainly is preferable today. But, I am saying it is possible to make it a go in the business without a degree. Take it from a guy who graduated high school in May,

1974...went to a "broadcasting school"...got his first part time radio job in October of 1974, and went full time 2 months later, and has been in it ever since. And I'm not the only one.

Today's on air radio station employee needs to know how to be a DJ, how to run a board, how to write and deliver a newscast. How to embed audio in his news copy program... how to do commercial production...how to do a podcast...how to write commercials, news, promotional copy...even the work of the time salespeople and how they go about selling ads. Sales, you see, is actually where the money is. Just look at any radio station parking lot. The beater automobiles belong to the DJ's. The Jaguars and BMW's typically belong to the sales people.

But, if you're really interested in getting in this business on-air, learn to be a "broadcaster". It'll be the best decision you could make. A true "broadcaster" realizes you're not just there to introduce songs and talk about the latest artist you met at a concert. When you're on the air, you're the listener's companion. And you have a responsibility to them. They depend on you to tell them what's happening. Being able to relate to their lives and try and give them what they want is the bond between you and the listener. Cement that bond, and you're a step above any "disc-jockey" who thinks their job is to just rattle their gums.

And, once you cement that bond, you'll also find you will have achieved at least a modicum of job security. Now, people get fired and laid off all the time...often for reasons that are not their fault. That is a tragedy. But, I can tell you, the old saying is, you haven't really worked in radio unless you've been fired at least once.

But, radio and broadcasting is also not a business where getting fired is necessarily the end of the world. If you get fired, you take it in stride and move on to the next job and next challenge.

Just recently, iHeart Media now out of a bankruptcy, and yet, still 6 BILLION in debt did some massive layoffs. The final tally isn't known, but has been said to be anywhere from 300 to 1,200 people. And it wasn't just on air people. It was receptionists, engineers, promotions people…a few people I know are looking for work today because of this. And there's likely to be, and has been, more.

The company is saying it wants to use artificial intelligence to make some of the jobs inside the station easier, and mentioned "music scheduling" as an example.

If you ask me, that's a bunch of hooey. If a music scheduling system is set up correctly, the music will schedule right, 98% of the time. BUT, setting it up is complicated and takes time and trial and error to get right. THAT'S what the problem is and this should be addressed by the people who make these software programs (which are for the most part extremely expensive anyway)…not a radio company.

Right now, here in Dayton, I am hearing some pretty awful "generic sounding" radio from most of their stations…basically…the ones with smaller signal footprints in town and now, no staff. Who the hell wants to listen to a bland station not playing the right music anyway that only refers to itself as "your Classic Hits station"?

Perhaps I'll be wrong, but this sounds like the beginning of the end of that company. And the company that followed them into bankruptcy, Cumulus, immediately announced some layoffs of their own.

Look, I get what they want to do. They basically want to return us to the days of the 1940's…when networks ran radio and the local station was there with "inserts" to the national programs. iHeart's idea is to become a national radio network of programming options for their stations…something the lesser signaled stations in cities can air. It's far cheaper to have to hire only 10 staffs of DJ's than 1,200 (iHeart's top number of stations once owned.) Spread those national air talents across the country with their bland, toned down, dumbed down programming and there is no doubt, there is a substantial amount of savings to be had.

What is lost, though, is local radio. One of the strongest cards in the deck. And they want to get rid of it. Good local beats bad national every single time. Because bad national won't tell you when the tornado is coming, when the roads are icy (and no, the "road sensors" in a computer program available online is NOT going to give you 100% accuracy on road conditions. They don't do that now and there are times even I have to ignore them when I'm doing traffic reports.) Having a local staff, even spread over three or four stations, is far better than trying to do it all from a central location somewhere in the country. You have to spend money to make money. And, right now, a few companies are trying to bite off their noses to spite their faces.

Moral of this story? Never, EVER, burn bridges. Because that manager who fired you or from whom you may have rejected an offer may, down the road, need somebody like you somewhere else someday. And knowing your work ethic and your experience may just put you in line for another job down the road. And sometimes, it might just be the best job you ever had.

It happened to me…and when it did, I was astounded by it.

Chapter 5 – My First Radio Gig

In my part of the Midwest, it was the days of the "Boogie Check" with John "Records" Landecker on Musicradio 89, WLS/Chicago. The heady days of the only Bill Drake Programmed "Boss Radio" station anywhere near my area in the 70's, the legendary "Big 8", CKLW/Detroit-Windsor. In Dayton, WING was still king, but upstart FM Top 40 rocker WTUE was coming on fast. It was right about that time that I received…the call.

I'd been scouring the area with resumes and audition tapes. But in Mid-October 1974, I got a call from the Program Director of WDHK-FM in Wilmington, Ohio offering me a part-time job on the air. I accepted (at minimum wage, of course!), and soon found myself working 6 days a week, but only 3 hours a day Monday Thru Friday from 10 am to 1 pm…and a 6 hour shift on the weekend.

Some people ask me, "Do you remember the first song you played professionally on radio?" I sure do. Don't laugh, though…it was "Jimmy Loves Maryanne" by the group Looking Glass, which was just a year or two from having had their biggest hit, "Brandy (You're A Fine Girl)". (And there's a You Tube video of singer Elliott Lurie recently singing it a'capella over Zoom. He still nails it.)

I was going to broadcasting school at night…and working days. I'd worked there about a month…maybe 60 days when I got a phone call from the PD again. The night DJ had been dismissed, and did I want to do 6 pm to 12:30 am full time? I said yes before I realized something:

I was still in school at night. So, I went back to the school to tell them I had to withdraw because I had a full time radio gig. At first, the school wasn't happy. "But, you haven't finished the course yet!".

I said, "Well, what's still left in the course?" The answer: "How to make a resume and audition tape!" My reply: "I made both…applied for…and got a full time radio job! Sounds like I passed that chapter in the course, right?" "Uh…yeah…I guess." was the answer on the other end of the line. "Let me get back to you, they said."

When they got back with me, it was, "We normally don't do this, Kevin…but all things considered, we can't think of a reason not to award you a diploma. So come back in February and pick it up."

The school is still in business in Dayton. But, it's expanded into a 15 month fully accredited Associates Degree program. I substitute teach radio broadcasting there today and program their internet radio station.

About that time, I learned the reason I had a job…the former nighttime DJ had been caught by the General Manager smoking pot in the studio. While I wouldn't say I never tried pot (because I have), I was about as far away from being a user then as any young guy could be.

It was fun in that first job. I had to take care of the UPI teletype (a black, lumbering machine stuck in a coat closet with the door taken off.) I hated changing the ribbon on that thing. You couldn't do it without your hands looking like you'd spent 20 hours in a coal mine by the time you were done!

But, I also was Music Director of the station…so I got all the new 45's sent in by the record companies to consider for airplay. Oddly enough, we had most of the major labels sending records. So, after a while, I only had to pay out of pocket for a few 45's here and there…out of my "princely" 80 dollar a week salary. (I should have stayed on hourly…I'd have made more money! But, I wasn't given that alternative.)

I also made the daily "news run". We had to meet every morning at 10 at the Sheriff's Office downtown where the Sheriff held court to the media and would read you the police blotter (which you had to copy longhand), that you took back to the station from which to right stories). This was not a private meeting. The reporter from the newspaper was there, as well as was News Director from the AM station across the street. He and I hit it off OK, despite being competitors.

He later became News Director at WHIO, Jim Barrett. I guess I'm the guy responsible for bringing him to town. I was working at WONE/WTUE in Dayton as a weekend newscaster. We had another part-time opening and the News Director at WONE, Kent Scott, asked me if I knew anyone who might be interested. I called Jim…he called Kent…Kent hired him. He'd work there for about 10 or 12 years before he'd go across the street to WHIO.

I did remote broadcasts, too. (For no more money, of course…it was considered "part of the job"…don't let my bosses get that idea today!) One of my first remotes happened on a Friday night in a local department store. As the remote began, a tornado was spotted on the edge of town. The police were going through the streets telling people on their PA in the car to seek shelter immediately.

I was careful in what I said during those first breaks on the air. That's when I learned why you should never…ever…give the microphone to the sponsor at a remote. Let he or she talk on it, yes…but don't give up control of it.

I introduced the manager and handed him the microphone. The first words out of his mouth? "Don't worry about the tornado, friends…Come on down…We have a BASEMENT!!!" (I wanted to sink through the floor…)

So, I was working, and all was well. I thought. Truth be told, I had noticed there weren't many commercials on the station Program Log. Before long, we learned the station was not doing well, financially.

Yes, WDHK was an Adult Contemporary station. But, it was also a Rock station (at night), an elevator music station in mid-days...and a Country station on Saturday mornings. Plus, we did plenty of religious programming on Sunday. That was the problem. We were trying to be "all things to all people". Some of that was possible then in a small town station...but our programming was far more spastic that most. No one could tell what type of station we were. And the Owner/General Manager whose old-fashioned ways then were more suited for the radio of 1954 than 1974, was beginning to feel the heat of only small dollars coming in the door.

There was also a growing concern among the staff about just how legal the station was. We had a remote link for the station audio (called a "Studio Transmitter Link, or STL) to the transmitter, but no actual remote controls for the transmitter. The General Manager told us that he and his family lived at the transmitter site, and since the whole family had FCC Operator Licenses, (which was true...the licenses were posted in the studio, along with mine) they were taking readings from there.

We realized it seemed like an odd situation, but we assumed the boss knew what he was doing.

A couple more things to know about WDHK. At the time, the station was in a converted 2 story home in a residential area in Wilmington that was also the studios and offices for the local Cable TV company. We shared one side...the cable company took the basement (for a TV studio) and the other side of the house for offices. The "living room" of the house was the office for the radio station. There was an office off of the living room (a bedroom that became the PD's office.) The kitchen became a conference room and studio. And a small production studio had been built between it and the main studio control room. The front and side yards became a gravel parking lot.

Oh yeah...the other station in town? It was on AM...1090... WKFI. Owned by a company called 5 KW, Inc...its parent company was (I kid you not!), the Gannett Newspaper chain. (You know...the people who today publish "U.S.A. Today?") A much better financed operation that we ever could have hoped to be, WKFI was kicking our ass because they had the News and Farm Information image...had a full time news and sports department...and DJ's that were a cut above the typical small town station.

I always thought Gannett used WKFI as a loss-leader, and I have lots of reasons to suspect that. For starters, for a small town station, WKFI had the very latest equipment coming out of their ears. They didn't play 45's on turntables...everything was recorded on a cartridge tape, and played over cartridge players. In 1974-75, that was truly state-of-the-art. Only the big stations had the capacity to do that.

And, my buddy, Jim? Well, don't tell Gannett, but supposedly, he was an expensive tape recorder in the WKFI budget. That's how they paid his salary. It was not a surprise when Gannett fired the WKFI General Manager later on.

WKFI also paid better (okay, maybe that was a matter of conjecture, but I do think Jim was making a little more than 80 bucks a week), and it also was the home at least part time of guys like my friend Mark Elliott who was just off his full time stint as "Jason Roberts" on WTUE. He would later move on to WKRQ-FM (Q-102) in Cincinnati which, at that time was owned by Taft Broadcasting. He did very well there and today is back in Ohio after many years traveling around the area and the country and continues work as (at last word) Operations Manager for WDJO AM/FM in Cincinnati while also consulting other radio properties.

It was while I was at WDHK that I played "donkey basketball" for charity at a local high school gym. Now, like at least some radio jocks, I was so totally un-athletic in high school it wasn't funny. If I had had to run up and down a basketball court for 40 minutes, I would have probably lost a lung. But, hey...I'm riding a donkey! He does the work...right?

Have you ever tried to guide a donkey? They don't refer to them as "jackasses" for nothing.

The game begins...most all of the donkeys head down the court. Not mine. Mine decides the easier thing to do is go toward the goal closest to it...the one at the other end of the court. And no amount of coaxing, urging, pleading is going to get that animal to go toward where everybody else is at. During the entire game, I don't think I even got the ball once.

I don't remember the score of that game, I think it has been forever blanked from my mind. And I never did it again.

It was also during this time, I got to call a high school basketball game. Once. You see, the regular play by play guy was sick, or out of town, so I was more or less the only person who could do the game.

Some people are great at this. I suck. I did show up ahead of time, tried my best to go over the rosters and tried to get familiar with the players. But the game just moves too fast...and I usually found myself calling the play of three plays ago.

I can read sportscasts of games fine. Just don't ask me to call the game, OK? Get an expert for that.

It was also while at WDHK, I was exposed to the country music industry for the first time. Of course, I knew what country music was. I grew up around the Midwestern Hayride (the regional television show that had acts such as Kenny Price and occasionally featured guests like Cincinnati native, Skeeter Davis who had a major hit in the 1960's with the song, "The End Of The World"). But, I had never been to Nashville...never had been to the Grand Ole Opry.

Lee Hendee was my close friend and co-worker at WDHK, who did a Saturday morning country music show on the station. One day, he came up to me and told me he had gotten from some record labels in Nashville to work on his behalf and got him some backstage passes to the Opry. He and his wife were making the trip there the following weekend and asked if I'd like to go with them. I said yes. We went on a Friday night.

I spent most of the day on Saturday with Lee walking up and down the famed "Music Row" knocking on doors at record labels and saying hello. Though a few were closed, we found more than a few who had people at work inside.

One such meeting was notable. A gentleman saw us in the lobby, and welcomed us into his office. He said his name was Barry. We chatted for a few minutes and it was about then, I noted that there was a gold record hanging on the wall behind the man...a gold record for the 1966 RCA album, "The Ballad Of The Green Berets". Yes, this was the man once known as "Staff Sergeant Barry Sadler", the man who recorded the song which went to #1. He'd have a tragedy later in life, but it was fun to meet him then.

That evening, we went to the "new" Opry House (the show had moved from its original home in the Ryman Auditorium by that time), and were welcomed backstage. The backstage area that evening was a veritable "Who's Who" of Country Music. Roy Acuff was here...I interviewed him and he threatened to "smack me upside the head" if I referred to him as "a legend" again. We laughed and I said, "But, you ARE!".

I talked NASCAR racing with Marty Robbins, said hello to Johnny Cash and interviewed several other stars of that day, including Little Jimmy Dickens.

But perhaps, the most memorable of those I met had to be Sarah Cannon...you know, Minnie Pearl? I met her in the Green Room...she was all dressed in her familiar stage outfit, complete with the hat with the price tag hanging from it. We spoke and a few minutes later she excused herself only to return about 15 minutes later. WOAH! Now, she's not in costume, but was in a gorgeous gold lame' dress and was definitely the most glamorous, most elegant lady I had ever met. I was sitting on the couch and Minnie came over to me with a drink in her hand. She had earlier asked what I was drinking...and had made me one! I said, "Minnie, you didn't have to do that!" Her reply, "That's how we treat our guests here in Nashville." It left an indelible impression on me. And she wouldn't be the last country artist who'd offer me a drink. More on that later.

It was a fun weekend and the next day, we all drove home and Lee and I went back to work. After I left WDHK, Lee and I would lose track of each other for a long time. We finally reconnected in the past 20-30 years and it was a joy. By this time, WDHK had been, eventually, connected with WKFI in a sale...and both were sold off. The stations still exist, but neither serves the local community...a face that doesn't sit well with more than few businessmen in Clinton County, Ohio. Lee and I tried, very hard to return local radio to that community. We had a construction permit for an LPFM there and had it on the air to a great positive response by the locals. But, it got caught up in a legal battle with a jerk in Grant County, Kentucky 90 miles away who claimed our 100 watts was interfering with his 3 KW commercial station. This guy kept throwing legal objection after legal objection at Lee. (He must have worked for Gannett at some point in his life). The stress of dealing with lawyers to try and battle this took its toll and Lee died of a massive heart attack, which ended our dreams of bringing local radio back there. (We were going to try and buy WKFI, add an FM translator and sell it to advertisers as an AM/FM combo. But, we couldn't come up with the cash or buyers to make the sale.)

As for the jerk, he bought a 50,000 watt FM station in Middletown, Ohio and is trying to be a country station that's a cross between modern and classic country. Tough to do halfway between Dayton and Cincinnati where they are at least a dozen country stations of all varieties. And his station is a cellar dweller in Dayton, but better demographically in Cincy. He has no local programming but is merely "repeating" the programming of his Grant County, Kentucky station on it. He does few promotions on the station. Frankly, I don't know why he wasted money on it...I figure he'll sell it sometime and will walk away with somebody's money. Until then, enjoy selling those spots, pal. You deserve it.

You aren't a player and never will be. And, at least one friend of mine knows him and says he gets his way by being a bully.

Believe me, if I COULD come up with the cash to buy a station, it would not be satellite, it would not be a repeater, it would be locally programmed. I believe in local programming. And I have always been right about that. And as long as you have a large enough business base within range of your signal, you can sensibly hire some local people and have a good operation. It doesn't have to be live 24/7, but just local. And in a small town with a good college in it, you can do internships to get some young people who are "paid" with college credit. In fairness, you give these students a paid shift on the weekend. It can all be done…and an operation such as this would go far to build back "a farm team" that would help stations in bigger nearby markets find potential employees.

Ohio still has "locally owned" and/or "locally operated" radio stations. One of my friends is a man named Lou Vito. Lou is the local owner of stations in Bellefontaine, Ohio (WBLL/WPKO). I respect him for one reason – iHeart has offered him millions of dollars for his operation. He's turned them down every time. He has a local staff. And their station is programmed locally.

It worked back then…and still can.

Chapter 6

What Do You Mean, I'm The "Acting General Manager"?

Yep. It began when I noticed our commercial logs seemed to be getting very light on spots. Before long, people were leaving. Quickly. First, the Program Director quit. Then, the Sales Manager. And one morning (I think it was a Tuesday), I am called into the General Manager's office.

"Kevin, as you know, the station's not been doing that well lately."

("Gulp", I'm thinking.)

"So, I have made a deal to sell the station to a new owner".

I asked, "When is all of this coming down"?

Says the GM, "I'm leaving the station and town today."

"And", I asked, "When does the new owner arrive"? "In two weeks", was the reply.

"Okay", said I. "So, who is in charge until then"?

That's when the bomb hit. The GM looked at me and said, "You are. You'll be the Acting General Manager until Dick Jones, the new owner gets here two weeks from Monday. Good luck." And with that, he went out the door, and I never saw him again until decades later when we communicated a few times on Facebook prior to his death.

So, at age 17 with all of about 6 months of broadcasting experience under my belt, I am now, temporarily, "The Boss". And what an education that was!

Paychecks were to happen that Friday. We still had 4 employees total. We needed about $350 dollars total to pay them. The station had exactly $20 bucks in the bank. So, I grabbed my coat and headed into town. I knew a few of the advertisers did owe us some money, and I went to visit them. They must have felt sorry for me when they found "the new kid" was trying to collect on bills. And by the next day, I had about $400 or so to put in the bank. So, payroll did arrive on time. And the checks were good.

I thought I had it made. I had no clue what was coming next.

I had just gotten done with my morning show on air at the end of week 2, and just before I got off the air, I saw a nicely dressed man in a suit and tie, standing in the hallway in front of the control room window. When I got done, I walked out to say hello.

"Good morning, sir". I said smiling and offered a handshake. "I'm Kevin Fodor, the Acting General Manager of the station".

He returned the handshake, then showed me his badge. "I'm, so-and-so. And I am an inspector with the regional office of the Federal Communications Commission in Chillicothe, and I'm here to inspect your station."

Okay…I knew this sort of thing could be expected. And I assumed most everything was in reasonable order. Note, I said "most" everything. But, I wasn't prepared for what was about to transpire.

Mr. Inspector first asked me to produce a week's worth of programming logs. I had that right there in the office. In fact, I had three years of logs as then required. I got them for him. And then he asked me for the past 6 months of "operating" (read: transmitter) logs. No problem. I was told all of the operating logs were back in the General Manager's office. I said I would go retrieve them.

So, imagine my shock when I went into the GM's office... opened the filing cabinet and found...one week's worth of transmitter logs. For three fricking YEARS of station operation.

That was trouble. BIG trouble. You were supposed to keep those logs for at least three years back then. And I had but 7 days of them.

You see, all of us who came to work there were told by the General Manager that there was no need for we operators to "take transmitter readings" as were required by law then every three hours. He said that he and his family were all licensed radio operators (true...all of their licenses were hanging on the studio wall with the station's license. So were mine and the licenses of the other DJ's). And he advised that the readings were taken by them because he and the family lived in a mobile home at the transmitter site.

That sounded reasonable to me. And if it had been true, it might have mitigated some of what was about to happen.

I showed the inspector what logs I had and explained what the General Manager had told all of us. What I got in return was a very stern look.

"Every licensed radio station that has a transmitter at another location is required by law to have a remote control to allow the operators to adjust power levels on the transmitter and to turn it off at sign off...and back on at sign on. I see you have a frequency meter here, so I can see the station is on frequency. But, there is no way for me to know if this is the correct reading... because I can't see what's on the meters at the transmitter."

"This is a totally illegal operation". He asked, "How do you turn the transmitter on in the morning and off at night?"

I answered, "We were told to leave it on, sir".

He replied, "That's also not legal". You've been leaving

a transmitter on the air with no programming being transmitted on the carrier being produced by the transmitter all night." (Remember, though there was automation back then, we didn't have an automation system. And computers were only in use by NASA at the time.)

I meekly answered, "Yes, those are the rules, sir. I know that. But, what can you do when the person in charge tells you all of this?"

He said, "Well, you can tell us. But, I can appreciate that might mean you'd lose a job." At that point, the conversation got friendlier if pointed. "You realize I could order you to shut this mess down right now, don't you?"

Crestfallen, I replied, "Yes, sir. I certainly do."

He paused, then said to me, "Well, I am personally convinced you had nothing to do with this. You were mislead by your owner. And seeing that you are so new to the business, I can understand your confusion with the conflicts you were seeing in the rules."

He went on, "Your new owner is a great operator. He has a long record of successful station operations and a stellar record of compliance with the rules. I am going to allow you to stay on the air until he arrives next Monday. And I am confident once he gets here that he'll get everything straightened out. Till then, go out to the transmitter site at least one or two times a day and take readings out there. Now, I am going to give you a citation for the rule violations I saw here. But, when it comes, give the paper to your new owner. He will send it to his attorneys who will reply in a letter as to what you told me, and the Commission will clear you of any responsibility. Now, get out there and take your readings... thank you, and I'll leave you now". With that, the inspector left.

I am now sitting in an office that now looks like a tornado hit it. Logs strewn everywhere. Paperwork on every desk. And I never felt so low in my life. I was practically in tears. How could this happen on my first job in the business? Damn it. I should have quit when everyone else did.

About that time, the man who owned the Cable TV company down the hall came into the office. His name was Fran Stratman. He had owned the local AM station for a number of years before he went into the Cable TV business he operated in an office in our building. Its TV studio was in the basement.

He asked what was wrong, and I leveled with him. Told it all and told him how badly I felt. Fran came over and put his hand on my shoulder. He said, "Kevin...you're forgetting something. The inspector is gone and your station is still on the air. He didn't shut you down. You can still operate and make money. You SAVED your station". Then, he said, "You don't realize this. But, you just gained five years of professional experience in one day. Great job!" With that, he turned and went back down the hall.

I've never forgotten Fran...or that conversation.

I admit it stuck in my craw for a while about why Ed would have gone through the battle he did to get the station, only to operate it in the manner he did. With all of the people he knew, you would have thought someone would have offered to loan him a transmitter control and some way to get the signal out and back from the transmitter. But, I realized he definitely had a lot of curve balls being thrown at him at that time. Today, of course, you can put your transmitter controls up on the internet and all it takes is a high speed connection which every station has today. You'd just need to buy the software.

The next Monday morning came and the new owner arrived and we were NOT on the air. I'm not an engineer and didn't hold a First Class License...and though I did what the inspector told me to do, the ancient transmitter we had kept drifting in power and kept going off frequency. (Apparently, it had developed a problem which I had no clue how to fix.)

The new owner's name was Richard Jones from Roanoke Rapids, North Carolina where he also owned stations. He and his family were moving to Wilmington as he had people in North Carolina capable of running the stations there. He asked why we weren't on the air and I explained to him as best as I could what was going on. (The transmitter, an ancient dog called, no kidding, a "Rust" was drifting in frequency and I didn't know how to fix it the night before. So, we gave a station ID, and I shut it down.) He nodded and said we'd go out to the transmitter in a little bit. Right now, he wanted a telephone to order new transmitter controls. I introduced him to his new office.

Ten minutes later with the transmitter control issue solved, he and I went out to the transmitter. Sure enough, there was a problem with it...and he called a contract engineer out to fix it. We were back on the air the next day and I had a new title...Program Director and Morning Show host. His family, who all had licenses could fill most of the other shifts for now, though we did eventually hire a young high school student to do 6 pm to Midnight...the "rock and roll shift" and would eventually hire others.

Dick began to teach me some of the finer points of radio programming. He would "pick" about 30 to 40 old 45's from our record library each day. Those were the day's "oldies" and those were the only ones we were to play that day, combined with the "current" and "recent" titles we had in another box. It was "pull from the front and put back in the back". For the oldies, it was "pull from the top and put back on the bottom". Simple enough.

We became an affiliate of the Mutual Radio Network (Dick would have preferred ABC, but WKFI had it at the time), and an equalized phone line was installed to run the network news and sports. We had a local guy, Mike Brooks, who was hired as News Director. And we had an UPI wire machine in the closet down the hall. He even bought a jingle package for the station. (Probably the dinkiest one I had ever heard, but, hey...they were still jingles!)

So now, how to fix the mess with no advertisers. Dick's answer was, frankly, brilliant and it's a lesson I have never forgotten.

Dick understood that there is no radio station anywhere that has "no listeners". No measurable ratings? That's possible. But, every radio station has at least a few stragglers out there who listen to it. The question is...how to get them to buy the products we're advertising...and how to grow that audience?

So his answer was: short, inexpensive commercials sold in dirt cheap package rates. Got $75 for a month? We'll give you 5, fifteen second ads every day 7 days a week! Got $150? We'll give you 10 thirty second spots a day 7 days a week. Got $300 a month? We'll give you 10 sixty second spots a day 7 days a week.

Considering WKFI was selling ads for 20 bucks each, OURS was an irresistible deal to advertisers. What Dick understood was: you have to get an advertiser to air enough spots per day to get his message out. Running enough spots per day (the "frequency" of the ads), regardless of their "rate", creates the "reach" the ads need to encourage a listener to go to the store and buy the product. And, the large number of ads in the packages quickly began to fill the spot clusters on the air and made us "sound" like a lot of businesses were advertising. That creates interest on the part of other advertisers about the station. ("What do my competitors know about them that I don't?")

It wasn't long till WDHK was quickly on the way to making money. Now, we hired a sales manager from nearby Washington Court House who hired a couple of other salespeople and we were rolling.

So, I was now living in a one-bedroom apartment about five minutes away from the radio station...and early one morning... the phone rang. I answered and it was my Dad.

"Son...it's 5:30 am...you've got to be on the air in 30 minutes!"

"Oh, God, Dad...I overslept. Thanks!", and I hung up.

I really didn't have time to get dressed, so I grabbed some clothes out of the closet, threw on a robe and shoes and headed to the car and to the station.

I got in the building at 5:45...just enough time to turn on the transmitter and let it settle down before applying "modulation" or audio. Those old transmitters needed a few minutes to run before you started gabbing on them.

We got on the air in time...but I was doing the first half hour sitting in the studio in my underwear with a robe over me. (Thank God they didn't have web-cams then!)

Mike Brooks, the morning news guy walked in about 6:15...looked in the studio window and fell on the floor, convulsing in laughter. I explained what happened and promised during his first newscast at 6:30 that I'd go in the bathroom and get dressed!

Now, it's worth mentioning that eventually, Dick did away with most of those cheap packages. WDHK eventually supplanted WKFI in audience and he could go sell spots the usual way, which REDUCED the total number of commercials heard per hour. This also helped listening. (Ahem...hey major broadcasters today! CUT YOUR DAMN SPOT LOADS! More on that later.)

One other thing happened, too. Dick bought WKFI from Gannett, which was now glad to sell it. So, in the end...FM triumphed over AM in Wilmington, Ohio, as it did everywhere eventually. In 1990, wanting to retire, Dick sold both stations for 3 million dollars. Not bad, considering he bought WDHK for $75,000 and assumption of debt.

Dick, as of the time I wrote this, was still around, though now in a care facility. I want him to know, I deeply respect what he did, learned a lot from him, and am very happy to have worked for him and made the acquaintance of he and his family.

    I continued to work for WDHK for about another year and a half. But, about three years in my first job was about as long as I thought I needed to be there. Of my friends from high school who were in the business, Tim Fox was already working at Q-102 in Cincinnati and then, went to Cleveland. Jeff Shade was working at WHIO-AM in Dayton as the producer of the morning show and a weekend jock. It was time for me to move on.

Chapter 7

Town To Town, Up And Down The Dial

From Wilmington, the long journey begins. I spend about 3 years as a weekend news reporter and anchor for WONE-AM and WTUE-FM in Dayton. Sure, it was a just a weekend and "fill-in" job, but the pay was $5 bucks an hour and I worked 20 hours a week. So, I actually made more money than Wilmington and could go back and live at home with my Dad...a good move since my Mom had passed away and Dad was having a hard time dealing with Mom's death. And, there were lots of times the full time news staffers went on vacation and I worked a full 40 hour week. My pay also increased to $5.50 an hour after the first year...and I had some benefits, too.

I loved working there, because I got to work with people I had listened to on the air there. Terry Wood was Operation's Manager for both stations. Terry recently was General Manager of a local group in Memphis, Tennessee, but I hear has now retired. I worked with morning man, David G. McFarland and we're still friends today. Dean Taylor did middays...we've been friends forever as did Lee Riley, another cool dude. Bobby Kraig was the night guy and I would work with him most often. He and his wife would invite me over for burgers on the grill. He eventually became a bigwig at Arista Records. I also got to work with the afternoon guy...who HAD been the original morning show host on WTUE in the early 70's when they were Top 40. Then, he was known as Greg Mason, but on WONE, he went back to using his real name on air.

Terry Dorsey was one of the funniest, most creative people I have ever worked with. And, if you've ever heard the "Hiney Wine" bit on your local station, you can thank Terry, because he created it at WONE.

The "Hiney Winery" was a fictitious business originally set in New Carlisle, Ohio, which, at the time, was a "dry" town...no liquor was sold there for a long time. The business was owned by the Hiney family which consisted of members like Seymore Hiney, Ophellia Hiney and lived by the slogan, "When life gets you down, grab a Hiney!" Terry would eventually syndicate the bit and made a bunch of money off of it, but not before leaving WONE and later, WING in Dayton and going to Dallas, Texas where he bounced back and forth between country stations and eventually ended back on KPLX-FM. He retired from KSCS-FM 20 years later and, sadly, died 30 days after that. I miss Terry a lot. He was a great guy and a wonderful talent.

On WTUE, (now an Album Rock station), I worked with morning show host Patty Spitler, a University of Dayton grad who eventually became a big time TV news anchor in Indianapolis before her retirement. I also worked with Alan Sells ("Big Al" of Texas radio fame), Alan "Mike" McConnell (now back doing mornings on WLW), and there was a weekend part time jock named Dan Pugh. You don't know him by that name, but if I said "Dan Patrick" to you...bet you know who I'm talking about. Especially if you listen to ESPN Sports radio. Lots of good radio people have come out of Dayton, Ohio. A guy named Chuck Browning was the PD (His real name is "James". He would, in later years, manage WHIO radio, and we are Facebook friends today).

This, to me, was a fun job. I did news, played around in the "old" WTUE control room, just off the elevator and the main lobby of the station. Played music trivia there one night with Terry Dorsey who, though he became a famous country DJ, loved 50's and 60's rock and roll. I worked there during the famous "Blizzard of 1978".

No one really thought it was going to be that bad of a storm...and I was off work the day it happened. I woke up about 2 pm and asked my father why he had let me sleep so late. His reply? "Go look out your bedroom window." YIKES! The snow was piled up so much against our front door that I had to dig us out. And then had to do it all over again the next day.

I mentioned Dean Taylor on WONE. His car had gotten stranded in Oakwood, a suburb about 5 miles out of downtown Dayton. He abandoned the car where it sat and walked the rest of the way to the station offices...and almost died of frostbite doing it. Everyone at work was very concerned about him when he arrived.

I had to go in early Saturday morning for a 6 AM to Noon shift. The roads were passable, but still not very good. (2 lanes open, the far left lane was still snowed under.) When I got into downtown, I saw that the entrance to the WONE/WTUE parking lot was blocked by a giant snow drift, no doubt caused by maintenance crews and their snow plows. What to do?

I did the only thing I could do. Turned 90 degrees and backed up clear across Third Street aimed at the drift. (Fortunately, there was no traffic in downtown Dayton at that hour of the morning.) I gunned the engine as hard as I could and plowed right through the drift, skidding sideways into the station parking lot. Well...at least I made it with no damage to the car.

The damage, though would be to me in the next few hours. Shortly after going on the air, I got a "tickle" in my throat. No big deal...we had a coffee machine for that. But, by 9 am...my voice was starting to leave my body...and by 10:30, I had a full blown case of laryngitis working on me...and no one to call to relieve me, because no one could get in at that time. I simply had to put up with it...and "croak" my way through the news. I was greatly relieved when fellow co-worker, Jeannie Lockhart, finally made it to the station at 1 pm from her home in Springfield (about 30 minutes away) and took over.

I went home...went to bed...and slept, literally, for about a day and half.

My boss was Kent Scott. He seemed very impressed in me...a young kid who came to him wanting a news job. I passed his pronunciation test and writing test and he hired me. I thought I may just have been on my way to a decent association with Group One Broadcasting owned by the Burk Family.

It was not to be. Group One, you see, also had a "Corporate Vice President of Programming". His name was Art Wander. And Art Wander didn't like me one bit. Now, I have never met the man, never had a conversation with him, never even written him. But, he judged me based on my "audition" tape, decided I wasn't any good and would NOT relent on that opinion. Not even after Kent worked with me on my delivery and knew I was showing big progress.

Kent was frustrated by Art's intractable attitude about me, and decided to do something about it. Next time he came to town, he sat Art down in his office and played him a recent tape of me, not telling him who it was. He only said, "Art, I've got a tape from a guy and wanted to play it for you and see what you thought about it."

Art listened to "my" tape, and replied, "That guy sounds pretty good. Why don't you that fire that idiot you have on weekends and hire this guy?"

Kent said, "Art, that IS the "idiot on the weekends"...he's made a big improvement in his on air delivery, don't you think?"

Most normal people would have agreed with that statement, but not Art. You see, Kent had succeeded in "putting one over" on Art, which pissed him off. He grunted, and left Kent's office, went back to Terry Wood and told him in no uncertain terms that, "As long as I am in my position in this company, that kid will NEVER go full time here. EVER!"

Eventually, Kent told me about all this...and said he wouldn't blame me if I moved on. Which, reluctantly, I soon did.

So, I auditioned for crosstown stations WAVI-AM and WDAO-FM which had an opening for a full time news anchor and street reporter. Don Mills was the News Director there. WAVI was a talk station. WDAO was the first FM radio station in America to air a format aimed at the urban, black community in Dayton. Don was a good boss, and we would work together again, decades later at WHIO. He was in TV at the time, I worked on the radio side.

WAVI/WDAO was a nice place to work, but the owner, H.K. "Bud" Crowl pinched pennies until they SCREAMED! They hired me at $165 dollars a week...I thought that was pretty good... until I got my first paycheck and discovered it was actually $125 a week...the rest was "overtime" for working a Saturday morning shift. Oh well. Still, it was a fun job...I did morning news on both stations followed by street reporting duties and, in doing so, met one of my boyhood idols, the late Astronaut and Senator John Glenn. (Who, later, on the recommendation of my friend Dusty Rhodes at WSAI in Cincinnati, got me hired to DJ the wedding of his Chief Administrative Aide in Columbus!) I covered car crashes, shootings, the Dayton City School's "busing" controversy...busing white students to predominantly black schools to achieve racial integration of schools.

I learned a lot of lessons about talk radio at WAVI that I've carried with me even today at WHIO. For starters, while most of the listeners are very fine people, there IS, however a segment of the audience that is more, well, passionate about the format than others. Passion to the point of radicalism. Passion that, frankly, makes me question their sanity at times.

But, talk radio WAS different back then. WAVI had a morning guy who was a Libertarian politically...a mid-day host who was Liberal in his beliefs, and various afternoon hosts who were Conservative in their beliefs. Made for some interesting conversations in the break room, let me tell you. The fans of the morning guy generally hated the equally the midday and afternoon hosts. The afternoon hosts sparred with the midday guy, ah politics. One of the WAVI "talkmasters" at the time was a 17 year old kid barely out of high school. You may know Mike Gallagher of Salem Radio Networks.

And, being the news guy…well, I can do nothing right in this type of situation. The Liberal listeners swear I'm a conservative. The Conservatives think I'm a Liberal. I'm actually an Independent who leans toward Libertarianism. I've voted for Republicans, Democrats, Independents and Libertarians. Guess that's why both sides hate me.

Of course, you couldn't do talk radio without a "delay" system because, of course, arguments on radio do go a bit overboard sometimes and those certain 4 letter words need to go. (All except for some of today's Hip Hop stations, of course.) Back then, stations had to go to great lengths to do it, because there was no such thing as a "digital" delay system then.

So, what the engineers came up with were two tape recorders mounted to a piece of plywood on the back wall of the studio. The left side machine recorded the programming…the right side machine played it back to the on air chain. But, reels of tape were not used. Instead, the engineers figured out how long of a "loop" of tape to make that would take 8 seconds to get from the "record" head of the left machine to the "playback" head on the right one and back around the two machines. And they made new tape loops every day. (The loop would literally wear out after about 8 or 9 hours of constant recording and playing on the air).

The "dump button" was actually a cartridge tape machine which sat within reach of the host's left hand. If a dirty word was said, you immediately hit the start button on the cart machine, which would play an instrumental version of the station's main jingle for 9 seconds to cover the word and prevent it from airing. During that time, you hung up on the caller, and took another call. When the 9 seconds was over, the recording rejoined with the new call and the "crisis" was averted. A "call screener" answered the phone and wrote down the caller's name, the line they were on and what they wanted to talk about and took it into the host. (Today, they do THAT all by computer).

I actually had to do a talk show there once...because the morning guy came in one morning with laryngitis. It was interesting. Because I had to start with enough "prep" material to do about 30 minutes without any callers. WAVI, you see was a "daytimer", which came on the air at Sunrise, and went away at Sunset. So, when you kicked the transmitter on and played the sign on, chances were good there was no one listening. The listeners would come to the party sometime in the first 30 minutes. And, if you had a caller 10 or 15 minutes in, you were doing good.

WDAO-FM, though, was a different station entirely. It was America's first FM station aimed at a minority audience. Till it came on the air in 1964, most all "black" radio stations were on AM... and most were high on the dial on what are called "graveyard" frequencies with limited signals. "Big 'DAO" on the other hand, was exactly what it said it was...a stereo FM with a 50,000 watt signal that blasted a signal from Dayton almost to Columbus... it rated in the Cincinnati market (much to the consternation of WCIN-AM), and even showed from time to time in the Columbus ratings, too (which WVKO-AM didn't like, either). In Dayton, WDAO was in double digit ratings by 1969, and sometimes, even beat WHIO-FM for the top spot...which was NOT easy to do back then.

It was an unusual situation in 1969. There, the FM made more money than the AM station. And, in the early 70's, station owners looked at WDAO's success and then looked at their FM stations and began to wonder if they shouldn't be counter programming the AM stations on FM. Some did, including Group One Broadcasting, who made WONE-FM (now WTUE-FM) a rock and roll station in 1970, adopting the new call letters in 1971. In other markets, it was the mid to late 1970's before this happened.

Once again, Dayton, Ohio radio was leading the way.

But, about 8 or 9 months later, our Chief Engineer turned me on to a potential job offer. WCIN-AM in Cincinnati was looking for a News Director. I'd run a 3 man staff (one of whom was part time) and, in doing so, would become, according to the organization then known as the Radio-Television News Director's Association as the youngest (at 23) large market News Director in American radio.

I covered auto crashes, plane crashes, local and state politicos, Congressmen, Senators and even Presidents. Jimmy Carter came to Dayton for a town hall, and I decided to cover it for us. I stood outside the Convention Center and walked inside behind the President and his Secret Service detail (as close as they would let us get behind the President, of course).

All was well…until about 6 months later.

I come home from work, flip on the CBS Evening News and hear veteran anchor Walter Cronkite open his newscast saying this:

"CBS News has learned President Reagan's assailant, John Hinckley, Jr. was apparently not just stalking him…but other leaders as well. This is a tape from former President Jimmy Carter's town hall in Dayton, Ohio…"

OK, now you've got my attention, Walter.

I watched the tape, saw the President get out of the limo… the Secret Service detail gathered around him and saw the gaggle of reporters (including me) walking behind them. Then, Mr. Cronkite delivered the shocking news…

"As the former President and his Secret Service agents walked toward the hall, our cameras caught a glimpse of President Reagan's future assailant off to the right near the front of the crowd."

Yes, I walked right past John Hinckley, Jr…and didn't know it. He had, apparently also done that the day before at Mr. Carter's appearance in Nashville. Thank God he wasn't writing letters to Jody Foster that day.

It was at WCIN that I met other movers and shakers. Senator Ted Kennedy, was at a Press Conference and I sat and saw then-Presidential candidate, Ronald Reagan at a separate press event. And, I also met…and spoke twice with…a University Of Cincinnati engineering professor by the name of Neil Armstrong.

Yes…THAT Neil Armstrong. The first human being to walk on the Moon.

I had found out about it from a news release mailed to me. It said that Neil Armstrong, the first man to walk the surface of the moon, would be appearing on a certain date at the Cincinnati Auto Inspection facility to urge fellow Cincinnatians to get their cars inspected.

Kind of a dumb appearance for Neil, I guess, but he DID have an endorsement deal with Chrysler Corporation at the time, and I have to assume it was Lee Iacocca who wanted him to do it. Yeah, it wasn't the way I ever thought I would meet him, but it was a way to do it…so I put it on my calendar.

I get to the Auto Inspection Facility on the appointed day and time and, sure enough, a brand new beige Chrysler Cordoba (you know, the one with the "rich, Corinthian leather") pulls up. A man gets out of the car and when he turned around, I could have recognized him from a mile away. ("My God! That IS Neil Armstrong!", I was thinking.)

Neil walks over to us, says with a grin, "Hi, I'm Neil. Who are you?"

Now, remember at that time Neil Armstrong was rarely seen in Cincinnati. He didn't speak to media at the college…he wanted to be left alone so he could teach engineering properly to his students, and I had heard he was a great teacher. That had sparked suggestions that he was a "hermit" who stayed to himself and never went out.

That was so far from the truth...and I can attest to it.

So, I was expecting a gaggle of media there. Nope. The only reporters there included a cameraman from WKRC-TV, Channel 12, a reporter from the Cincinnati Enquirer and...little ole' me.

Neil shook our hands and we did the obligatory interview and I was completely expecting that, when the interview was done, he would turn on his heels, say thank you and take off.

Nope. You see, Neil's car wasn't done being inspected yet. So, he just stood around and started shooting the breeze with us. We asked him a little bit about the Moon (Of course! Wouldn't you?), and he again said it was "the greatest experience of my life". He called it "a tougher landing than I expected". (If you'll recall, he had to take over the controls of the Eagle when he was coming in because the auto-targeting was taking him into a crater field.) But, he did remark of the "beauty" (his words) of the surface of the Moon.

I left that event thinking to myself, "My God! What a thing to be able to tell my grandchildren!" Of course, I never had grandkids because I've never been married to have kids, but my nephew has sure heard the story over and over and over!

The next time I had any chance to speak with Neil was at the tenth anniversary of the Apollo 11 flight...at the University of Cincinnati. I got the last question.

"Neil", I asked, "If you had the chance to do it all over again, would you?"

Neil flashed a grin at me and replied, "Sure. When do we

leave"?

THAT, my friend, was the real Neil Armstrong. The day he died, I was on the air and I was devastated by the news. And to learn later that it may have even been a case of malpractice...still shocks me today.

I am so grateful that I had the opportunity to meet him.

I also had my first brush with health problems while on that job.

You see, I was, at the time doing morning drive newscast anchoring, which required me to be up in the morning at 3:30 am, drive 40 miles from my home to Cincinnati and be in the office by 4:45 am in order to be on the air with news by 6 am.

Usually, because I was, more or less, "the news department" at WCIN (for reasons you'll read about in a minute), I spent all day covering news conferences, city council meetings (and, at that time, Cincinnati City Council was the biggest collection or strange people I have ever met in my life. Good people, but the collection was odd). I usually headed for home about 4 or 5 pm, got home at 6 and was in bed by 9.

On top of that, to make a little "extra" money, one or two nights a week, and most often on the weekends I spun records in a disco near my home...Mother Rucker's Speakeasy Disco was the name and during the disco craze of the late 70's, it drew good crowds for a while and I made $25 dollars for being a disco jock from 9 pm to 2 am.

Yes, I was burning the candle at both ends. But, I was 23 and you can do that at that point in your life. But, it did catch up with me.

I was headed home one evening after a very long day at work...I went into a grocery store near my home to grab something to fix for dinner (most likely a box of Kraft Macaroni and Cheese

– THE evening meal of starving radio people). I didn't get far into the store when I apparently collapsed and was told later that I had a seizure. Medics and police were called...I did come to and a police officer was kind enough to drive me home, since I lived just around the block from the store.

Now, I have no recollection of any of this. But, here's where the story gets funnier.

At the time, I lived in a 3 bedroom apartment with 2 of my high school buddies. One of whom came home about an hour after the police officer got me back to the apartment. He found me sitting on the couch, intently "watching a show on TV". There's quotes around that because...well...the television wasn't turned on. I was sitting there in front of a blank screen telling my roommate how great the show was.

My buddy, Dave, quickly noticing this was not a normal thing for me, became concerned and called my Dad who lived up the street in the same apartment complex with his recently "new" bride. (My mother had passed away a few years earlier right after my graduation from high school.) The conversation, I'm told went something like, "Al, you'd better come over here quickly. I think your son has just lost his mind!"

Dad came over and before long, he too was convinced something was definitely wrong with me. So, they put me in a car and drove me to Miami Valley Hospital in Dayton.

You see, I had recently had a bout with Mononucleosis. I went to the doctor and was off work for about 4 days taking my medication and getting my lung's scanned. On the fifth day, a Friday, the doctor, not knowing the crazy hours I was keeping, cleared me to go back to work. Had he asked about my hours, he probably would not have allowed me to go back for about another week.

So, we get to the hospital and now, I decide, I am tired.

(Well, sure. Remember, I got up at 3:30 that morning and it was probably 9 pm or so). So I want to go to bed. And I made the point of, pointedly and using some choice 4 letter words, informing all around me about that. Admitting hurried up and took me upstairs so I could go to sleep.

The next morning, I awaken to find a nurse standing next to the bed I was in. "Mr. Fodor, do you know where you are?", I was asked. I looked around and said, "Well, it looks like I'm at Miami Valley Hospital." The nurse said, "Yes. That's right. Do you know how you got here?" My reply? "Uh, no. Would you like to tell me, please?"

About that time, my Doctor came in and told me about it all. He kept me in the hospital for a couple of days and then, sent me back home with strict instructions to take the rest of the week off and rest.

They never were able to completely explain what happened. They just assumed that I had worn myself out. And, when I walked into the grocery store, my body temperature apparently "flashed" way high and, in effect, temporarily shorted out my brain. A night's rest and I was OK. But, I apparently was exhausted. So, a few more days off the job and I was able to go back for good. Fortunately, I did have health insurance with that gig and it paid for almost everything.

But, back to the office and my job. Unfortunately, WCIN's owner was almost as cheap as WAVI's. So tight with a buck was he that I was only allowed 2 other news people…and one of them was lazier than hell. He hid behind the union rules to keep him from having to go cover news stories…refused to use his car to go cover stories (despite a very liberal policy of gas mileage reimbursement from the company), and looked at me and said that "only God could tell him what news to cover" (citing the union rule that said I couldn't discriminate against his religion).

We discussed this with the man behind closed doors in

the General Manager's office and he was just as adamant and stubborn as he ever was. When he left, the GM told me, "Don't worry...We'll get rid of him. But, we'll have to build a case against him for about 6 months so we can get the union on board with us."

So, for 6 long, grueling months, I was basically covering ALL of the news for the station. I was morning anchor, street reporter, and occasionally had to help the Chief Engineer, Kurt Farmer rebuild my newsroom from Army Surplus equipment...all the owner would let him buy. We also installed a telephone line into the P.A. system in Cincinnati City Hall's Council Chamber, so I wouldn't have to physically be at every meeting, I could just record it from the newsroom.

We did, eventually, fire that news reporter...cost us literally a year's salary to get rid of him. He immediately went to the union complaining I had "discriminated against him because of his race". But, once we gave AFTRA all the documentation, they sided with me.

One day, the Program Director popped his head into the newsroom and said, "Hey, Kevin...thought you'd like to meet somebody. Say hello to Michael Jackson!"

Oh, my God! In walked this very shy, unassuming young man who shook my hand and said hello! We chatted briefly for a couple of minutes and I told him how much I liked and admired his music. This was 1979...when "Rock With You" was topping charts. Who knew that just 3 or 4 years later, he was going to set the music business on its ears with "Thriller"?

I never believed the accusations made against him later, and still don't. Having met Michael, it is impossible for me to fathom him ever, EVER harming a child. He respected everyone, and I truly believe for him, it was all about performing and the music. His death was a total shock to me, and a real tragedy for music fans everywhere.

There's a lot of talk in radio today about something called "collaboration". This is where stations share staff and content across their stations and platforms. It can be very successful. And, out of sheer necessity, I kind of "pioneered" the idea.

If you know anything about the Cincinnati Radio Market, then you'd know it is...and always has been...very competitive. WCIN had challenges, mainly because of a horrifically bad nighttime signal (we were a full 5,000 watts daytime, but had to cut back to only 500 at night and on an extremely directional nighttime pattern that only barely covered what the ratings people call the "High Density Black Area" (consider that the area of town where the audience was mostly minority listeners). And, I had a terribly small staff that just wasn't going to get bigger. The owner wouldn't give it to us.

Fortunately, for us...there was another station in town that also had the same issue. It was the BIG country FM in the market, WUBE-FM. I remember being at a luncheon with their then-News Director, Doug Anthony. Both of us were complaining about the situation among ourselves. Then, Doug had an idea... each of us gets on the phone every morning and runs down the major stories for the day. He sends his reporters on some stories, I go do others. Now, we WERE both union shops, so we couldn't trade voice reports from our reporters (in my case...ME). BUT, neither stations AFTRA contract forbid the trading of "actualities" (voices of newsmakers). We could still trade actualities over the phone to each other and "sound" as though we had a reporter there.

Doug spoke with his General Manager...as did I. It was legal. And, it would benefit both stations. So, my GM said OK, and so did Doug's. Our news staffs roughly doubled in size overnight! And our local "content" increased greatly. And, no one would really know what was going on. You see, not a lot of black listeners in those days listened to country music stations. And, not a lot of country music listeners crossed over to listen to the local R & B station.

What the big stations in town who had large news departments, (stations like WLW or WKRC or WSAI), couldn't figure out...is how WUBE and WCIN were getting actuality material from news conferences and on stories where we obviously weren't there! What they didn't know...could...and did...hurt them a bit. But, the audiences of WUBE and WCIN DID benefit from the two stations working together!

The bosses loved the arrangement. The owner of WCIN didn't. But, he was from out of town. He called me, "unethical". I called him "cheap". Today, I would have won the argument about collaboration hands down.

WCIN got a new Program Director around that time. Though he and I clashed initially, we both figured out we were trying to get the station to the same place...so we formed an alliance...and he actually got me a new part time news person which helped me...I no longer had to go out on EVERY story. The part timer would go out for a couple of hours a day. I hired a young black teen straight out of high school whose name was Ken Kilgore for that slot. He had a good broadcast voice given how young he was at the time. (He sounded much more adult than I did...even then!), AND...he could write, had a great command of English and Speech and picked up on the workings of radio news very quickly.

Now, news wasn't what he really wanted to do. He really wanted to be a DJ. But, he was willing to DO news to get some experience. I was glad to have him. My other full time slot was filled by a young black lady from Toledo. Her name was Jill Frost. Now, SHE WAS a journalist. Very good writer, very savvy at news. She replaced me when I left...and won a TON of awards for WCIN's news operation. I couldn't have been more proud of her.

And, Ken Kilgore? He finally got his shot at being a DJ when WCIN acquired an FM signal in nearby Hamilton, Ohio north of Cincinnati. It became known as WBLZ-FM at 103.5. Ken became an afternoon drive DJ there...and about 2 or 3 years later left and went to a radio station in Chicago! Good for him! I've not spoken to him since, but if he reads this, Ken...way to go! You did it!

So, now we had a new Program Director. His charge...to get the ratings up. And he had an idea. Combine the popular R & B songs of the day with a few of the more popular pop and rock songs of the time. There were some great ones that DID fit the format. WDAO in Dayton was playing Grand Funk's "Some Kind Of Wonderful", and the Average White Band...they even played the Bee Gees from "Saturday Night Fever". So, why couldn't WCIN play "What A Food Believes" by the Doobie Brothers?

Great idea. The PD's reasoning was, "Why should I give my audience away to WKRC or WLW?", (Which is what was happening. Black listeners would go THERE to hear those particular songs, then switch back to WCIN for the R & B.) Couldn't an R & B station have 3 or 4 crossover tunes on their chart?

It made sense to everyone, except the black "tip sheets", which went to R & B radio programmers. To the tip sheets, to play a song by a white group was unthinkable! Why, that playlist slot could go to a struggling black performer! Our PD, who was black, by the way, just was making a business decision. He wanted ratings.

Well, he got them. The small influx of white teens who now came to WCIN for the combination of music, and the black adults who now trusted the station because it had good, credible news coverage pushed the ratings to a 5.6 (about 2 or 3 points higher than they ever were in the past). So, now the struggling AM had about half the ratings of WLW. What do you think that meant to the station's advertising rates? Now, add the ratings of FM sister, WBLZ. We were now a force to be reckoned with. Well, for a while, anyway.

After a while, though, I was gone, and the PD went to Atlanta where he did what he had done at WCIN and made WVEE-FM in Hot Lanta a monster!

I may have worked my butt off at WCIN. But it was a great experience, personally. I learned about a different culture of people who welcomed me and respected me as a broadcaster... as I did them. I was glad to have been given that opportunity.

So, why did I leave?

Fun times, indeed, but radio was changing. There was something called "deregulation" coming in the form of an FCC order called "Docket 80/90". The original plan I agreed with, which was to reduce the ridiculous amount of paperwork involved with radio station license applications. But, what also passed shortly later was a ruling that said radio stations no longer had to "pledge" a certain percentage of their weekly airtime to news and public affairs.

For me, that was a problem. If stations no longer needed to do that, they could get rid of their news departments entirely. Some music station scrapped all news. Others just kept one person to rip and read from a wire service, with local news re-written from the local newspaper. And it was another nail in the coffin of AM Radio as stations which once proudly sported 5 man, 10 man and even in one case, a 20 person news department (CKLW/Detroit), slowly got rid of everyone.

What was wrong with all of this is: people who listened to AM radio expected to also get news and traffic and sports and weather and information. Abandon that and all you had left to compete with was music. And the music sounded better on FM. So, most AM stations started dropping like flies then, leaving only one or two in the market to survive. And slowly, even they started seeing their ratings drop. That left one AM station standing with "acceptable" numbers. Now today, most AM stations can't get a 2 share of the market. Sure, WLW is #2 in Cincinnati, and #1 when the Reds are hot. But, for how long? It seems like their numbers are slowly eroding and I know their audience is getting older and older by the minute. It's only a matter of time.

By 1982, WABC-AM, the preeminent Top 40 radio station along the eastern seaboard fell to talk radio. In 1986, 93/KHJ-AM, "Boss Radio" in L.A. fell. In 1989, Musicradio 89, WLS-AM went talk.

For me, it was time to go back to being a DJ. And so, I did. But on FM.

First to Xenia, Ohio to be a country DJ for about 5 years on WBZI-FM. It was an independently owned AM/FM station. The AM was a daytimer kept in the basement of the home which was home base for the stations. It ran hillbilly gospel music. The FM was upstairs.

Sure, the pay was lousy and there were no benefits, but it was, at the time, the only FM country station in the Dayton market, so it had that going for it.

Unfortunately, the General Manager, Dick Moran, seemed to want to do everything he could to keep from spending money. He would not spend a dime to promote his station. (He did get some free "trade out" television ads at 2 in the morning, but that was it.) His Sales Manager, Dave Richley was a nice enough guy, but seemed accepted to the fact that Dick wasn't going to spend money and just tried to make the best of it.

We had the support of the record companies, so we could get some albums to give away. Every once in a while, we could get some concert tickets, too, but that was about it.

Despite the frustration of working in this atmosphere, we did have fun.

I did bar shows, and the occasional concert. And despite Dick, I got the station some national publicity a couple of times.

First, when I, on my own dime, of course, got on the Agenda Committee of the annual Country Radio Seminar in Nashville and made a couple of annual trips to Music City to work with the Committee to plan the event, and get guests to speak for it. I had been asked to do this by Lon Helton, now a long time syndicated country show host who, at the time, was Program Director for KHJ in Los Angeles, which had now "gone country". I am still Facebook friends with Lon today.

I got invited to be on a panel one year on the topic of "the future of country music". The reason? WBZI aimed at a younger audience than most country stations did. Why? There were more young people on FM at the time.

My point on the panel was that I thought the attempts to lean country music to a younger audience was a good thing for it. At the time, new groups were exploding as a new movement called "Urban Country" was taking over Nashville. There was a new group WBZI had promoted in Dayton called Alabama whose early hits were rocketing up the chart. Hank Williams, Junior was hitting it big on discs and in concerts, was raising hell by adding ZZ Top music and later A/C-D/C music to his concerts. Young country listeners were eating it up, even if their parents hated it and wanted more Johnny Cash and Elvis.

There was another new singer, too from Texas…George Strait. I emceed a show of his in a bar in Middletown, Ohio in 1981…on the heels of a new song he had released called "Unwound". He had the tightest band I have ever heard in Ace In The Hole, and I had no doubt he was going to be superstar. Today, he IS country music.

I told the panel that "country music MUST do everything it can to attract a younger audience. They ARE the future of the business, and if we don't do this, there's a good chance in 10 or 15 years, we're going to be seeing declining record sales and labels closing their doors. And…stations changing format."

That was in 1982 or 1983…it happened in 1988. One year later, guess what? New artists came along. Clint Black, Alan Jackson and some guy from Oklahoma named Garth Brooks. I knew something was up with him when I was doing a dance at a middle school near Dayton and the kids wanted to hear this song called, "Friends In Low Places". I played it with a bit of suspicion…and wound up having to play it 3 times more that night.

For decades now, Country Music has been the top radio format in America. I'd like to think I had something to do with it. But, I'll be happy enough knowing that some people were actually thinking the way I did and programmed their stations accordingly.

We really weren't a "news station", but there were times we had to step in and do news, which at times satiated my desire to report on big events.

It was early in Ronald Reagan's presidency and one afternoon, Dave Richley, the Sales Manager, came running up the stairs with a piece of teletype paper in his hand. It said "Shots have been fired by a lone gunman at President Reagan as he was leaving a Washington D.C. hotel after giving a speech before a trade union group. The President was reportedly not hit by the gunfire and is on his way back to the White House".

Of course, that's wasn't true as we all now know. And it wasn't more than a few minutes later the whole story began to change…as word came the Presidential limo had changed course and was now at George Washington Hospital. We were told the President had walked under his own power into the hospital, but collapsed shortly inside it and was carried into an exam room by his Secret Service detail.

I was reporting on all of this in between songs as we could get more information by the teletype, and now by a small television we had brought up and turned on in the main office off the studio. I believe we were watching ABC's coverage.

Then, came word that, in fact, the President HAD been shot, had a bullet in his chest and would soon be taken to surgery.

The side story, of course was that of Presidential Press Secretary James Brady, who was hit in the head by a bullet. He would survive the act, but was severely brain damaged in the attack and would be severely disabled for the rest of his life.

It also didn't help the media's case when several outlets erroneously reported that Brady had died. They had to eat crow big time on that...(you don't report on anything without two sources of confirmation...and I just think they "ran" with the story to be first to report it...of which our media is often guilty).

So, here I was playing music and giving bulletins as word came of the identity of the President's alleged assailant. A young man named John Hinckley, Jr. who was from the state of Colorado.

Of course, I got that information right as the music rotation had me playing an "oldie"...John Denver's, "Rocky Mountain High"...a beautiful song about the state of Colorado. The phones lit up with listeners accusing me of "wishing for President's death" by playing that song. Hell, I didn't know of Hinckley or where he was from. John Denver was just up next in the music rotation and playing when I GOT the information. Needless to say, we dropped that song for a while.

It was a long time before we learned just how close President Reagan came to death. He almost didn't make it, because the bullet he took was in a place that was hard to find. It could have resulted in an embolism and instant death. But, it didn't. And at least some in the world breathed a sigh of relief as he returned to the White House and, over the next few weeks, resumed the duties of his office.

WBZI was also where I, by accident, learned about "payola".

I was doing a remote from a bar in Franklin, Ohio during

which time, a man came up to me, said his daughter was putting her first country song out and asked if he could give me a couple of copies to listen to for possible airplay. I said, sure. Never saw the man again.

When the remote ended and I got ready to leave, the bartender handed me an envelope left by the guy. I felt 45's in it and assumed it was the record he wanted us to listen to. I took the envelope from the bartender, left, got in my car and went home.

I didn't open it until I got to work the next day. Opened the envelope and dumped the contents. Unfortunately with the 2 copies of the 45…also dropped out three one hundred dollar bills. Oh…gee. I knew instantly why they were there.

Scared to death, I went straight to the Dick Moran, gave him the records, the cash, the package…everything. Told him I didn't intentionally take the "payola" and asked him what I should do…

Dick was very nice about this. He told me, "Kevin, I know you weren't trying to take this…You're too straight up to do it. So, here's what I want you to do. Take the records and the cash, seal them in an envelope and send them back to the guy certified mail and ask for a return receipt. You'll never get one, of course… but you will get the card back as proof that the postal service attempted to return it. That keeps you in the clear with the law." I told Dick I would do it that on my lunch hour.

As I got up to leave, Dick asked me to shut the office door and sit down for a minute or two longer. I did and he lowered his voice and said, "Kevin…let me give you a little fatherly advice. Should the time ever come that you decide you want to sell out"… he paused, and then, pointedly said, "FOR GOD'S SAKE, DO IT FOR MORE THAN THREE HUNDRED DOLLARS!!!" I laughed, saluted and told him, "Yes, sir" and left.

Not long afterwards, we did a remote broadcast that was more fun than I had ever had. One of our salespeople, Jack Rutledge, had heard where WLW/Cincinnati had broadcast play by play of the then World Wrestling Federation matches, and he thought that might be something good for us to do.

So, he calls Titan Sports in Connecticut and gets Vince McMahon on the phone. Sure enough, Vince gave us permission. Then, he called several clients and got commitments in minutes for $3500 in advertising for the 90 minute broadcast. We took the plan to the boss.

Dick Moran said, "There is no way in HELL we are going to broadcast professional wrestling matches on this radio station." That's when Jack showed him the signed contracts of the advertisers. (You see, the station had NEVER made $3500 hundred dollars in 90 minutes ever in its history.) Dick slowly looked up and told us all, "Well...I suppose we will broadcast professional wrestling on this station!"

Next thing I know, we're at Hara Arena in Dayton figuring out how to make the broadcast link between Dayton and Xenia happen. It was a "double hop" technique. A Very High Frequency Transmitter with an antenna strapped to a small microphone stand that sent the signal up to an apartment on the top of the arena's roof occupied by the maintenance man and his family. We placed an Ultra High Frequency Transmitter near the window in the kitchen and ran the antenna cable out onto the roof, from where we walked out on the roof and aimed the antenna on a stand toward Xenia. It worked.

So, that night, my old high school friend, Rob Ellis and I are at ringside live calling the matches. I still don't know what I said to tick off Brad "The Hitman" Hart...but he got in my face big time. He was in a match with Kamala, the Ugandan Headhunter. After body slamming the Hitman, Kamala comes out of the ring and runs to the broadcast table, where he grabbed the chair Rob was sitting in and yanked in out from under him, dumping him on the floor in a heap...and running back into the ring with Rob's chair to smash over Hitman's back. The two of us were convulsing in laughter on the air.

And, it was while I was at WBZI that I got some national attention for a song parody.

You remember when Ronald Reagan dared Congress not to mess with his idea for tax cuts by "borrowing" Clint Eastwood's line from the movie "Dirty Harry". You know, "Go ahead...make my day!" ?

Warner Brothers Records had released a novelty song about that movie, and we were playing on the air at that time. Then, it hit me...rewrite the song and use President Reagan's "Make My Day" where Clint Eastwood said it.

I did just that. Put it all together and planned to air it the next day. Out of courtesy, I called my record rep at Warner Brothers and played it for him. He listened to it and said, "That's good... have you considered calling the White House and playing it for them?" I told him I hadn't. He said, "You should". So, I did.

I dialed 202-456-1414 and asked for the press office. They answered the phone. I told them who I was, what I had done and wanted to play the song for them and they said, "Sure...play it for us". I did and the lady said, "Hold on. I want to get somebody on the line". Apparently that "someone" was President Reagan's Press Secretary. He listened and said, "Wow. That's neat. Can you send us a copy?". "Uh, sure", said I.

So, back to Dick. I said, "Dick, I need to overnight something". Dick said, "My God! Do you know what that will cost? Just where does this package need to go?" I said, "Would you believe...the White House?" I explained what was up and not only did he give me permission to overnight the package, he started calling the TV stations.

Next thing I know, I'm on the evening news and actually did a brief, lip-synched video of the song. It made all of the local TV stations. I started getting phone calls from stations across the country asking for a copy of it, which I sent out.

At the time, my high school buddy, Tim Fox, was the Program Director at WKTI-FM in Milwaukee, Wisconsin. He was walking into the station listening to it on the overhead speakers when he heard a voice...and realized it was ME. And I was singing a song on HIS radio station. Tim ran into the WKTI control room saying, "Hey! I KNOW that guy. I went to school with him. What's he done?" His morning show explained it. Next thing I know, Tim's calling me. The station was getting multiple phone calls from listeners wanting to hear my song. So, for a couple of weeks, Tim added me to his station's playlist.

I wish I could say it made #1, but, like all novelty songs, it died after a couple of weeks. But, hey...I got a song on a chart once!

But, WBZI, though was not all roses to work for. As I said, I was not making much money (about $200 a week) and was having some personal issues with a family member with a medical condition who was my roommate for a while. I needed a break. My friend, Tim, found it for me. A station in nearby Richmond, Indiana (WQLK-FM) needed a night DJ...the station was owned by a Tennessee company called Brewer Broadcasting, said they were a good company and called them personally to recommend me. I contacted the station and was hired on the spot.

I began working there as the 7 pm to midnight jock and later was promoted to Assistant Program Director, Music Director and did afternoon drive.

We had a consultant at the time whose name is Bill Hennes. Bill, it turns out, was the Program Director about ten years prior at CKLW in Detroit. A good guy, and a great jock (he was known on as "Wild Willie" and, so I hear, had a reputation of being just that off the air.) though, like all such consultants he was human and wasn't perfect on his music picks. (I remember him pushing us hard to add Linda Ronstadt's version of "When You Wish Upon A Star", you know, the Disney song…and it just didn't fit us. But, that's OK. You see, consultants are there to consult. For the most part, they aren't there to "run" the station as a "Super PD".) So, our relationship with Bill was always good. I recently reconnected with Bill on Facebook. (I only wish I could have worked for him at CK). Bill, is also the man who hired Gary Burbank (then PD at WNOE in New Orleans) to be CK's "Morning Mouth".

Our Program Director, Dan Osborne, known on air as "The Captain", did mornings and always looked for those stunts and games that would put us on the map and get attention with the listeners. One such stunt was a hoot and it got us national attention.

Remember, this was around the time of "We Are The World" and the earliest of "Farm Aid" concerts which were held then in Indiana. John Mellencamp was exploding on the music scene…and he was from Seymour which was not a long drive from Richmond.

So one day, Dan sees this article in the Richmond Paladium-Item (the local newspaper) that said the schools in Mobile, Alabama were so broke financially that they couldn't afford toilet paper and were urging parents to send a package to school for their youngsters to use when nature called.

BINGO! Dan comes up with idea that we would collect packages of T.P. from our listeners. We'd keep it all in our conference room and, when the promotion ended, he arranged for a local industrial firm to lend us their private plane and pilot for a day and, then I would fly to Mobile on the plant to "deliver" the Charmin, so to speak (while not "squeezing it", of course).

The name of the promotion? "Roll-Aid". (The pun was intended.) Our theme song for the promotion was the 60's instrumental hit, "Wipe Out". (Another horrible pun.) And it wasn't long before the K-96 FM conference room was loaded to the gills with toilet paper!

So, on the appointed day, I met up with the pilot at the 6 seat single engine plane. We loaded the back of the plane almost to the point of no return with toilet paper and off we flew to Mobile. I flew in the right seat (I HAD done a little bit of flight training as I said earlier and had soloed in single engine planes, so I could act as a co-pilot and was capable of landing such a plane with a little help from flight controllers if I needed to.)

Of course, a fatalistic thought came into my mind. "If this plane were to happen to go down, what would the people who try to rescue us think surrounded by God knows how much toilet paper?"

We landed the plane at the airport in Mobile and there were three local television crews there to see us arrive. It was big news there. I was interviewed for the local TV news shows and the next day, I did the morning show on an FM station there where we formally presented the paper gift to the school system. Part of the show was carried on K-96 as well. The station, in return took us out to dinner, put us up in a motel and sent us back with some great seafood, which was happily accepted by the station.

Remember that episode of "WKRP in Cincinnati" where Dr. Johnny Fever gets drunk on the air to (supposedly) urge people not to drink and drive ahead of New Year's Eve? He wasn't the only to do it, and with pretty similar results.

Dan gets this idea in his head for us to do it (us meaning "me") on the air one afternoon about two days before a giant New Year's Eve party we were going to have with about 12-hundred people at the Kuhlman Center in town. The station asked me for my drink, and I picked Jack Daniels. They got a fifth of it…and my job, assuming my liver was up to the task…was to drink it all in in five hours. We'd have an Indiana State Police Officer in studio with the breathalyzer, I had friend in studio to drive me home, and by the time I got off the air, I was supposed to be snockered.

At first, we thought, I could drink a shot every 20 minutes and that would do the trick. Uh, no. I guess I could hold my liquor better than that, especially because I did go to lunch that day and was drinking on a full stomach. By 4 pm, I was only registering a 0.2 on the machine.

Dan comes in the studio with a stern look and says to me, "Look we need you to get drunk in order to make the point to our audience. So, DRINK, DAMMIT!" OK, boss!

So, now I'm pounding shots of Jack Daniels on the air... and by about 4:45, it was becoming obvious that the booze was beginning to have an effect. By 6 pm, it was obvious to anyone listening, and to me, that was pickled beyond belief. That last hour must have sounded hilarious. I do remember some kid calling me on the request lines asking if I was drunk. I replied, (slurring my words), "Yeah, I think I am". I don't remember my last breathalyzer reading, but judging from my speech, I'd have been in handcuffs for sure. I was told it sounded pretty funny. I don't know if it was or not, because, well...I only remember parts of it today. And, that last hour is pretty fuzzy.

After I departed the studio, Dan wanted to have a little fun at my expense and called a 7 pm staff meeting in the conference room. I suspect he wanted to let the alcohol settle a little bit as we discussed the big party 2 nights later. After that, I was driven over to the party site to "look it over" and make sure the staging was what I needed it to be. This led to a funny exchange the next day between our Sales Manager and the client.

The station did have a heart and let me sleep in and I wasn't expected to be at work until my show at 2 pm, so I was able to sleep until around 10:30 that morning. I felt OK and wasn't TOO hung over. (And no, I never "got sick"...not even once.)

The Sales Manager came into the studio and told me that the client had called with some big concern in his voice. He said the client told him, "Everything's all set out here, but I do have a concern. Jason (my air name) was out here last night and, well, I don't know how to say it to you. But, Jason was DRUNK!" The Sales Manager told the client, "That's ok, he was supposed to be drunk" and explained what was going on. The client had a good laugh about it and the next night, we had a huge party, I spun the tunes and everyone had a great time.

And no, outside of one glass of champagne at midnight, I did not get drunk. Well, not until we got back to the hotel after the party, anyway.

Richmond, Indiana and K-96 was a great time. I dealt with record reps, made connections, helped put together the station playlist (which I "counted down" every Saturday morning). I not only got my head cleared from the bad experience at WBZI.

It was while I was in Richmond that I would meet my best friend. And be adopted by a family that is still my "extended family" today.

I had casually known a man by the name of Don Eggenschwiller. He lived where I lived in New Carlisle, Ohio and I met him at a remote broadcast there. Told me he had 5 children, three of whom were triplets. He told me they were going to have a cookout at his house that Sunday, said his boys were all rock and roll music fans and thought they would get a kick out of meeting a real disc jockey…someone who actually knew some of the stars (which, frankly I did) and the record labels.

So, I went to the house Sunday for dinner and met all the family and the boys and yes, we became very good friends immediately. In fact, some nights, I'd get off work from the radio station and go over to the house (where I was allowed to come at any hour, day or night)…and would jump into the top bunk of triplet Dean's bunk bed and wait for them to come home from "drink and drown" night at one of the U.D. bars. (Drinking laws were different then in Ohio.) Dean would come in later and we'd hang out before retiring in our bunks.

I came home from a gig early in the morning of November 17th, 1985 to be told to get back in the car and hurry to Miami Valley Hospital in Dayton. My father had shot himself in the chest in an apparent suicide attempt...and was barely hanging on to life. I rushed to the hospital...but by the time I got there, it was too late. My father was gone. My mother had died from cancer about ten or so years earlier. I was now an orphan.

I didn't understand any of this until after the autopsy. Turns out my father was riddled with cancer. He had literally waited until he knew that I was out of town and unable to stop him. That didn't make it easier. Nor, did the remembrance of our final conversation...a screaming argument on the phone about my decision to get into radio.

You see, Dad could never understand how I could work in a job which, back then, offered no health or life insurance, no pension, and money which, at the time, frankly, sucked. I tried to explain, but to no avail. Dad hung up on me. And we never spoke again. It's my one regret in life.

But, the next morning, I just had my first cup of coffee in my hand, when into my mobile home bursts Don's son, Dean. He had just been informed by a mutual friend uptown what had happened to my Dad. He rushed over to me, grabbed me in a bear hug and said, "Kevin, I'm so sorry to hear about your Dad. I'm here for you, buddy and I'm not leaving. In fact, I'm moving in with you."

It was the beginning of a friendship that lasted almost 20 years.

Chapter 8

Stunts and DJ Games

It's inevitable when you're a disc jockey that you'll be involved in all kinds of stunts, and will get your listeners to do them as well.

In my case, my first "stunt", as I've mentioned was playing donkey basketball at a charity fundraiser in Blanchester, Ohio.

Next came the 80's "bar game" known as mud wrestling. Why any human being would want to wrestle anybody in mud is beyond my capability of understanding. But, yet, I was asked to do it for charity. My opponent was one of the women's mud wrestling team called "The Chicago Knockers".

"Dear Lord, what have I gotten myself into?", was the first thought that came to my mind. Then, I learned the "Knocker" I had been assigned to grapple with was a third degree Black Belt in Karate. We were instructed to definitely "not touch" the women during the match. Don't get me wrong, I love a good looking lady, but I am NOT going to try any hanky panky with someone who could dismantle my head from my shoulders in about ten seconds. Needless to say, I lost that match in record time.

Karaoke? Been there, done that, got the T-Shirt to prove it.

On the other hand, I had another experience with professional wrestling that turned out to be more fun than I had ever had.

We got a phone call at WCOL one morning from Turner Broadcasting in Atlanta, owner of World Championship Wrestling... they were doing their "Thursday Night Thunder" broadcast across the walkway in Ohio Center that night and could we send over a DJ to welcome the crowd before the broadcast? The PD asked me if I was free that evening and might like to do it. I wasn't busy that evening and said, sure...I watch the show. Be glad to.

So, I walked over there at 6:30 (about 90 minutes from air), checked into the backstage area. While signing in, I noticed a rather large arm coming over my left shoulder and it was pointing at the girl at the check in table. "Hi, Macho!", said the young lady.

I looked over my left shoulder and realized the arm resting closely to my neck was that of "Macho Man", Randy Savage. I gulped and said, "Hi, Macho. Don't kill me...please?". He turned, gave me one of those infamous "Oh, yeah's" and walked off.

It was, to say the least, interesting with that group of characters backstage. I found myself playing rock and roll music trivia with Mr. Fuji. And, of course, Hulk Hogan was lurking around saying hello to everyone. And yes, the so-called "mortal enemies" backstage are often, in fact, good friends. Though, even I admit, on occasion, those friendships get a bit strained.

You see, there are two types of pro wrestling matches, or so I learned. You have what's known as a "work", which is where both wrestlers follow the pre-determined "script", if you will (though it isn't exactly that), and the expected winner happens when he or she gets his or her finishing move on the opponent.

But, then you have what is known as a "shoot". There, anything goes...and anything does. And people can get hurt...or even killed...as a result.

I am friends with a guy who owns a wrestling promotion in town called Rockstar Pro Wrestling. They, basically, train local men and women to be pro wrestlers. And, they are a feeder program to WWE. It takes about two years for them to get somewhere... but they do. First, perhaps to New Japan Pro Wrestling (that part of "sports entertainment" is big in Japan), then perhaps to some other promotion and that may, eventually, lead them to the big time.

But, it is NOT easy and NOT fake at all. It takes athleticism to do it and anyone from their late teens to their 60's is, in my view, an athlete. Don't believe me? Get in a ring, and let yourself be body slammed by a 200 pound guy who then launches himself squarely in the middle of your chest...and see if it doesn't hurt.

So, at the appointed hour, I stood at the edge of backstage and heard the ring announcer introduce a "great friend of World Championship Wrestling"...and heard my name.

I come through the backstage curtain and about 10,000 people begin to boo the hell out of me. Not surprising, of course. Turner Broadcasting, you see, being from Atlanta worked often with country radio stations. Columbus, Ohio ain't Atlanta. This was a rock and roll crowd and I was about as expected and as welcome as a palm tree in a snowstorm.

I walked up the steps to the ring, climb under the ropes and the announcer hands me the wireless microphone with a sheepish "God, I'm sorry you have to go through this" look on his face. I take the microphone and, at first, decided to walk around the inside of the ring staring down the crowd. In my mind, I'm thinking, "OK...I watch this damn show like you do and you as sure as hell not going to do this to me." But...how to deal with this?

Then, it hit me. I had to make the crowd understand I was one of them.

So, I gathered my courage...and did my best Ric Flair impersonation. "Welcome", thundered I, "to where the Big Boys play" (the catch phrase of WCW at the time). "Tonight in this very ring, before these cameras and before not only the United States but to fans everywhere in the entire world, the Superstars of World Championship Wrestling will be here to thrill you with their impressive skills." (Now, the crowd has shut up...and is as quiet as a church mouse.)

"And in the worlds of the FIFTEEN TIME, HEAVYWEIGHT CHAMPION OF THE WORLD, Ric Flair...tonight, Columbus, Ohio, you're going to be" (now I'm imitating Ric Flair's dance moves) "stylin' and profilin' better than you ever have...and remember...to be the man, you've got to beat the man. WHOO!".

The crowd started cheering me...I threw the microphone back at the ring announcer, climbed out of the ring, down the stairs and back down the aisle with people applauding and cheering ME. I started working the crowd, shaking hands as I walked back.

Looking up near the TV booth, Bobby "The Brain" Heenan was hanging over the back of the booth, giving me a "thumbs up" and yelling, "Nice job, guy! Nice job!".

I couldn't resist...I pointed back at him and yelled, "Heenan... YOU! I want you!" He laughed.

I got backstage and Hulk Hogan walked over to me. "Brother, I never saw anything like that! They hated you going out there...and you turned them around and had them eating out of the palm of your hand when you got out of the ring. Most DJ's can't pull that off...that was one hell of a great job!"

"Thanks, Hulkster", I said.

I must have done well. I got the approval of Hulk Hogan on that one.

And, yes, sometimes the listeners got in on the act. We once did the "What would you do for concert tickets" bit? Now, one station did that to horrible results...leading to the death of a listener.

It was called "Hold your wee for a WI" (the computer game). And it never, EVER should have been done.

The idea was that the contestants would binge drink water...

and the first one who could hold it the longest would win.

The problem is a medical condition called "water intoxication". It's very real...very dangerous and completely deadly.

And, sadly, it bit that station squarely on the butt that day.

Listeners who were doctors and nurses were calling the station's morning show that day, alerting them to the danger... some were even pleading that they call the contest off. The morning show, stupidly, laughed at these people. Some of those calls were actually put on the air.

The contest ended, and one of the contestants went home, and died a short time later.

Folks, the first rule of radio promotions is simple: Thou shalt NOT KILL a listener doing a radio stunt. The station, rightfully, got the hell sued out of them and it doesn't exist today. The FCC was about to revoke their license, but the company agreed to sell the station and changed the format and so Uncle Sam relented.

No way was any station I was programming going to do that. On the other hand, fun stunts were fine.

So, we had a listener tell us she was willing to step in a wading tub and turn herself into a human ice cream sundae on a street corner for concert tickets. Sounded fine to me. We sent our "stunt guy" out and we proceeded to surround her with gallons of ice cream, poured hot fudge on her head. Topped it with about an entire can of whipped cream and put cherries on top of her head. The honking of horns at the intersection told us exactly who was listening to us (and there were a ton of them). And, yes, she got the concert tickets.

I walked to work one day on the air to make a point about the need to stay healthy. Left my house at 5:30 am...and got to work at about 8:45...just in time to say goodbye on the morning show. A nice, brisk 6 mile walk with cellphone in hand. Point made.

Oh yes, and when you work in a city with a Zoo, there's always a zookeeper who wants to come over and bring animals with them over to the morning show.

I have had small, young Bengal tigers in my studio (which as infants are just about like bigger versions of kittens and are fun to play with and feed). Monkeys can be fun to be around, but only when they're young. They become horrible pets when they grow up.

I don't like snakes. But, I've had a boa constrictor wrapped around my neck before.

Spiders? YUCK! My morning show host, Kelly Quinn on Star 107.9 hit the studio door on a dead run when the Columbus Zoo's Jack Hanna brought a tarantula in. And not a small one, either. This one was as big as a man's hand! It walked all over our studio console while I grabbed the microphone and kept a respectable distance.

Oh yes, then there was the day that a skydiving instruction company came on the air with us…and Kelly decides she wants to skydive…on the air!

Well, actually putting a microphone on her that would work in a skydive was not really feasible technically for us at that time. But, we had our Promotions Director, Becky Walnoah, on the ground with a wireless to describe Kelly's dive and run up to her upon a safe landing.

Our General Manager…and myself…both thought she was crazy. Look, I've piloted planes before. Soloed and even done what's known as a "Dual Cross Country" flight before as pilot in command. I've flung myself thousands of feet in the air and gotten myself back on the ground in one piece…even if I bounced once or twice. But, I always landed safely. And there is no way on God's green earth that you're going to find me jumping out of a plane, unless the decision is jump or die.

The skydiving place was about an hour away from the station, so we had to do all of this on a cellphone. (The station had one as did I...and I still have the number of mine).

Kelly is given the instructional lesson that all prospective jumpers get...then put on the parachute, got in the plane, and took off.

I noticed our General Manager had come into the studio to hear this. He had bullets of sweat on his brow...and so did I as Becky described the scene. We knew how many people in Kelly would be seated...so we knew when she came out the door and into the air. And out she came, plummeting to Earth.

Bill, our General Manager, was a devout Catholic...and I think he and I set the world's record for the number of times the "Lord's Prayer", and the "Hail Mary" could be quietly said.

But, Kelly made it...and rushed to the microphone to tell of the experience. It was great radio, even if my PD's heart went into my throat as it happened.

I think Kelly has kept her feet on the ground since then.

When I got to K-99.1 FM in Dayton in 2004, they were still doing a free summer country concert in a park in Huber Heights, Ohio. Called "A Day In The Country". They had been doing them for about 5 years and they were great events. But more work than you can ever imagine.

The idea was simple. Pay for a headline act and a secondary act (which being a reporting station with the trades will get you some help with the record companies in obtaining the services of the artists), then let the record companies give a promotional appearance to a young up and coming act and get a local act to open the show for a promotion). So, you have about a 5 hour event (with downtime between acts for stage set up). Sell, beer, soda and water on site, have an official "burger" "pizza", and "hot dog" vendor. Then, a month before the show, give away about 70,000 free tickets to the show.

These things turned into some real productions and we had some soon to be BIG names as headliners. Aaron Tippin, Toby Keith, I think Alan Jackson did one...Clint Black, too.

And the crowds were IMMENSE. Usually, you get about 60 percent attendance with free tickets. Ours was more like 90 percent.

On a good year with warm weather and low humidity, we would have 60,000 people show up. No kidding. We'd be at the park at 7 AM, would open the gates at 11 and the concert would start at 12 noon...wrapping up around 5 or 6 pm. We all took turns introducing the acts, but then all of us would be on stage to help bring on the headliner.

The station gave us T-shirts every year with the correct logo and artist names on the back...plus lanyards with "All Access" badges to identify us to security and stage management.

And, we never had to buy food there, we had access to the backstage food tent for the crew and acts.

Over time, though, the shows got more and more expensive, and the budgets kept getting cut.

Now, we on the programming staff had to go out the week before, pound fence posts into the ground and set up the snow fencing for the show. Sometimes in extremely high heat and humidity. It sucked. We had to set up all the chairs, too. But, we did it. Because we knew the listeners appreciated the show.

I even got to open the show with my band one year...but, not on the main stage. We played in the parking lot before the gates opened at 11. That was fun. But, it turned out to be the last year the station did the event. So, I supposed you could say I "killed" at Day In The Country. (smile emoji here).

What really sucked more...my band was such a hit that the Operation's Manager told me after the show that if we DID do the show next year, my band would open it. He said we were much better than the local act that opened it.

Ending the free concerts, needless to say, was NOT a hit with the listeners.

I never heard such complaints in all my life. We "ruined" their lives, they said. They took vacations around the concert and said the show was "their vacation". But, the reasons the free shows came to an end was understandable.

First, when the station started doing them, NO country acts came to Dayton in the summertime. There were few, if any venues around to do a show of that magnitude. Now, you had Fraze Pavillion, Timberwolf Amphitheater at King's Island and the giant "Country Concert" in Fort Loramie, Ohio (an hour away from Dayton) all doing country shows. It was making booking a decent show very difficult, because the contracts of many artists prohibit them from doing a show within 60 miles of the show 6 months before or after it.

The station didn't want our show to devolve into 2 baby acts and a karaoke contest. It wouldn't have drawn enough listeners to make the sponsorships worth it to the advertisers. So, it ended. For a while.

Recently, though, we were able to restart it, though this time as a paid concert. Still a reduced ticket price (in the $40 to $70 range. You might not think that's a deal, but have you priced tickets for an Eagles concert lately? Top ticket is around $500. Or Paul McCartney? Heck, I recently paid $200 for a front row seat to see the surviving members of the Monkees!)

But, last summer, on the 30th anniversary of the country format at the station, we had a BIG show. We promoted it and it was virtually a sell-out. This is why I know radio isn't "circling the drain". At the end of the show, WE were all brought out on stage to shake hands like the performers do with the people in the front rows and get "high fives" from everyone! Our headliner came out and did selfies with all of us on stage with the crowd behind us.

You want to talk about a fun night? And feeling about ten feet tall? The listeners humbled us with their love and appreciation for what we do.

And ALL of us were there. Including, the couple of out of town voice trackers. That's another way you deal with voice tracking. We paid to bring those guys in from out of town, put them up in a hotel and had them at the show talking with listeners and hanging out with the advertisers, too. This simple gesture makes those guys one with us in the minds of the listeners.

It's a once a year expense for the station. But, it pays back in ways you can't imagine. And it is well worth the money. You see, we got a cut on the ticket sales and were allowed to keep 100% of the money from listener, advertiser and staff catering on site. The venue kept a portion of the ticket sales and 100 percent of the beer, soda and general food sales on site. A win-win for everyone. And, I just learned, this year's show is going to be even bigger…a bigger venue, more tickets to sell and who the heck knows who the headliner is going to be? Well, the PD knows, but she ain't saying right now. I don't know…but this one may be over the top.

Promotions are essential for making money with a radio station. Of course, companies such as iHeart have taken it national with their "iHeart Music Festivals" which are held in places like Las Vegas. It is done with the intention of doing these major shows to give away tickets on the air and sell them locally…allowing the stations out of town to "fly" people in for the shows.

A nice idea. But, now the law is beginning to question just how the acts are being obtained, alleging the possibility that the artists (or their managements) are paying the stations or supplying the acts in order to get airplay for the artists...payola, pure and simple.

I hope this isn't the case. Surely, they can't be that stupid. But, who knows? Payola has happened before. It can happen again.

Chapter 9

My First "Dream Job"

So, in 1986, I get a call from Rob Ellis…that friend I had known who was a year or two behind me in high school (and the guy dumped on his butt by Kamala, the Ugandan Headhunter)… who was now working at WING-AM in Dayton. He said they were looking for a 7 pm to midnight DJ and was I interested?

Now, you gotta understand. WING, in those days was an "oldies" station playing the hits of the 50's, 60's and early 70's. Basically the old Top 40 music that the station played back then. I was a BIG WING listener as a child. My parents got me a tour of the station at age 10. It was my "dream job".

And you're damn right, I was interested. I interviewed and got the job that day. Just 2 weeks later, on a Saturday morning, I sat down in front of the studio audio console, turned on the microphone. (An old Shure "bullet" mike which was later, upgraded by Engineering with a newer Shure SM7-B.) And for the first time in my life, I heard me saying in my headphones (with that awesome reverb underneath my voice), "Oldies 14-10, the legendary WING." I couldn't believe it. I was finally working for the radio station I grew up listening to as a child. The station I'd dreamed of working for. I was in Hog Heaven.

For a while, that was a really fun job. The Program Director was a man named Steve Warren. Not the man who wrote something called "The Radio Programmer's Manual"…that was a different Steve Warren. This Steve was a nice enough guy, but he wanted to "experiment" with WING for a format he wanted to do. It was a derivative of the oldies format, but was aimed at the kids who were in high school in 1955-1963…the older fringe of the listeners. For him, the hit songs were "Standing On The Corner" by the Four Lads and "Washington Square" by the Village

Stompers. It might have been a decent idea, but it completely missed the center of the oldies universe at the time, which was 1964-1969...the Beatles era. And though WING was big in the early 60's (it changed to Top 40 in 1960), it was a MONSTER post Beatles. That was clearly the direction the station needed to take, and Steve resisted. Finally, Steve Warren was given his walking papers (with a little "shove" from longtime morning man, Steve Kirk to the G.M. who asked, "Alex...how far do the ratings have to drop before you do something here? Do we really need to go to a one share?"), and my friend, Rob Ellis was made P.D.

Rob's first decision was to make me "Music Director" of WING, and quasi Assistant Program Director (there was just no money in the budget for one). His first order to me was "You know what this station is supposed to sound like. Go, make it happen!"

The first challenge was going to be the music library. Frankly, WING did a terrible job of keeping up its music library over the years. They had SOME greatest hits albums in a cabinet, but the 45's were a mess. Some were barely playable, others were not. So, Rob got me a $3,000 trade out with a local CD store. And I went out and spent every dime of it getting copies of CD's that contained the correct original versions of the hit songs. And I proceeded to dub over 2,000 songs to cart from CD. Not that I intended to rotate them all, but wanted to play the hits and still have a library that would make it virtually impossible to get "stumped" on a listener request on our request shows that I did.

We changed the station's imaging and got former KHJ and CKLW morning man Charlie Van Dyke to do it. We got the old Bill Drake Top Hour musical stager the station used to use and added Van Dyke's voice saying, "And now, Ladies and Gentlemen, Jason Roberts!", etc.

Radio jingle freak that he is, Rob got us a huge jingle package from Jam Creative Productions in Dallas. This was the biggest jingle package I have ever seen before, or since. It came on 2, ten inch REELS of tape and it had everything. Jock Jingles, Year Sings, Jock Shouts, Year shouts. Jingles with music beds, traffic and weather jingles, hundreds of cuts. I added some "period" jingles on my evening show, too which added to the nostalgic sound of WING.

Then, we hit the road. The station "vehicle" was an old Winnebago bus that was called "The Legend" that we had confiscated from our sister station in Springfield. I eventually learned to drive that behemoth and our first "event" was a Friday night live 3 hour long broadcast from a place called "Hamburger Heaven" on Woodman Drive in Dayton. The place featured a massive burger as big as the plate…and yes, I ate one every Friday night. They were delicious. And people came out in droves. Guys in their classic cars…women in their classic cars. They all grew up with WING. And in the middle of it was me…the guy who also did the same.

We did public service events like the "National Night Out" with Dayton Police. One year, that was a funny one. We showed up at the day and time requested, but no one was there. Seems the cops got there early and left without us. So, we called them, they sent a cruiser back to escort us to where they were and off we went.

Little did I realize the officer was going to turn his lights and siren on and high tail it to the place where the event was being held. So, here we are, me…Rob…midday jock Kim Faris and others, and we're doing 60 or 70 miles an hour on the city streets in a 20 foot long Winnebago. The cop took one turn at about 55 miles an hour, and I did the same, almost going up on 2 wheels in the process. Everybody thought I was about to kill them, but we all survived.

Another great annual event I had taken part in for years was the annual Jerry Lewis Telethon for Muscular Dystrophy. We did it at WBZI for years, (Rob also worked there for a while) and we wanted to continue the tradition at WING. It was seen on WKEF-TV, Channel 22 with longtime host (and former WING Air Personality) Johnny Walker. I never saw a guy work harder for a charity than Johnny. (About the closest comparison today is K-99.1's Nancy Wilson...she's the Program Director, and Morning Show Host, does events everywhere almost daily and hosts the station's annual Radiothon for Children's Hospital, which raises hundreds of thousands of dollars each year. So did the Jerry Lewis Telethon.)

Johnny would call me and ask me to go help M.C. bar nights to raise money for MDA which I gladly did. I have no idea how many I did...it was dozens a year. Everywhere from Kettering and Centerville to Coldwater and back again. And I would broadcast from and appear on the annual telethon to urge people to give.

When Johnny left Channel 22 to run the now defunct Hara Arena, station staffer Joe Smith stepped in to host the telethon for many more years. And aside both was the station's "friendly ghoul", a huge bear of man named Barry Hobart...who, in monster makeup was known as "Dr. Creep". He was a great friend of mine.

One time while at WING, living in New Carlisle, Barry called me at work, said that he had a couple of tickets for the World Wrestling Federation show that night at Hara and asked if I wanted to go. I said, sure. He said he'd pick me up at the house and I gave him directions.

Now, I was aware that Barry owned a hearse that he would drive around when portraying the Good Doctor. I didn't know he was coming in costume and make up and in the hearse that night.

The appointed time came, and I could hear something coming down the street. It was Barry...the hearse...and literally EVERY kid and adult in the neighborhood and they all converged in my driveway. The word spread fast that "Dr. Creep was in the trailer park". Barry got out, took pictures with everyone who wanted one, signed every autograph and then, when the crowd took off, he and I got in the hearse and went off to the Arena.

And I became the neighborhood celebrity. Nobody knew I was friends with Dr. Creep.

Barry was another Channel 22 staffer who gave time, energy and probably blood to that Telethon. He was at every event and spent 30 hours during the telethon going to the regional donation centers and sitting in the "fishbowl" where kids would bring their change in return for saying their names on television. I wasn't on camera a lot, but I was in the middle of it all.

MDA, in my view, made a big mistake shutting that telethon down a few years back. Sure, Jerry Lewis was getting long in the tooth then and it was time to modernize things. But, that could have been done. Had TV been a little more ahead of the game, it could have televised the show on air and online. The world would respond. We'd all like to see that demon exorcised from society.

My last telethon appearance was a few years back. The show was now done at the Wright State University's Nutter Center. And, that year, it was a nostalgic theme. The segment they asked me to take part in was a "reunion" of the cast of the station's kids show, "Clubhouse 22", complete with its puppeteer and the puppets.

I was never a part of the cast of "Clubhouse 22" (though my high school rock band auditioned to play on it once), but what they wanted me to do was to help Barry. He was not in the best of health at that time and it was getting very hard for him to get around. I was only happy to assist. Off camera, I let him grab my arm and we walked together to our marks on the set. When the cameras were on, we laughed and joked and cut up on the air with the puppets who threw stuff at us…and we threw it back. It was three minutes of live television and was a blast. When it was done, I helped Barry back to his seat and realized, I was never going to experience something like that again.

Not long after that, Barry died. I went to his visitation and he was out of makeup, of course. I'm sure that's what his family wanted and that was fine. Somehow, though, in the back of my mind, I think Barry would have wanted to be buried in his cape, top hat and make up. You see, Dr. Creep was more than a TV character. He was an institution in Dayton. He was larger than life. I was happy to nominate him for the Dayton Area Broadcaster's Hall of Fame and he was inducted.

If you ever want to see what all this was about, go to You Tube and search for "Dr. Creep" or "Shock Theater". There's some of his shows there.

Working with Steve Kirk was one of the greatest thrills of my life. Steve was WING's morning guy when I was a kid. And he was a radio institution in southern Ohio, as was WHIO's morning man, Lou Emm. And, though there were competitors, both were good friends.

Steve, you see, had worked in Columbus at WCOL-AM (1230), AND in Cincinnati at WSAI-AM (1360) BEFORE he went to work at WING. So, he drew audience from all three cities at WING. And, at their height, his ratings were astronomical.

And how do you tell all of that? Just go a concert or two with the guy, which I did twice.

Steve invited me to a private corporate show with Frankie Valli of the Four Seasons. Incredible show and Frankie was in GREAT voice that night belting out all of their great hits like "Sherry", "Big Girls Don't Cry", "Let's Hang On" and his incomparable hit, "Can't Take My Eyes Off You". I think Steve and I both got to say hello to Frankie, too.

But, before and after the show, everyone in the audience wanted to meet with the OTHER star in the room...Steve Kirk. And, he was kind enough to introduce me to his friends and listeners at the show.

The second time was at Riverfront Stadium in Cincinnati for The Rolling Stones. Both of us had dates that night (I think Steve was between wife 3 & 4 then. He's now on number 5, I think.) Before the show, at the intermission and after the show, Steve drew crowds from all over that stadium. Listeners from Cincinnati, Norwood, Hamilton, Middletown, Dayton, Springfield, Kettering, New Carlisle, Oakwood all came up and wanted to say hello and get an autograph.

And, of course, the Stones were unbelievable. I had gone to get a hot dog and coke when I heard the opening strains of "Tumbling Dice" coming from the stage. It caught me by surprise. I remember thinking, "My God! That IS the Rolling Stones on stage!" Hit after hit after hit. If I remember right, it was about 2 or 3 hour show. And they are still playing shows as this book was written. I wouldn't be surprised if Keith Richards outlives ME. (Of course, nothing can kill Keith Richards. He'll inherit the Earth after the nuclear holocaust!)

Sadly, though…it all ended way too soon with WING, and through no fault of mine.

Great Trails Broadcasting (owners of the station) was once upon a time a GREAT employer, and some great jocks worked for their stations. At WING, Steve Kirk, Jim Quinn (who became a legend at KQV-Pittsburgh…the same station that, love him or not, hired a DJ named Jeff Christie who later did a talk show under his real name…Rush Limbaugh). Fred Winston who'd make his mark at WLS-Chicago and is one of the funniest people ever to crack a microphone worked there. Al Morgan…who went to L.A. in the 70's to work for 93/KHJ under his real name, Al Connors. And the late Terry Dorsey who'd take his "Hiney Wine" bits to Dallas to radio and syndication. At sister WKLO/Louisville, you had Bill Bailey who would later go to WAKY in Louisville and would give some radio advice to a funny young buck named Gary Burbank who did mornings on WAKY for a while. Most of you should know what happened to him. He later went to WLW in Cincinnati and did first, a successful morning show and then afternoons until he retired. Great Trails also once owned WRIT in Milwaukee and WBOS in Boston and WCOL-AM/FM in Columbus.

But, by the late 80's, it was down to WING, WIZE in Springfield and WCOL AM-FM in Columbus. WING was, effectively, "mothballed"...and everyone, but Steve Kirk was to be let go. Which meant, I was going to be looking for work.

Didn't quite turn out that way. I learned later that Steve Kirk marched in to the owner's office and proceeded to tell him that, if I was let go, the owner would "rue the day he did it". And Steve persuaded the owner to let me move down the hall full time to an open position on sister CHR, WGTZ-FM ("Hot rockin', flame throwin' Z-93, Eaton Dayton and Springfield alive!"). The next afternoon, I was hired onto the FM staff.

I hated to leave WING...but I LOVED working for Z-93. It was a market leading 12 share MONSTER at the time. Request lines that rang off the hook, even at 3 in the morning. (And, don't let anybody tell you kids don't listen at 3 AM. I can tell you for a fact, they did!) I did remotes, even did a live midday show on a wireless microphone placed inside a zip lock bag since I was up to my chest in the wave pool at Kings Island Amusement Park.

And we still did promotions. Concerts, CD and ticket giveaways, flyaways to destinations for listeners to meet Van Halen, Aerosmith and others. Easy to get that stuff from the record companies when you're #1 in the market.

I had been assigned to emcee the Milli Vanilli concert at Hara Arena for Z. Unfortunately, the week before the show, the "scandal" erupted in Cincinnati. For those of you who don't remember, Milli Vanilli was 2 guys who were somewhat like The Monkees, but even worse. Seems Rob and Fab not only lip synced their records on stage...they didn't even sing on the records at all...at least the Monkees sang and eventually played on their records.

It all blew up in Cincinnati. When the pair went on stage, the record was started and the lip syncing began. Then, the record stuck. "Girl you know it's...girl you know it's...girl you know it's...girl you know it's" over and over. The pair was booed off the stage and that was the end of their careers.

But, even Z-93 was feeling the pinch of the company's money issues. I was called into PD Jeff Ballentine's office one afternoon and given an interesting offer...middays at WCOL-FM in Columbus...a station that was moving into an oldies format just as WING had done.

Did I want to leave my hometown and move 70 miles east? No. Was it a bigger market job? Oh, yes it was. Columbus was market 35...Dayton, at the time, was 46. So, I agreed to take the job...at my present salary, of course.

Jeff stood up, shook my hand and said, "Congratulations on your new gig...and thanks for taking it, because your position here is being eliminated."

It turned out to be the best career move I had made so far.

Chapter 10

From Oldies to Country to "New" oldies

So, I get to Columbus and find myself put up inside a large hotel for a week with the company paying all my expenses. (I would decide though for a while that I would commute back and forth from my home in Clark County.)

And, we did take the station into the oldies format. But, first we had to put the old station to sleep. Boy, did I feel bad about that.

WXGT-FM (92X) was, at one time, the big CHR station in Columbus. It ruled the roost with night jock Suzy Waud. (Yes, that's her real name...pronounced "Wad".) Stereo Quad Suzy Waud is much beloved of the 80's generation there and always will be. She is the local version of the original M-TV VJ's. (And, I actually know and have had contact with, a couple of the original VJ's.)

But, 92X had gotten long in the tooth. Though Great Trails continued to put every available dime into promoting the station, it wasn't enough. They began getting out promoted by crosstown rival WNCI-FM, programmed by a former 92X staffer...Dave Robbins who had cut his teeth in Chicago with WDJX/Dayton's former PD, Buddy Scott at B-96.

92X would announce a big weekend promotion, and Dave would "cover" it at WNCI and throw a thousand dollars on top of it. WNCI was the overall listening leader in town, so they got the credit for the promotion with the audience. 92X tried to come back by saying "WNCI Lies!". Dave returned with "WNCI Lies... spot the lie this weekend, tell us about it Monday morning at 7:15 on the Morning Zoo and grab your grand!" There was just no way 92X could win.

So, Rob and I walked into the WCOL building with a staff who knew they were losing their jobs in ten days (they were all being paid a lot of money, much more than the company was willing to pay us). And, needless to say, Rob and I were the perennial "turds in a punch bowl" and knew it, so we locked ourselves in an office while we got ready for the new format.

WCOL's call letters were magic for oldies music because its' sister AM station was the Top 40 powerhouse of the 1960's there. We had the heritage in Columbus and remember, that's the strongest programming card there is, remember?

We hit the air. The audience loved it, and frankly, so did I. The station put on "package" oldies shows and that's where I got to meet and M.C. artists like Martha and the Vandellas, The Crystals, The Platters, Tommy Roe, Lou Christie, Original Temptations Eddie Kendricks and Dennis Edwards, Peter Noone of Herman's Hermits and many others.

The concerts were incredible. One night, we had the original lead singers of the Temptations there. Eddie Kendricks showed that he was a masterful showman. Walking off the stage and into the crowd singing "Just My Imagination" while shaking hands, kissing women and got right back to stage center just in time to sing the last notes of "running away with me." He held that last note…and that was when the bass player hit the opening notes of "My Girl" and it brought the whole house to its feet cheering. Not long ago, I spoke with the sole surviving member of the group, Otis Williams about that. He agreed with me about Eddie's showmanship. He was one hell of an entertainer.

On another night, Peter Noone was the headliner, and we had Martha Reeves and The Vandellas and The Crystals on stage among the other acts.

Normally, we closed the show by bringing out all of the acts, who would then sing the Spaniels hit from the 50's, "Goodnight

Sweetheart Goodnight".

I bring out all of the acts, dutifully took a step back as the DJ emcee and led the applause as the entertainers sang. Suddenly, I see Martha coming back to me with the leader of the Crystals.

"Sweetheart", said Martha, "You're the DJ…you're supposed to be singing with us!"

"But, but…but…you're the stars!" protested I.

"Nonsense.", said Martha…"you come up here and sing with us!"

Well, okay, I thought. I knew the lyrics of the song. I walked up to the microphone and began singing the lead part of "Goodnight Sweetheart".

That's when Martha and the Vandellas on my left…and The Crystals on my right began singing backup in 6 part gospel harmony…with little ole ME as lead singer.

I'm thinking to myself, "What in the hell am I doing HERE?"

We stole a Fourth of July fireworks event from Saga Communication's Sunny 95 (WSNY). The first year we did it, they tried to crash our event with their helicopter traffic guy flying his chopper onto the grounds.

We had gotten inside information that they were going to try and do it. And we wanted to keep them out. Our "new" PD (Rob had been let go) came up with the answer. Michael Cruise realized that the fireworks were being set up in the field in the park that afternoon. Flying a helicopter onto those grounds while fireworks are being set is dangerous to the fireworks crews. Electrical energy from the landing of a helicopter, at least theoretically "could" set off the fireworks.

So, Michael called the local office of the Federal Aviation

Administration, explained the situation, and got them to issue a "Notice To Airmen" restriction of landing in the park that afternoon.

I was on the air from the park promoting the event when Sunny's chopper arrived overhead. We called the FAA on our cellphones telling them the WSNY helicopter was trying to land. The FAA controller immediately radioed the chopper and informed them of the flight restriction. The pilot complained to the control tower that they had always done it before. The tower told them, it doesn't matter, it's too dangerous to let you land. So, he had to fly away. And, we just "smiled".

It was a great time...and we were a great station, but then, an unbelievable thing happened.

Crosstown station WBNS-FM, a "beautiful music station" which definitely needed a new direction decides to flip to oldies and start a war with us.

Understand, this never happens in that format. First in wins, and everybody knows it. The problem was, Great Trails had gotten a "reputation" of turning tail and changing format at the drop of a hat the minute it got some competition. That's one of the things 92X did that helped its demise. The boys at 'BNS, knowing they had a lot more money to spend than we did, thought it could outspend us, and we'd flip format.

They didn't realize the crew at WCOL NOW, wasn't going to put up with that anymore. We were insulted...and frankly, mad at their move.

Why? There was a better and more lucrative alternative available to them. There was no full signaled country FM in Columbus. And a well programmed 50,000 watt in town FM station would have easily wiped up the out of town signals and, with just a reasonable amount of marketing and because of the immense popularity of country music in 1992-93 would have easily rocketed to #1 in Columbus.

RadioOhio (owners of WBNS) chose NOT to go after the brass ring, despite the fact they could afford it. No, they had to "pick on the little guy", and were willing to drop dimes to pick up pennies in advertising money just to try and "get a win". They were being bullies, and there is one way to stand up to a bully.

Our General Manager, Bill Cusack, you see, is a Marine. I say, "IS a Marine", because when you're in the Corps, you're in it for life. And, he may not have looked it in his 60's, but Bill was, if not anything, a fighter. And he wasn't going to put up with WBNS's crap.

So, the next morning, we arrived to Bill's office to find it filled with Army fatigues, fake artillery shells, fake hand grenades, Army mosquito tent netting and more. We were instructed to take some of all of it and that Army fatigues were now officially the "uniform of the day". And, we were expected to be in uniform every day. (And, consider this…in how many "ordinary" jobs does something like this happen?)

With the help of Dayton's GM, we got hooked up to a consulting deal with Critical Mass Media…the consulting arm at the time of Clear Channel Communications and a company run by the notorious programming genius, Randy Michaels.

I was on a conference call with Randy that day. His message was very clear…"You guys have "cume advantage". (Cume, pronounced, Qum – long "u" - is a ratings term that means "body count"…how many people in your format are listening to you each week?) As long as you have it, you can say what you want to say and, if you say it often enough, people will believe you and not WBNS. You also have "heritage", another big reason for them to believe you. They have trusted those call letters for generations. Now, you're back. You ARE their station. BE it."

Randy gave us Joel Lind as our consultant and together with PD Michael Cruise, they re-directed our playlist and re-deployed it. Actually, we had 2 lists. The "A" list that we played during the week. But, on the weekends, we added a "B" list...filled with hundreds of familiar, if not the best testing songs...but nothing that would hurt us if it was "sprinkled in" on the weekends. That gave WCOL "depth" that WBNS didn't have.

And that included some GREAT lesser known titles by the Beatles. Songs like "Tell Me Why" from the movie "A Hard Day's Night" and "Hold Me Tight". Stuff you almost NEVER normally hear on an oldies station.

WBNS tried for playlist "depth" with their night guy...but it was another "swing and a miss". He was a former weekend jock on WTVN who called himself "Chucko"...I think his actual name was Chuck Taylor. He was an abject joke...a wannabe 1950's jock with a flannel mouth, screaming and yelling at the top of his lungs, while he honked horns, rang bells on air and played, mostly, forgettable stiffs. B-sides, never wases, stuff only the deepest of record collectors would remember.

Chucko was a caricature of a 1950's jock. Guys like Weird Beard on KLIF and Wolfman Jack were tops at doing that kind of "character" radio. Chucko thinks he could pull it off...but, really didn't do it very well, and the music he played made it worse. The car collectors in town LOVED him, said he was going to be "the biggest thing on Columbus radio" and predicted "WCOL is toast". I have mellowed in my feelings toward him over the years, but he's still out there, trying to convince people on You Tube what a big guy he was.

Joel told me car collectors and record collectors are but the smallest portions of an oldies station's audience. I've always found that was right.

One of my favorite weekend promotions we did while I was there: we had come in contact with some old reel to reel tapes of the station's DJ's from the 1960's. They were not edited, but were entire program hours which included the DJ's, the newscasts, the commercials, all of it.

I "equalized" the tapes for best quality possible (remembering, of course, that is was a recording of an AM radio station). And then, proceeded to edit the sections where the old DJ's introduced songs...edited the newscasts as separate entities (some really good historical stuff was on them, such as the 1967 Six Day War between Egypt and Israel).

From all of the tapes and tape cassettes we had in house, I was able to come up with about 10 hours of "old, vintage" programming...which we could, of course, rotate from 6 am to Midnight Saturday and Sunday.

We called it: The WCOL "Reunion" Weekend. We took the old station and put it back on the air. Now, we didn't air AM quality radio all weekend. The "jock talk" was actually matched with the quality CD recording of the song that we had in house...and it, and the song were placed on individual cartridge tapes which were interjected at several spots in the hour. Vintage newscasts were aired at :20 minutes after the hour and :20 minutes before the hour. Since, the station DID do "Columbus 20/20 Newswatch" at one point in its lifetime.

This weekend was an absolute SMASH with the audience... and with the families of the DJ's and newspeople. They were hearing their favorite DJ's, their fathers, their husbands back on the radio in their prime. Some of whom, of course, were no longer with us. I received a tearful letter from the wife of one of our newspeople thanking me for including his newscasts on the weekend. She said she hadn't heard her husband on the radio in years...and cried tears of joy being able to hear him on air again doing what he loved so much.

The end result? We killed WBNS in every rating book, except for one...and, in that one, we still beat them by two tenths of a rating point. And Chucko lasted about 18 months. He was finally canned when he objected to WBNS pre-empting his show for the Beatles Anthology. He wanted to do his special to the

Kennedy Assassination. Sorry, Chucko...the Beatles became a hit because they lifted America out of their grief from the loss of the President. Beatles over Oswald every time. You're out.

We also did something fun later on WCOL-AM, which was airing a talk radio format at the time. We were going to change the call letters to WFII and call it, "1230, FYI" (the call letters WFYI were not available, but identifying the station as 1230, WFII, Columbus would make the whole thing legal. As long as we identified at the top of the hour, we could call it anything we wanted.

So to kick off the call letter change, we stunted by doing a talk radio format we called "Blah Radio". Every word that every "host" said was substituted with the word "Blah". So, we created a half hour of talk radio all made up of the word "Blah". The talk show hosts would prattle on "Blah blah blah...blah blah blah blah." We did an "impression" (though we didn't carry his show at the time) of Rush Limbaugh by playing his "theme song" from the Pretenders and having a very pompous sounding host "Blah-ing" away. We did a newscast of "Blahs". You could tell it was a newscast because we used the famous Bill Drake news sounder and put a phony teletype under the "Blah Anchorman". We had a sports opener and a sportscast of "Blahs". Complete with the interview of an athlete...that was obvious. Why? Because HE said, "DUH-blah, DUH, blah blah blah", etc. And we just ran that half hour all weekend long. (The "blah" Drag Racing commercial was a scream!)

What was crazy about it all...after listening to it three or four times, the "blahs" started making sense to the audience. They told me so. They "got" the joke. And were being entertained by it. Go figure.

But, then around 1993 came word that Great Trails was selling WCOL to local owner Nationwide Communications.

Normally a station sale is nerve wracking for DJ's...because many times the air staff finds itself looking for work as the new owner wants to change format.

Not at Nationwide. The company's motto was, "You win with people", and they meant it. They kept EVERY on air staffer who wanted to work for them. They told me the format would change to country. I had no objections because I had worked in country radio before. So, now, Nationwide was in control and I was preparing, along with Michael Cruise to make another format change.

The afternoon of the 6 pm format change, I am in the corporate office on the top floor of One Nationwide Plaza in Columbus as Assistant Program Director of the station and was there with PD Michael. Nationwide Communication's President Steve Berger told us something I had NEVER heard before out of an owner.

"Guys, we want this radio station to be #1…and we're going to give you every tool you need to do that. We're kicking it off with a 300 point per week television campaign, billboards and bus cards. When you launch the format this afternoon, we'll play 10,000 songs in a row…we'll be commercial free for 23 days. And, for the first 6 months of operation, there is NO budget. ANYTHING you think you need to make us #1…no matter the cost…tell us what it is, and you've got it."

As we're going back down the elevator, I turned to Michael and asked, "Did you hear what I think I just heard out of Steve? We can spend whatever we want for 6 months?" Michael smiled and said, "Kev…that's how a winner works."

First, we had to blow up the oldies format. At Friday 5 pm, we said goodbye, I believe with Don McLean's "American Pie". And, went to a computerized "countdown". A metallic voice counting down the "seconds" to the new format, interspersed every 30 seconds or so with an announcement reminding people to "Tune here Monday night at 6 when a new, clear radio station will appear on this channel." That led to a funny situation Monday morning.

I was standing in the reception area of the office at WCOL when a Columbus Police officer walked in and asked to see the General Manager. Being the only "manager" in the building at the time, I asked the officer if I could be of help. He told me, "We're getting some calls from concerned citizens about this "nuclear radio station" you guys are saying is coming. What's all this about?"

I said, "nuclear radio station?" The officer nodded his head. I couldn't help it. I broke out laughing. "What's so funny?", asked the cop. I said, "It's not a nuclear radio station we're promoting, but a new…clear radio station, referring to our 50,000 watt signal!" Now, the cop was laughing too. "Oh, that IS funny…I'll go back to the station and let everybody know!"

Crisis averted, (and no mushroom clouds over the corner of Broad and Young Streets), I went back upstairs to put the finishing touches on the "kickoff promo" to the new format which would air ahead of its first song.

That audio is still on You Tube somewhere. Jim Merkel, our new station "voice" said something to the effect of : "This is WCOL-FM; Columbus, Ohio. In just a moment, we're going to introduce you to a new radio station. Over the past months, we have been researching the market, trying to determine what Columbus radio listeners wanted in a radio station. And in the past few weeks, it became clear that what Columbus radio listeners wanted was a station plays the kind of music THEY want to hear. And what Columbus radio listeners want to hear is America's Music" (cue in Collin Raye: "That Was A River"…a subtle dig at crosstown competitor, WRVF-FM "The River" programmed at the time, by my friend Rob Ellis".) "And, because we know you want to hear a lot of music, here's the first…of ten thousand songs in a row. That's our way of introducing you to Columbus's NEWEST radio station...Continuous Country Favorites, 92.3"...(jingle sings: WCOL-FM, Columbus!)...

And off we went playing music.

I was the first DJ heard on the "new" Continuous Country Favorites, 92.3, WCOL. The first song was Alan Jackson's "Chattahoochie". And away we went...with no commercials...for 23 days. When the 23 days was over, we formally launched with a staff that included Dixie Lee and Skip Mahaffey in mornings, Buckeye Bill Tanner in middays, John Boy Crenshaw afternoons, me in the evening and Miss Lisa (Bryant)...another holdover from the oldies format) for overnights.

And the station exploded like the Saturn rocket. The first monthly ratings trend had us moving from #6 in town straight to #1...and that's exactly what the first rating book showed when it came out, too. Good Lord, we had beaten WNCI!

Of course, the promotions money helped. Nationwide gave us $80-thousand dollars to give away to listeners the first full rating book, and we handed out every dime of it in checks to listeners in increments of $1,000 dollars to a grand prize of $10,000 dollars to caller 92. I think we melted the phone exchange that morning.

I started making better money and fast. I had gotten increased to $25,000 while GTB owned the station. Under Nationwide, I was quickly moved up to $35,000 and was given a "bonus" arrangement that said every rating book that I was #1 in my time slot, I would get $1,000 cash. I was #1 for the next 13 rating books. That's over 3 years of bonuses and $13,000 dollars. And I got around $250 to $300 for every remote broadcast I did.

I got to work with the best damned radio consultant who ever lived...the late Rusty Walker from Mississippi. Rusty gave me my air name...Rowdy J. Roberts. Told me it would be easily remembered in the ratings. He was right. Twice.

I also got to work with our Head of Country Programming, Bob Moody…you know, "Cosmic" Bob of CKLW fame as I mentioned earlier.

I loved the job…but I was beginning to get the "itch" of wanting to move from Assistant Program Director to PD. And frustrated, because I was passed over twice despite having been APD for 8 years. Though, I respected greatly the guy who was hired, a very talented programmer named Gary Moss, I also knew there was good reasons, I thought, for me to move up when Gary left. After all, I clearly knew where all the "bodies" were buried in that operation.

My answer came from a man who became one of my biggest mentors…and one of the best friends I ever had in the business. The late Dave "Rock and Roll" Robbins. Dave was now WCOL and sister WNCI's General Manager. He would move on eventually to become a V.P. at the CBS Radio Group in Chicago.

Dave told me, "Jason…I think you'd make us a GREAT program director, but you have one problem. You have never programmed a station in a competitive market situation before. And that's makes it tough for me to "sell" you to the upper level corporate office. So, here's what you have to do…go find yourself a station in a rated market…any station in a rated market that will give you the PD's job. Make it work for a couple of years…and you'll be set. You'll never have that obstacle again."

I understood, but was frankly amazed that my boss was TELLING me to leave and find a PD's job at another station. Many GM's would never tell a market leading DJ that because they don't want to lose that kind of talent. But, that's the kind of manager and person Dave Robbins was.

So, I quietly put word on the street that I was looking for a Program Director's job.

And the first offer that came would be a life and career

changer. One I never expected and what happened has given me a bit of notoriety in the business that I would have never traded for anything. I was about to, in a sense, "invent" a radio format. One that has now lasted for over 20 years. I don't claim paternity for it…but I sure did play a role in it. And, it's a format that is STILL on the air in America today. One no one thought would work. One I got laughed at for trying. But, today, the last laugh is mine.

It may just turn out to be what people might "remember" me for in radio when I am gone from the scene. And it all started with a business discussion at a neighborhood bar.

Chapter 11
What Do You Mean...A "New Kind Of Oldies"?

It all started one afternoon when I got a phone call from my former PD, Michael Cruise. He was programming then a smaller station in suburban Delaware, Ohio...called WLYR...or...Light Rock 108. (We called it "slight rock" because the ratings were anything but impressive). But, remember...Dave Robbins told me to take the first PD's job from any station that would give me the chair. And Columbus, of course IS a rated market.

Anyway, Michael wanted me to meet with my former Oldies 92.3, WCOL boss, Bill Cusack. We met at a tavern nearby and Bill handed me a "monitor" of a station in Cleveland run by Clear Channel Communications (yes...the "Evil Empire"). He said, "Jason...look this over and tell me what you think about it".

I looked at the monitor of songs this station was playing and saw something unusual in it...about 85 percent of the music on the list were all hit songs from between the late 1970's to the very early 1990's. I said to Bill, "Well, one thing's for sure, no station here is playing music like this except for WNCI's "Friday Night 80's" specialty show". Bill replied, "I know. So, what would you think might happen if a station took that music and made a format out of it? Do you think it could work?" I thought about it for a minute, and said, "It would be a format of a new kind of oldies... oldies for a younger generation...I don't see why it wouldn't work".

We agreed to meet again about this idea and would two or three times. I'd meet Bill in the parking lot of his station. We'd get in his car and would drive around talking about the new station idea.

We decided to make it 100 percent gold based, as opposed to Cleveland whose music mix included about 15 percent current and recently based hits. And decided the name of the station would be "Star 107.9". The slogan? "The Best Of The 80's…and more". And, that is when Bill asked, "Okay…so, do you want the job? He said he'd pay me $38,000 to start, plus benefits (health insurance, etc.). And I said ok and put in my notice to Dave Robbins at WCOL. I kept the format change under wraps from Dave for a while.

What really amazed me was that so many people thought it couldn't work. That it was a fad, that the music was "burned out", and that it couldn't last. They had said the same damn thing about the Oldies format. It worked…why couldn't this?

You see…nobody had ever done this type of format anywhere. There were no rules for "how" you do it, as it is in CHR, Country, Oldies or any "established" radio format. I had to make it up as I went. If you do this today, it's actually quite easy. You can buy a music list from a consultant, get a jingle package made up, hire your staff, follow the instructions and…bingo! You have a radio station!

So, the first thing I had to do was come up with a playlist. So, I went north to Delaware, Ohio and locked myself inside a production studio at WDLR-AM-FM radio there (owned at the time by Star's Chief Engineer, Mark Litton), and began to record music into the computer we would be using on air. 700 titles taken directly from the Joel Whitburn book of charts from Billboard Magazine. It was quite a job…locked in a production room for eight or ten hours a day recording music. Today, the software allows you to automatically "ingest" the music into the computer hard drive. You can even buy a music library that ingests by itself into your software.

And, it turned out what I was doing was exactly the WRONG thing to do.

I also bought a jingle package done by Thompson Creative Productions in Dallas, Texas and sat in by phone as the recording session for the jingles was being done. It was the next best thing to flying to Dallas and being present at the session. I would like to have done that, but we didn't have the budget. Still, though, the jingles had punch and fit the station well.

Now, who would be my air staff? Well, for starters, I have never believed in "cleaning out" an entire staff and starting over. These are human beings who have to put food on their table. I didn't want to make staff changes unless I had to. And, as it turned out, only one staffer didn't want to work for the new station. He may have regretted that decision later. In his place, I hired a young jock who took the name of a Los Angeles DJ…Billy Burke… to work afternoon drive. He was up tempo, very into the music and turned out to be a great choice. He works for THE Ohio State University's TV station today.

There are a number of air checks of the station on You Tube…and some that "claim" to be of me, (air name: Jason Roberts) which are not me. But at least one on there IS me. There are also air checks of Mike Dunn, a.k.a. Billy Burke doing afternoon drive on You Tube as well. And, an interesting video of the station itself where you will see Bill Cusack, Jerry Kemp (Jay Stevens) and others.

We'd start off with me and my former WCOL news person now working in Delaware, Kelly Quinn. (It was to be temporary as I didn't think I could be PD and morning show host…and it turned out I was right). Middays were handled by light rock staffer Jay Stevens (who I told only needed to bring his delivery up a notch or two to do what I wanted to hear and did very well). Evenings were a multiple number of people over time. Overnights were voice tracked locally by part time staffers such as Deborah Bonner who also worked live on the weekends and Robin Young (who became known as "Flounder")…just like the "Animal House" character.

Now, how to shake up the market when we came on the air

with the format? We didn't have the biggest of promotion budgets, though I did have one. We decided on buying bus cards because they were cheap and could be traded for advertising. Our Sales Manager, Tim Stinson came up with a good idea…a plane that we could put in the air anytime that would tow a gigantic banner with our logo on it. The cost was only $300 bucks for a couple hours of flight…and we flew it over Ohio State football games and outdoor concerts. No other radio station was doing that…but when they saw us doing it, they quickly became copycats. Eventually, the air traffic over these events became quite congested. We were the trend setter with that.

One last thing. We weren't financially able to afford going 23 days commercial free. But, Bill Cusack and I settled on 5-thousand in a row that would allow 12 or so days of non-stop music. That was OK with me. It was long enough to make an impression.

I got everything recorded in the computer by Thursday afternoon, May 30th, 1998. The day before, I met with the air and sales staffs and told them what I was about to do to the radio station. We were already "stunting" the station by playing "Wheel Of Formats"…the sound effect of a spinning wheel would play in between songs…with a station voice asking "What music will the wheel stop on this Friday at noon? Be listening to find out". And after that a totally different song style would play. It was, to put it loosely, an eclectic mess. From a heavy metal song…to Frank Sinatra…to the Beatles…to the Go-Go's…to an Urban song…to Top 40…to classic rock. Imagine…Dean Martin's "Volare" into Led Zeppelin.

I was frank and honest with the staff. "There are literally no rules to this format. No one has ever done it before. I have no clue how to do it either and we're going to be making it up as we go. I am sure we will make mistakes…lots of them. The ratings are going to go up and down…but should stabilize as we figure out the best music mix to play." What Bill Cusack gave us…God

Bless him...was the ability to fail, and the time to figure out how to correct the problem.

I sent everyone home that night...and told them to be back at 10 am the next day.

I did not realize that we...and I...were about to make broadcast radio history. In more ways than one. And that what I was about to do might just be my legacy in the business.

Why? I am still remembered for it. And, I can say I was the first to program it on a station that intended to make it a format. Even my boss at work today acknowledges that I did it first. Why? He was the third person to do it. And today, WOGL in Philadelphia is doing it...and, I might add...the legendary WCBS-FM in New York is doing it. So, too is KRTH (K-Earth 101) in Los Angeles, the former KHJ-FM.

But, I did it first.

Chapter 12

Launching A "Star"

Columbus, Ohio radio history will note that Friday, May 31st, 1998 at 12 Noon will be forever marked as the day a new radio format never before heard, began at 107.9 on the FM radio dial.

And yes, every station in town was listening at that moment to hear what we were going to do. They were worried about us... because they couldn't figure out what the heck I had been up to since "leaving" WCOL. I had literally "vanished" for two weeks.

The station that worried the most? WNCI. They had no format competition, you see and were ripe for the picking. And we didn't have to "beat them" to win. All we needed to do was be competitive and knock them down a few points in their target age group of listeners and we'd make money hand over fist with competitive ad rates.

At the stroke of 12 Noon...the Wheel of Formats ended... we aired a brief launch promo announcement and then, the sounds of Huey Lewis and The News and "The Heart Of Rock and Roll" were heard. "The New Star 107.9...the best of the 80's and more" was on the air and rocking.

Some stations were overjoyed. Some laughed at us, saying, "What a joke! This music is all burned out and no one wants to hear it." A lot of Program Directors in the industry said this, too as the format announcement hit the internet on the "All Access" website. Some WNCI staffers said, "Oh, crap"!

As I've said before...they said that about "oldies stations", too. Like my old boss, Dick Jones in Wilmington. He truly believed that music from the 60's would never be heard on radio again.

I, instead, had the last laugh. And I am still laughing about it today.

Three months later, when the first rating book came out, some radio managers in Columbus got a rude awakening. Star 107.9, a weak signaled Class A radio station with an antenna on a tower 10 miles north of the northern most Interstate outerbelt... debuted in the Top 10 of Columbus radio stations with a total audience rating of 3.1. In demo, the station was easily in the Top 5 and was already beginning to nip at WNCI's heels. The ratings on the station, especially in demo had NEVER been so high.

Our Sales Manager couldn't be happier, because the phones started ringing with advertisers begging to be on the air immediately.

What a fun job this was...before long my staff and I were doing remotes and personal appearances...and concerts...I got to M.C. the first...before a sold out house at a nightclub that held over 500 people who came to see Rick Springfield. You know, hits like "Jessie's Girl", "I've Done Everything For You", and "Don't Talk To Strangers". And WE were responsible for it. Kelly Quinn and I met Rick that night, and I still the photo of it at home.

Sure, WNCI got the biggest of 80's shows because of their record company connections and their monster signal and ratings. But, we got ad buys for them, gave away tickets, and I interviewed artists like Kate Pierson of the B-52's and John Mellencamp...also the bass player of Duran Duran, John Taylor. We'd fly the banner plane over every concert and our banner outshowed WNCI's. Most people in the crowd thought it was our concert when they saw the plane because we had the biggest banner. I remember doing a concert outside Polaris Amphitheater and broadcasting before the show on Star from there.

WNCI had their inflatable "boom box" on site and, while I was on the air, the boom box came undone and started rolling down the hill. I called the station, told them to call WNCI and tell them that their boom box was headed toward Interstate 71

North! They had to scramble and send some interns out to find the boombox and save it, and all the drivers on I-71.

Six months later, the second 80's station came on the air in the U.S.. It was called..."The 80's Channel"...WXXY and WYXX in Chicago. Bill Cusack flew me up there for a day to listen to the station and have lunch with their Program Director, Chris Shebel (a former WLS DJ). It was there, I got to meet one of my idols in the business, Fred Winston, one of the funniest men to ever turn on a microphone. I told Fred I had listened to him as a child on WING in Dayton. He leaned down and said in a quiet voice, "I think the statute of limitations is up on that one". We both had a good laugh about that. And, not long ago, I caught up with Chris Shebel at the "Celebration of Life" for Dave Robbins in Columbus following his death.

"Don't you find it a bit ironic, Chris...that the format that you and I programmed in the 90's that everybody said was a fad and could never last...is now called "Classic Hits" and is on the air in just about every radio market in the country?"

"Yeah", said Chris. "How about that?" Indeed.

I did eventually get off the air mornings and moved myself to afternoons. Getting up at 4:15 in the morning, and getting off work around 5 or 6 pm is no fun at all.

Somehow, around that time, I happened to come into a list of the home phone numbers of the stars, and thought maybe there was a good morning show bit to be had with this. I spied the home phone number of Davy Jones on it...you know, the cheeky, short lead singer of the Monkees...he was living in Pennsylvania on a farm he owned at the time.

Now, we NEVER sabotaged any star we called. We always called ahead of time the day before to ask if we could do the bit and to arrange a time to call and do it. Sometimes we got hung up on, but most of the time whether the star agreed to do it or not, they did tell us they appreciated our respect in calling them first.

In the case of Davy Jones, we actually spoke with his grounds and housekeeper first. Davy was out of town for the weekend doing a show. But, the gentleman told us that if we'd call back Monday morning at that time, he would let Davy know that we were going to call and when so that he would be ready for the call and would answer it.

We called on Monday and sure enough, Davy answered the phone and did 20 minutes with the morning show. Couldn't have been nicer. And I have always respected him for that. Some people claim to have had not as great an experience with him, but he was OK in my book.

80's stations came on the air in Birmingham, Alabama and Dayton, Ohio where 95.7, The Point was launched. I would eventually program it, too. Today, The Point is WHIO-FM. I'm still on the station today, and our sister station, The Eagle is an "80's Station".

And all of this, because I agreed to try and be the first guy to program such a station. It is something for which I am truly proud. And don't you ever believe the small handful of "know-it-alls" out there who say we weren't a success because we only lasted about three years.

The fact was: we took 4 million dollars out of the Columbus, Ohio radio ad market in a little less than 3 years. That's an average of about 1.5 million dollars a year…on a signal challenged FM in a large market with limited promotion and research money. I defy ANYONE to call that "a failure".

Now…about the music. Why was I wrong to program according to that chart book? Well, because you can split up the music of the 1980's into categories…not all of them good. The early 1980's saw the music go very light and fluffy. Air Supply was big, you had a lot of ballads make the charts. Why? Because

AM radio was beginning to die off in audience in favor of better sounding FM. So, it began targeting adults. In Dayton, top 40 gave way to "Adult Radio 1410, WING".

In 1983, though, Michael Jackson shook the world with an album called "Thriller". And THAT brought teens and young adults back to a new version of Top 40 Radio called "CHR" (Contemporary Hits Radio). High energy DJ's playing outstanding music that was being actually driven by the popularity of something new called "M-TV" (or, Music Television). The first TV channel to program music videos 24 hours a day. Now, remember, some of those early M-TV videos didn't actually do well on the music charts. Some songs such as "I Melt With You" by Modern English peaked in the 30's and 40's on the charts. But, they are SO memorable today because of the video play that M-TV gave it. And they had some great V-J's, too…Nina Blackwood, Alan Hunter, Martha Quinn, J.J. Jackson and Mark Goodwin kept young viewers entertained around the clock.

They would not only be responsible for new trends in music. M-TV was responsible for bringing back classic artists…like the Monkees. They brought their TV show back for a weekend. And the response was so big that the Monkees had to do a new album of (mostly) new material. "That Was Then, This Is Now" hit the charts around 1986…it reached #20 and the group was back on the charts for the first time since around 1969. The Monkees (minus guitar player Mike Nesmith) went out on tour and played to sell-out crowds. I couldn't believe in 1986, I would be playing anything NEW by the Monkees, but so it was.

In 1986, the Monkees played Universal Amphitheater in Los Angeles and Mike Nesmith agreed to join his fellow simians for the concert there. His part of the show came at the very end… when…after singing, "Daydream Believer", Davy announced to Micky that they had a "special guest" to bring out. Micky said, "Who?" and Davy announced, "we have MIKE!". Micky, of course joking as he usually does, asked "Michael Jackson? Michael

Jordan? Who?" Davy replied, "Michael Nesmith!" And on walked Mike onto the stage.

"Where've you been?", said Micky to Mike. "I was lookin' for my HAT!" (referring to the green wool hat he always wore on the show) And, he would play about three or four songs. Then, all together, they played "I'm A Believer" and the show was ended.

So, you see...M-TV and the 80's format now known as "Classic Hits", was actually groundbreaking in many ways. It made new artists and it brought back others who have become legendary musical acts because of it.

It was a heady time for sure. But storm clouds were forming. And I was about to weather a storm like I had never thought I ever see. In the end, my time at Star came to a close, but my biggest challenge lay ahead. One that would be a triumph for me...but one which came to a frustrating end.

Chapter 13

What The Hell Is A "Stop 26/Riverbend"?

The call letters I selected for Star 107.9 were WXST-FM. The "ST" of course, stood for "Star" and the "X" was a nod to the CHR station most dominant for most of the 80's decade in Columbus, Great Trails Broadcasting's "WXGT" or "92X".

And despite being competition, oddly enough, one of the biggest fans of my station was my old boss at WCOL, Dave Robbins. Dave loved the format…thought it could be extremely viable. We had lunch often (with sincere thanks to my former employer). And, up until the time of his death, Dave and I still communicated by Facebook. I asked him if Star could be considered the first "Classic Hits" station. Remember, at the time, he had just retired from CBS Radio…which jumped into the format first with WOGL in Philadelphia, then with WCBS-FM in New York". Dave thought it was entirely reasonable to think Star was the first in. Somehow, I suspect he was thinking about us when CBS was getting ready to debut the format in Philadelphia and New York.

What fun we had! We were flying by the seat of our pants doing a format that, basically, nobody knew how to do.

We gave away Ohio State football and basketball tickets. (We never had a lot of them, but the station did buy some).

We got novel on our outdoor advertising. Our Sales Manager, Tim Stinson got in touch with a man who towed banners with an airplane. But, these weren't just any banners, these were about 20 feet long by 30 feet wide in size….big enough to make a sign, a billboard. We put our logo on it…and they would fly it for an hour over an event.

In our case, we flew them over concerts and Ohio State

Football games. Now, imagine, being in the horseshoe and having a flying billboard with your station's logo on it flying around the stadium for an hour being seen by around 90,000 captive potential listeners. It wasn't long before every station in Columbus copied US.

One contest that worked well for us was something many stations did called "Insurance Policy Games". The idea behind them was this: The station buys an "annuity" (a life insurance policy indemnifying it from actually giving away the grand prize, which mathematically was not easy to do), BUT...if by some fate of God someone actually hit the grand prize, the insurance company would pay the prize. Our station DID do what a lot of stations didn't do...we always gave away a gift certificate for each contest play and registered everyone who played the game for a "second chance" prize of $5,000. That way, I felt we would avoid ill feelings from listeners who may well have thought their time was being "wasted" listening for a radio contest that gave away nothing.

We "built" the excitement of the contest over a period of 6 weeks, never announcing just how far the contest would go. Week one: our promotional announcement said, everyone who played the game had a chance to win $1,000 cash. (Why $1,000? That was the "typical" amount given away by big stations like WNCI at the time).

At the end of week one's final contest, a new promo: "Well, that was fun, but one thousand dollars just doesn't feel like it's enough. Next week, every time we play the game, you have a chance to win $5,000 cash!" The phones rang a little harder the second week.

End of week, two, same end of week promo except the third week's prize amount was $10,000! Now, we had some of the market's attention and the phones were ringing off the hook. End of week three, the grand prize amount went to $25,000. End of week four, $50,000...and end of week five...every time the game was played, it was worth $100,000 dollars cash! I think we may have caused severe disruption to Columbus's 821 trunk telephone exchange that week.

No one actually won the grand prize, of course...but one contest player won five grand and every player got a $25 gift certificate from somewhere, so it was fun.

I am writing this on January 1, 2020, and a lot of the talk on this day is of Y2K day this day 20 years ago. Everybody will tell you that "nothing happened" that day where it had been predicted that everyone's computer would crash, there'd be major blackouts as the computerized equipment at power stations would go out and there would be general hell everywhere from it.

It figures that Star 107.9 and its sister station, WOMP AM/FM in Wheeling would have the only Y2K problem in America... well, maybe not, but who knows? (I have since heard that other stations did have some "funnies" happen that day.)

December 31st, 1999...we were live at a place called "The Elephant Bar" in Columbus having a massively huge on air New Year's Eve bash...(and yes, we did play Prince's "1999" a few times that night).

Midnight came...and we pranked the radio audience. Counted down "5...4...3...2...1...Happy New Ye..."(silence on air). We had turned our microphones off. Left them off for about 15 seconds, then turned them back on and said "Just kidding", and went on with the music and the party!

It all came to an end at 2 AM, and everyone, including me, had breakfast there. Afterwards, I got in my car to go home. Turned on the radio and got a shock! The DJ who was on the air was playing the right songs, there was just one problem.

She had resigned about 6 or 8 months earlier and no longer

worked for us!

I turned my car around and headed back to the station not knowing what I'd find. I was sure she had given me her key when she left, so...how in the world was she on the air?

I got to the station, went up the elevator to the third floor and opened the office door. All the lights were out except the one or two we left on for security purposes. No one was in the studio... or anywhere in the station. The screen on the on-air computer was showing the right schedule...but still, the wrong schedule was playing. It was one of the weirdest things I had seen in my life.

I grabbed a CD, put it in and rebooted the computer. When it came back up, it was playing the right schedule and I put it back on the air and everything was fine. To this day, I have no idea where in the bowels of that thing it had that old schedule...but everything was fixed and I went home and nothing like that ever happened again.

We would "tweak" the guys at WNCI from time to time, all in good natured fun. But, one day we discovered...the station had "given up" doing its Friday Night 80's show. That meant...we had Friday night, and the 80's audience, all to ourselves! Of course, we immediately adopted the "Friday Night 80's" name, daring WNCI to send us a "cease and desist" order. They wouldn't, of course...because once you stop doing the show, your state "Service Mark" on the name is over. We were "the new home of Friday Night 80's, Star 107.9!"

And, while we were around, Dave Robbins always had a message. "You're playing too many songs. Cut the playlist!" I'd eventually figure that out. But it took time, trial and error, and dealing with a number of consultants handed to me by the station.

The first consultant, Pat McMahon wasn't around long. He had no interest in the format, so he left and Bill then gave me a local area consultant...former 92-X Program Director, Tom Gilligan. I would be very critical about Tom and his advice for a while, but have mellowed about that. He was, I discovered, a disciple of another oldies consultant named E. Alvin Davis. E's "oldies" format was about 15-hundred titles strategically deployed and, quite frankly, I'd eventually tweak that format slightly and would become very successful with it on a low powered FM operation in Logan County, Ohio.

The only issue with Tom is that he wouldn't stop "adding" songs to the playlist. Now, in fairness, his intentions were that, eventually, we would stop adding songs, deploy them differently and properly and move on from there.

The only problem that caused for me: the bigger the playlist got, the lower Star's ratings went. You see, folks...and for you people who believe radio stations should play thousands of song titles, when you get above a certain level of titles, your "time spent listening" goes down because people are not hearing "the hits" often enough.

And that wasn't good, because, as the ratings fell, we started losing advertisers and money.

I was at my wit's end. I went to Bill Cusack and leveled with him. "Bill...what's up with this? I know you're a tight playlist guy. I've seen you fire PD's and consultants who couldn't justify a big list. Why are you letting Tom do this...it's really putting us in the hole?"

Eventually, Bill cut Tom loose and brought in a former jock of his at another station, a former WNCI staffer named Pete Dylan to act as an "advisor" to me and help me deal with the playlist.

One day, out of frustration, I called Pete. "Pete...why are we playing all these songs?" Pete said, "I thought you wanted to play them." I said, "Pete, all I want to play is what works. I don't care how many songs it is, but I want to play the hits often enough, so we don't get our heads bashed in when the ratings come out."

So, Pete came in that afternoon and, together, we came up with a solution. We'd get rid of nothing. But, we would re-deploy the library into a short list of "hits" that would play most of the day...about 450 titles. The other songs were used for "specialty" and "request" shows.

And we did a number of them. "Rock Of The 80's" aired from 10 pm to midnight Monday thru Thursday. That was where a lot of the hard rock played...everything from Saga's "On The Loose" to Motley Crue's "Girls, Girls, Girls" and Skid Row's "I Remember You" played.

There was "The Deep End" on Sunday nights. That was where a lot of the alternative deeper tracks from groups like R.E.M. and others played.

We did a "Saturday Night Dance Party", where a lot of the lower testing dance music and early hip hop played interspersed with hits by Prince, Madonna, Information Society and others were heard.

Deployed in this manner, where the audience could "understand" why the music was being played, worked...and the numbers began to nudge upward.

But, then, a short time later came a bombshell announcement that Star 107.9 was being sold for 11 million dollars to Liberty Media (Yes, John Malone's company who is apparently trying to buy a bigger interest in iHeart Media today). But, Liberty Media was spinning us off and selling us to local attorney Percy Squire and his company, "Stop 26/Riverbend, Inc."

Who???? What???? The company owned at that time another Class A in Johnstown, Ohio, WVKO-AM in Columbus and eventually picked up an FM in Lancaster, Ohio. I was welcomed by the new owner and staff...but kind of disturbed by what was said at the time..."We've never had a REAL Program Director before!" "Gulp", thought I. We were told that major black athletes such as Magic Johnson and others were going to be investors in the new company.

Turns out, Mr. Squire didn't have the financial backing he thought he did when he committed to that 11 million dollar purchase price. None of his investors wanted any part of the deal. And his company already had one foot in bankruptcy court.

Paychecks started bouncing (though, to his credit, Mr. Squire always made those checks good from a personal account). Bills stopped getting paid. I started getting angry phone calls from our vendors over the problem. Percy assured me there was another investor around the corner and the problem would go away soon.

It never did. One by one, most of my staff left and I couldn't blame them. I was able to hire others, but most didn't last long. The ratings kept tumbling because promotional money dried up. I got so tired of having to "beg" Percy for money to pay for our computerized music scheduling program, Selector, which was $300 a month. We had to have it...or I'd be doing the music by hand.

We did have an idea, though. ("We", meaning me and my new "advisor" Pete). We wanted to take the Johnstown station to a CHR format designed to impact WNCI's demographics. We could take the combo ratings of both stations and sell them that way. The two stations, together...if they got Star's average of a 3 share...would be a combined 6 share in total audience. WNCI was getting about a 9 or a 10. Theoretically, one down book for WNCI and we "could" have beaten them, at least in demo.

And during that period of time, the FCC was allowing stations to "sell" airtime to record labels for "spins" of new artists. Though considered payola if a DJ did it on his or her own, this was a case in which the station "sold" the three minute block to the station for the song, and the record company could, legally, recompense the station with concert tickets, backstage passes, giveaway product, T-shirts, etc. We decided we would only do this on overnights, but, it was a way for us to come up with promotions for the new station. They were called "Program Length Commercials" and they had to be logged on the station's Program Log, but that was no real issue to us. And we were talking with some of the old 92X jocks to voice track the station's airshifts.

We got Star's ratings back up to the top ten and at its highest ever…a 3.4 share total audience and even bigger in demo.

It would have worked. The sticking point? Percy.

I have worked for a number of black radio owners and still see the same disturbing problem. All they want to program are stations aimed at the minority audience.

Now, before you call me a racist…I have no issue with that desire. In fact, I admire it. BUT…the problem is…they take these stances even when it makes no sense from a business perspective to do so. You are NOT going to make money programming the #5 rated black FM in a market. Particularly not if #1, 2 and 3 are owned by a deep pocketed big consolidator such as Radio One and you have no money to put into your stations.

Our Johnstown FM was a programming mess. It was a different format every daypart. Urban Adult in the morning, usually a syndicated show such as Tom Joyner. Black News-Talk middays with Jesse Jackson. Hip Hop afternoons…and jazz at night interspersed at any time by a speech by Columbus black Mayor Michael Coleman (a really nice man I like a lot), but it was terrible programming. You never knew what you were going to hear when you tuned the station in. And the bad ratings showed it.

Unfortunately…I later figured out…that mish mash was also to be placed on 107.9.

It was the beginning of the end. I just couldn't take it anymore. I had received an offer from crosstown competitor Saga Communications, through their Program Director for their "oldies" stations, my long time best friend and high school classmate, Tim Fox...to program WKIO-FM, a 25,000 watt FM station in Champaign, Illinois which had some programming and ratings challenges at the time. I was sure that I could fix that. I took the job and, honestly, was in tears resigning to Bill Cusack. I knew I was leaving him in a lurch. But, he understood.

You see Percy was doing everything he could to make Star fail. He signed deals (without telling me or Bill) to air syndicated urban radio shows. I was getting calls every few days from ABC Radio asking me why we were negligent in returning commercial affidavits for one of their shows. I replied, "We don't air that show...we're not an urban station".

Bill didn't know what going on...and couldn't get an answer from Percy, either. In the meantime, Percy DID give Star one thing it desperately needed. Six months of service from a research company that had a new kind of music research...a system of research done over the internet. It's common place today...but not heard of when we did it.

With it, I was able to "test" the music in our library...40 songs at a time. After a couple of months, I began to see a trend in the research...the hard core "urban-dance" songs were all (with just the exception of a few titles by Madonna and Prince) at the bottom of the list, pop songs by artists like Michael Jackson, Cyndi Lauper and Huey Lewis were middle to upper middle in the pack. At the top...the rock songs. Mellencamp, Aerosmith, Def Leppard and the like. Heavy metal was a cypher and so, too were most alternative titles.

Using that music research information, Pete and I were to recraft the music on Star 107.9...and the ratings started to steady themselves and began to climb.

The next book, we were well back in the three and a half share range, and the demos were great.

It was all for naught, though. Because Percy was intent on destroying us. Before long though, Star was Urban Radio...and Stop 26 went bankrupt. More on that later.

Chapter 14
Putting My "Child" To Sleep For The Last Time

It was time for me to go. Percy was moving Star into the basement of his legal practice in downtown Columbus. Not bad studios...but somewhat of a weird facility to be sure.

The offices were decent, too. But, I had signed up to run a competitive radio station and it was obvious to me that, with Percy Squire's constant interference with the programming, there was no way that we were going to be competitive. None of his stations could be. Not in Market 34...which is what Columbus was at that time. His stations did better in Youngstown, I'm sure through no real assistance of his. And it turned out that he later was sued for apparently never even making ONE payment on the purchase of Star 107.9. His company was liquidated later...but, last I heard, he was still around in Columbus. (He still owns WVKO-AM there. Fortunately, though, he did make one good decision...he's hired my friend, John Anderson, to program it. And John tells me, so far, he's keeping his hands off the programming.)

Percy, should you ever read this, please understand, I respected you as a person and still do. You weren't a bad "boss". However, had you stopped and listened to what we were proposing...really listened to us...we could have made you a LOT of money. And perhaps, your company would never have needed to be liquidated.

The worst part of it all...I had to put on a game face to my staff like it was all going to be OK for the sake of the company when I had grave doubts about it personally.

And slowly, but surely, a lot of people began to leave. And I had to scramble to fill their positions, knowing full well, the format could be yanked by Percy any day.

The phone calls just kept coming from networks of Urban Radio shows wanting affidavits for commercials for programs we weren't airing. I kept going to Bill, but he had no answers for me.

About that time, I got a call from my high school friend, Tim Fox. He had been programming KIOA-FM in Des Moines, Iowa for several years (another legendary station there) for Saga Communications. Seems Saga recently purchased WKIO-FM in Champaign, Illinois. It was an oldies station and Tim asked if I might be interested in talking with them about possibly being the Program Director?

Saga is a good company. And despite all I would go through with them, I still think they are a good company. They are run much like the Cox organization and believe, as I do that "you win with people". In other words, hire good people, get out of their way and let them do their jobs.

I drove over to Champaign one weekend and they put me up in a hotel, expenses paid and asked me to listen to the station and take notes. I did, and listened hard. The following Monday, I would meet with the General Manager about the job.

I was listening on the way in already. And I heard the "issues" Tim had described to me with WKIO. It was clearly "all over the road" when it came to oldies...was WAY too "deep" and the music scheduling was terrible. I heard the station transition in a segue (that is with no station identifier or jingle in between) from Nat "King" Cole's beautiful song, "That Sunday, That Summer" straight into Madonna's "Lucky Star". YIKES!

The original Program Director of the station is a guy who, frankly was then and still is a legend there, Mike Haile. He is a deep playlist guy. He had worked at WKIO when it still played some current Top 40 hits in with the oldies and felt if it was an old song, it fit WKIO, regardless of "genre". Well this created a bunch of what we programmers call "train wrecks". Mike, wanted no part of WKIO under Saga, because it meant that he would have to program the station according to the wishes of the new owners, which meant he would have a corporate office over him... and he would no longer have ultimate control over the station's programming. So he left and went across town.

Look, I know music has changed over the decades. But, you simply cannot play "Dream Lover" by Bobby Darin directly into "Bust A Move", by Young M.C. The flow just isn't right.

Saga did a local music test for WKIO (at a cost of around $20,000 I might add). So, we had a good idea of what music would work. The format just had to be implemented correctly. And I knew I could do that. I had a great conversation with the G.M. (who previously had run WNCI in Columbus, ironically.), and I returned to Columbus where I heard nothing from Saga for about 6 months.

One evening, though, WKIO's Manager called. Did I want the PD's job there? Heck yes, I did... I saw danger with Star 107.9 coming and wanted out. I was hired during that phone call, said I would be a given an employment contract (something I had never had before) and would be paid $40,000 a year to start. It was decent money for a small market like Champaign and I was told there were ways to live on that money.

I was willing to do it, but I wanted to seek a little programming advice from a guy I didn't know, had never meant... but from whom, I thought I could get some good advice.

I had gotten the e-mail address of Ron Jacobs. Ron was the original Program Director of 93/KHJ, "Boss Radio" in Los Angeles. And, in later years, he would go on to help "invent" the show known as "American Top 40" which would make Casey Kasem famous.

So, I e-mailed Ron and explained what I was doing and asked if he could give me some advice. I was expecting maybe a nice paragraph or two. Imagine my shock when Ron sent me 10 PAGES of advice…he outlined the complete strategy behind "Boss Radio", told me how to deploy the music, told me how to make the station "larger than life" and to maximize every promotion so it fit that goal.

Wow! This was like getting God's radio programming strategy. Ron told me to e-mail him anytime…and if my station needed advice, he'd gladly be our consultant. That never happened, of course, but I was honored he'd ask. (And, believe me, had we needed a consultant, Ron would have been the first person I would have called.)

Among the things he told me: Don't ignore ANY daypart, especially the overnight show. The all night person, he said, is often ignored by programmers…and that staffer needs to know that his or her work is respected and appreciated. He told me to get out of bed at 2 in the morning at least once a month and listen to the all night show. Then, send a note or e-mail to the all night person and give them some love and advice.

He told me a good PD is a father, a place to go when a staffer needs to vent or when a staffer has some doubts about their performance and needs advice. A good PD is meticulous and strives for perfection in making music logs and helping his staff achieve greatness…who anticipates problems and deals with them before they become major issues.

He didn't have to do all that, but I sure did appreciate it. Ron died a few years back and I cried at the news of his death. He created one hell of a radio station. And Bill Drake created a format that has never been touched. Most of his principles still guide radio stations today (all but his advice on commercial loads). What Drake did was to understand that people are not listening for flannel mouth DJ's. They're listening for the music. The best of the business, whether you worked for a Drake station or not, understood this and tailored their shows accordingly. I mean, think of all the greats who worked for Rick Sklar at WABC.

Dan Ingram NEVER got too wordy. And NONE of those guys ever did. Sure, Larry Lujack talked sometimes with his "addresses to the nation", but they were bits. Over the intros, Larry was as concise as they come. Sometimes too concise.

The best in this business, know "shorter is better" and "shut up and play the hits". I can say more over a 15 second intro than a lot of people. And it works whether you're a jock or a news guy. When doing news, I am always paying attention to "word conservation". Look at an AP headline these days, and sometimes, it makes you wonder who in the world would just rip and read this stuff. You don't need to call the President of the United States by his or her full name every single time. But, that's the AP stylebook and they are wedded to it.

You don't need to speak "The King's English", either. Speak like a real person does. Write like the listener thinks. You can communicate in fewer words that way and fewer words improves your story count.

You can even, within a few boundaries, write like CKLW's infamous "20/20 News Team" once did.

I do all the time. Billboarding an outrageous story by saying, "This story might just make you mad. A man is waking up staring at gray bars, all because police say he led them on a high speed chase down I-75 that has left a family of three dead. Cops tell WHIO news 38 year old Joe Blow of Nowhereville robbed a convenience store, and took off when patrol cars arrived. Careening down the interstate at speeds of 125 miles an hour, Blow slammed into the car containing the family when a tire blew, pushing them into the path of an oncoming semi. Investigators are still trying to piece together what caused this shocking tragedy".

Hits you in the face, doesn't it? Life has a way of doing that, too.

So, now I had to move to Illinois.

I packed a U-Haul truck...had a "moment" with my then ten year old nephew who had known me practically from birth. The night before I left and his parents were taking him home...he ran over to me on the couch, jumped on my chest...grabbed me around my neck and couldn't stop crying. Clearly, he didn't want me to leave. I cried, too.

He's in his 30's today and lives at my house. You see, his father, sadly, died when he was in his early teens in 2003 and his mom lives in West Virginia. He graduated high school there, but had apparently no intentions of living there because there's just very few job opportunities in "West, By God". So, he moved in with me...went to school for a time at a local community college and today has a good job working working for a name brand manufacturer of ink cartridges Regardless...he'll make it at something. I couldn't be prouder of him. His Dad would be, too.

I drove west to Illinois, 300 miles out of state to live for the first time in my career. Found an inexpensive duplex in nearby Rantoul in former housing from the now shuttered and redeveloped Chanute Air Force Base. Only $500 a month and much better on rent than in Champaign, where the 6 figure college professors were paying about $800 plus a month...and it was only a 15 minute drive to work.

And what an education I was about to get. And not all of it good.

Chapter 15

How To Win In The Ratings...Lose Money...And Your Job.

I was greatly welcomed in Champaign. I arrived to find a big party in my honor at the station, with burgers, hot dogs and beer on the patio.

I found the way to my office and dug in. Again, I kept all the staff, replacing the former Program Director. A young man who, frankly, just couldn't see the forest for the trees.

And, here we'd go.

I kept the staff...Lon and Patti mornings (Patti was a holdover from the previous owner), Jerry Morefield middays and my promotions co-ordinator, I did afternoons, and another young holdover from the previous owner named Rob Stone did evenings. We voice tracked on the weekends, which enabled all of us to have a five day work week.

I had a promotions budget of $15,000 per rating book. We were a 2 book a year market, Spring and Fall, so I had about $30,000 a year to spend. We bought billboards with slogans like "Wake, Rattle And Roll with Lon and Patti Mornings" and the "Oldies 92-5" logo. And we gave away about $8-grand either in money or prizes every book.

Cash was the first book promotion...it was already underway when I got there and it gave us a good bump in the ratings. We gave away University of Illinois Football Tickets, too. Why? We got a ton of them.

I got in my office one morning and the General Manager, Dale walked in and thunked a heavy manila envelope on my desk.

"What are these, Dale?", I asked.

"Oh, they're your football tickets. We get a lot of them to give away because, frankly, the football team isn't that good".

Good Lord, there must have been 100 packs of season tickets in there. I gave some to my staff, took one myself. I had to stop the practice later, because the IRS changed some rules and insisted that such "gifts" be taxed as income.

But, then, the unexpected happened.

Like everybody in this country, no one was prepared for what was going on happen on September 11th, 2001.

I was driving into work that morning listening to the morning show when I heard the initial report. I immediately, switched to WLW Radio in Cincinnati. I could usually pick them up on Interstate 55 going south into Champaign…and it allowed me to get a taste for what was going on at home in Ohio. So, as I did, I heard them go to a sister station in New York City, who vaguely described an airplane that had flown into one of the towers of the World Trade Center.

Like a lot of people, I thought they were talking about a small private aircraft like a Piper or a Cessna. I drove into Champaign, and was stopped at the last traffic light before turning on the road that, a short distance later, put me in the station parking lot. It was there, that "Cessna" became a "passenger jet". "Holy Crap"!, I thought. Looking both ways and finding them clear, I ran the red light and barreled into the station parking lot, running in through the back door and down the hall to studio where I just managed to make it in time for Lon and Patti and I to witness the second jetliner flying into the second tower.

I got chills down my spine. I looked at Lon and Patti and said, "Guys…one plane is an accident, but not two. I think we just went to war". And I went out the door and back to my office.

The day was a whirlwind. And I was stunned getting a call from my boss at corporate who told me to go down the hall and "tell" the General Manager that, on his authority, we were to stop playing commercials IMMEDIATELY, and not put them back on the air until advised by corporate to do so.

The last time that sort of thing had been done was when President Kennedy was assassinated in Dallas in 1963.

I got a phone call from my extended "brother", Dale who was standing outside Wright Patterson Air Force Base in Ohio. He was telling me about fighter jets scrambling outside the base and taking off.

We were going "all news" until further notice as were all of our sister stations. That posed a problem. Like many big companies, we did away with news network affiliations a long time back. We simulcast a local TV station, until they went to network coverage and was advised that, we couldn't air the network programming. By afternoon, we had a deal with CNN and our engineers scrambled to rig a "standby" satellite connection to CNN while they sent us a permanent satellite transponder to do the job. By late in the afternoon, CNN was on the air. (No insult intended to any conservative or Republican person out there… back then, CNN was the leading cable news station in America. Fox News would upset that box of apples later in time).

We were all news all day and into the next morning. Our morning show went on the air next morning at 5:30…I broadcast live from a hastily formed American Red Cross fundraiser in a parking lot on campus at the University Of Illinois. I told Lon and Patti, in my view, the best thing for them to do was speak from the heart, take phone calls and let the listeners vent. If they cried…let them. In fact, cry with them if they wanted.

Then, came the moment I will never forget. A few days later, I'm on the air and read online that former Beatle Paul McCartney (who had watched the towers burn sitting on the runway at JFK airport) had expressed his shock and sadness over the attack and told America to "hang tough" and that as soon as he could get his band together, he was coming back to do concerts all across the country.

Wow! The Beatles, of course, helped America recover from JFK's murder. Now, here was at least one of the surviving group members coming back to help us recover from this tragedy.

Our little "local" fundraiser collected an astounding $350,000 for the Red Cross in dimes, nickels, pennies, dollar bills, tens, twenties and even some 4 and figure checks from people. Sir Paul was about to raise even more with his, "Concert For America" in New York City which featured about everybody who was anybody in the music business.

First, I heard Paul had scheduled a concert in Chicago. Fine, I thought, but it wasn't going to help us much…oldies stations had little connection to record labels because we don't play current music…and don't report to trade publications. Those were the stations that could easily get tickets for that show.

But, then…I came up with the answer. A concert was scheduled a couple of weeks later in Cleveland. The light bulb went off over my head. I called my staff in on the Saturday morning tickets went on sale for the Cleveland show. Told them to bring their credit cards with them. You see, there's a little trick you can use to get tickets for a big show. You simply call your LOCAL ticket agent office when the tickets go on sale out of town. Few people are calling the local office for an out of town show. You get right in and can buy tickets before they sell out.

So, that's what we did…and about 90 minutes later, I had 40 pair of tickets for Paul McCartney in Cleveland. (And yes, my staff was reimbursed by my promotion's budget.) Then, we picked up the phone and traded 22 hotel rooms (one station rep was going and our driver), we rented a bus from a local bus company, and got free half day admission for everyone to the

Rock and Roll Hall Of Fame.

I spent about $8,000 total on the "Magical Mystery Bus" Tour to see Paul McCartney in Cleveland. We did the contest for about 3 weeks...listen at 7:15 mornings for the approximate time, the "Beatles Song Of Day" would play and the name of the song would be announced. Listen back around that time, when you heard it, caller 9 wins a pair of tickets on the trip which included show tickets, an overnight stay at nice hotel with a free breakfast the next morning and a half day visit to the Rock Hall before riding back to Champaign and arriving around 7:30 that night.

I was there as the listeners boarded the bus for Cleveland and was there when arrived back home the next day. Two very hoarse ladies got off that bus. Said they had been upgraded by a "representative of Mr. McCartney's" right into the front row of the show. Holy Crap! That had never happened to any listener of mine before...and you want to talk about how to win over a listener for life? That sure did it.

And it got the attention we had hoped for. That was obvious in January on ratings day. I figured the numbers would be good. But, was not prepared for the new General Manager, Kristine Foate to walk into my office and say, "Congratulations, Jason. You've got the number one station in Urbana-Champaign!" Double digits! A 10.2 share of the audience...and ratings that went from #6 straight to #1! Boy, did we party that night. And every air staff member was included.

Had one issue with the new General Manager, though. Steve Goldstein called me in late November, 2001 and was concerned. He had noticed I hadn't spent my entire promotional budget yet. I told him, I was just trying to be frugal with the money as the station was just getting off the ground.

He replied that I had to spend that money. If not, I'd lose it and never get it back. He asked me if my staff had any jackets? We didn't. So, Steve told me to find someone in town that could make letterman's jackets to make ten of them...have each jock's name embroidered above the right breast...with a small sewed patch of our logo on the left breast, and a GIANT station logo on the back. So, I did. I spent $3,500 dollars to the penny on the jackets and every one of my jocks was thrilled at the unexpected Christmas gift from the PD.

The GM wasn't so thrilled, and called me into the office for a dressing down. After she calmed down, I told her it wasn't my idea...that it was Steve Goldstein's idea...that he told me to spend every penny of my promotional budget, and advised her to "take it up with the Vice-President of Programming" if she needed to discuss it some more.

That must have been one hell of a conversation between the two of them. And, I think Kris lost that argument.

We did other great promotions. One summer promotion was called the "Crushed Classic". I would drive over to Des Moines on the company's dime for a day and went to an auto graveyard where I would buy 2 cars...a good, well running classic automobile that would be the "giveaway car". It would get a new paint job if needed and an interior touch up. The first year, it was a 1965 Ford Mustang GT!

The other car, well, would be a hunk of junk. Inoperable and just perfect for what I was about to do it. I sent it to the crusher. (You see I had to go to Iowa to do this first for contest security reasons and secondly because the damn state of Illinois would not do such a thing. If you'd like to know why I think Illinois' finances are such a mess, I could talk about it for about 3 or 4 days. They will NEVER get out of debt until they take some radical measures to do it. Measures they can't stomach. Their answer to their problems are always higher taxes and more spending. Eventually, Illinois will go bankrupt and I feel sorry for the fine people who live there...because I also feel strongly they should NOT be bailed out by the Feds. They need to take their medicine.)

The crushed car was made into a "cube" and put on a trailer which I pulled with the station van. The contest car was driven back to Champaign.

When we got it back, the trailer with the crushed car was placed in a barn where we went to work on it. We removed all seat belts and "identifiable" markers on it (name plates, VIN numbers, etc.), and spray painted it silver.

We announced the contest...and sold remotes where we would "reveal" the crushed car for 92 minutes (our frequency was 92.5). We would have a rope surrounding the trailer with the car people could come out, take pictures, take video of the car, they just couldn't touch it because we weren't going to let them get that close.

Their job was to determine the make, model and year of the crushed car. And the first person to correctly do that, won the giveaway car.

It was pretty easy to sell those remote broadcasts because every car crazy within 50 miles would come out to see it. And, despite what you may think, we always had a handful of people who would get it right.

That brought about a "Classic Car Reveal" party, which we sold during which time, we announced the make, model and year of the Crushed Classic. And we had all of the people who correctly guessed there. They were given a number we threw into a hopper and from that, we pulled the winning ticket. We announced the winner...and gave everyone who took part some consolation prizes from sponsors and fed everyone who showed up lunch.

We promoted mostly via billboards. We eventually teamed with a local television station to have station meteorologists. Our station cluster was often #1, #2 and #3 in the market, though just WHO was 1,2, and 3 bounced around. But, I didn't mind as long as it was all in the family.

I had really good people working for me, even though they weren't all the most polished of announcers. And I respect every single one of the.

Champaign was on the edge of tornado alley. And spring and summer was not fun. I spent months sleeping with a NOAA weather radio next to my bed. If a tornado warning was issued, I had to drive into the station to alert the public as the Emergency Alert System box was the only way to do it when no one was there. So, the 2 AM wake up calls were not really that fun and many spring and summer days, I arrived at work bleary eyed. Sometimes I was there when the morning show arrived.

My sentence of purgatory on tornado duty ended when my 7 to Midnight guy, Rob noticed the bags under my eyes one day and said, "Jason…here's my phone number. I'm up generally until 3 or 4 in the morning. Just call me at home and I'll go in when there's bad weather." I was very indebted to him for that.

We had lots of those station parties and many burgers were cooked on the grill out back. Dave Robbins was right. Get somebody to hire you as a PD, make it work for a couple of years and from there on, you're set. WKIO was a great place to work.

A short time later, my buddy Dale actually decided to move to Illinois and join me. He had fallen into a bad relationship with a woman and thought moving over there and in with me would help him get over the relationship.

Not only did it do that, but both of us started making friends who lived in towns and cornfields nearby. There was a great Amish cafeteria south of town, a fantastic family restaurant IN town and, in Rantoul was a breakfast place that featured something called a "haystack"…picture this: a cheeseburger without the bun, set between biscuits, a couple of eggs and hash browns with sausage gravy poured over all of it. Yes, it's a heart attack on a plate...but well worth the time to eat one every now and then.

My friend, Dale and I hooked up with a drummer...and formed a bar band that played on the weekends in some of the local gin mills. We were pretty good and gathered a bit of a following.

The nearest White Castle was an hour away...but, missing the taste of those sliders, we sent the morning DJ's "danger boy" up to Kankakee in the station van to get a case of them on the air. Yes, it was worth it.

And, a half hour away in Danville, there was a "Big Boy" Restaurant...an off shoot of the local "Frisch's" chain here in Ohio...where I could still get the Chili Spaghetti and Big Boy sandwiches I loved from there.

Oh, and pizza? OMG! There is a place there called Papa Del's. It features deep dish, Chicago style pizza...and it's to die for. These pizzas weigh about a pound each and are absolutely delicious. You can even have them shipped to you in dry ice. Every time my friends, or I go to see other friends there, you can bet 2 or 3 of those pizzas come home with us.

WKIO was number one in the market. I was actually beginning to like working away from home. After all, I had decent vacation time and always spent it back in Columbus. I thought I was set. I was wrong.

Chapter 16
Losing The Gig

It wasn't long after having that big rating book at WKIO that I began to learn a brutal truth about the radio business...and the oldies format. I had always known everything in radio revolved around ratings. But, I didn't realize how much of it was determined by audience demographics and the whims of advertisers and their ad agencies.

We were #1 age 12 plus AND among adults age 25-54 and 35-64. Those are all very desirable demographics to be #1 in. But...seems some advertisers and agencies believed our audience, despite its size and the realities of today's seniors, was "too old",

There's a belief out there largely promulgated by college professors who never spent even one day in the radio business that says older Americans have less money to spend than their younger counterparts, are less likely to spend it (because their money is supposedly all tied up in investments for their old age) and are too unwilling to change brands based on a radio advertisement.

That was true of my parent's generation. But doesn't even come close to describing mine. Consider this: As I write this, I am 63 years old, now 8 years out of that "demographic mainstream" the advertisers and agencies want to talk to in radio ads. I own a house, bought a brand new car last year, spent over $15-thousand dollars in cash fixing up my house and I darned sure DIDN'T only buy at businesses with which I am comfortable. It was radio commercials by Lowe's, Home Depot and Menards that influenced me on where to buy what I needed.

Today's seniors are FAR more active, tend to live longer and enjoy retirement and their later years in far greater numbers than ever before. I ride bicycles, I hike, I fish, I swim, I camp. Heck, I'm even training in martial arts…jiu-jitsu and wrestling primarily (where I have already submitted, beaten and pinned guys in their early 20's. Before too much longer, I expect to be down in weight almost to where I was a year or two after I graduated high school. But yet, to some advertisers and agencies, I should be ready for a walker. The hell with that! (And thank you to Ohio Congressman Jim Jordan – you were my inspiration for the martial arts and wrestling training.)

And, former KHJ/Los Angeles Program Director John Sebastian understands the changing older demographic, too. He's debuted a new format in Phoenix, Arizona called "The WOW Factor"…a format squarely aimed at 55 to 72 year olds. It is NOT specifically an oldies station, kind of a combination of oldies, classic rock, classic hits, some smooth jazz and even a few country crossover and Adult Contemporary recent hits. Though it's too new to tell right now, his format appears to be gaining some steam and I'm betting it will find an audience. His station's ratings continue to improve…and I am hearing commercials on it, as he is now streaming across America.

WKIO found itself out of the Top 5 stations in the market only once. And yet, we were losing 50 cents for each dollar made the entire time I worked there, because the advertisers in Urbana-Champaign only wanted to go after the College students.

And it's not like the students don't want to know about the 1960's. I was invited to come to a class at the U of I and lecture the students about the Beatles and their impact on society. And I did.

I even got to see Paul McCartney in Indianapolis for the first time. I have never seen any of the Beatles before. And, when I went with my friend, Dale, I did something I had never done before. I went a concert, didn't move, didn't eat, didn't even get a beer. I was fascinated at the music I was hearing. It was like I was hearing the Beatles on stage again. (Paul's band is incredible...they literally can recreate the sound of every song the Beatles ever made...something the original Fabs were never able to do because of the limitations of equipment and sound systems then.)

I can't believe I cried at a concert. But, I sure did. I was like a school kid again. Paul once said in an interview that he walks on stage and sees a lot of older folks in the audience...but, two or three songs later, we all start looking younger. Yep...I can relate to that. You hear him play songs like "All My Loving" and "I Saw Her Standing There" and see if you don't get tears in your eyes. And no one in the arena is NOT going to sing along with "Hey Jude". What a fantastic experience that was for me!

But, back to radio. What, to me in hindsight now was worse about dealing with agencies and demographics – though I still believe Saga was then and is today a great company for which to work, they simply wouldn't listen to me when I brought up the possibility of including music from the 1970's and 80's into our format. I had experience programming it on Star in Columbus and SAW personally the age of the listeners it attracted...listeners exactly the age the local businesses wanted...the college crowd and those just graduated into adulthood.

What was I told? The music of the 70's and 80's was "burned out" on people...(which of course, didn't explain the 80's lunch feature and weekend features on our sister station Mix 94-5). Eventually, they DID let me add a few songs from the mid 1970's right toward the end of my time there...but I still contend they were playing it far too conservatively for that particular market. And that's why the station lost money.

Now, Mike Haile...if you ever read this...though I know I was very critical at times about the way you programmed WKIO all those years, looking back now, I think you actually may have had the right idea...even if you "deployed" those 80's songs incorrectly with the train wreck segues.

I believe today that Saga, at that time, was guilty of "Failure of Imagination". They simply couldn't believe that "oldies" could actually transcend generations and reach other age groups. They believed, as many did, that the format would die with the listeners. And the proof of that failure...the company today programs MANY Classic Hits stations all over America. WKIO in Champaign, now on 107.9 FM (Star's EXACT frequency) is now playing 80's music! So, Ed Christian (President of Saga and my "big boss")...you took my advice only 20 years too late, but I'm glad the company eventually came around to my way of thinking. Had only we had done a new music test locally and included 80's titles in the mix, we would have found the answer to our demographic and financial issues.

The ONLY ratings book where we really fell was in the fall of 2003. For 3 years we weren't out of the top 3...and that OK because #2 would be Mix and #1 was WIXY...all company owned. But fall of '03, we dropped to sixth place. Next thing I know, I'm the boss's office trying to explain it. And, a couple of weeks later, I was quietly but politely informed it was time for me to submit my resignation as Program Director. It didn't help that my morning show somewhat went off about me with MY boss, VP of Programming Steve Goldstein, either. Their complaint was that I didn't "critique" their shows often enough. True, that I didn't do one every day. But, I listened every morning to them and if I heard something out of place, it was certainly mentioned to them. I just thought they were both professionals and felt the best way to handle a pro is to get the hell out of their way and let them do what they do best.

I should also add that Steve Goldstein called me a few days before I left and told me that he didn't want me leaving with the thought that I had failed in my job. In fact he told me the company had failed me. He said, "You did everything we told you to do.

And you took the station to #1 and kept it right around there for years. That's not failure, Kevin. I want to you know that. I am proud to have been your boss...and I would certainly have you back in another position."

That impressed me. You see, Steve was Assistant Program Director at the legendary Top 40 station, 77/WABC in New York City on the night John Lennon was gunned down and murdered outside his home at the Dakota apartments. Steve had to go into Manhattan at Midnight and unlock the station's music library so the WABC DJ's would have John Lennon and Beatles music to play that dark night". He didn't have to say those things to me... but I always appreciated that he did.

So, now faced with needing to leave the job in about 60 days, I had to think about what I want to do next. The first thing I really wanted to do was go back home to Ohio.

I had contacted Cary Pall, who was now programming my old station in Columbus, Star 107.9 as an oldies station. He was looking for an APD and afternoon drive jock and was willing to hire me to do that. I also remembered an interview I once had with a friend of mine named Nick Roberts, who almost hired me for a country station in Springfield, Ohio, but we just couldn't come to terms with salary. Nick was now the Operations Manager of Cox Radio in Dayton which was running K-99.1 FM (country), WHIO AM (Newstalk), WDPT-FM in Piqua (80's), and WZLR-FM 95.3 (Classic Rock). We got together while I came home to Ohio for a week at Christmas 2003. He gave me a tour of the place (that legendary facility on Wilmington Pike in Dayton I had first walked into as a Cub Scout visiting the children's show hosted by a man named Joe Rockhold...as "Uncle Orrie").

At the time, Nick said he really didn't have anything full time, but said he certainly had part time work I could do for him while I continued my job search. That was, of course, better than nothing, so I agreed to stay in touch and said I would contact him after I got back home and got a place.

So, back to rent another U-haul, load it up and drive back to Ohio...which I had to do in a snowstorm. I almost lost my van outside of Indianapolis when I started to fishtail in the snow. (It was kind of funny. I had my cat Ringo in a carrier in the seat next to me. Every time I would pull the wheel one way he'd meow, the other way and he'd meow again, as though he was protesting my driving.) By the time I got to Columbus (where I decided to land first because of the expectation that I would go back to work at the old Star for Saga), the snow was about a foot deep and I was doing 20 miles an hour on I-70 as I made it to Hilliard. I got a place there and moved in that week...my actual employment though was still uncertain.

I called Cary as requested, but got some very bad news. His budget had been cut by the company and he could no longer afford to pay me what I needed. (Crap!) So, my next call was Dayton and Nick Roberts at Cox. I explained the situation and he quickly replied, "Hey...I've got an idea. I've got to discuss it with my General Manager. But, give me 48 hours. I promise I'll call you back on Thursday." I said OK, and waited.

Thursday afternoon, Nick called back. "So, are you ready to come to work for us?", he asked. I said, "For part time, you mean?" He said, "No. Full time. I just realized I had two part time jobs open here that, with the right person, could be combined into a full time job." I had to take a small pay cut to start, but Nick assured me he would get my pay raised within a short time to where I needed to be. So, I asked, "Ok...when would like me to start?" Nick said, "How about Monday morning?" (Three days hence). I said, "I'll see you at 10 am, boss!" He replied, "You got it. See you then!".

I had been unemployed for exactly 4 days...the ONLY 4 days I have been unemployed in my entire career! Talk about luck! That's why I tell my broadcasting students to never burn bridges with employers.

You see, later I learned that Nick had gone around to the people on staff...on the air...in sales, etc. He asked if they knew me and if they said yes, he asked what they would think about me coming to work there. God bless them. Every single one of them didn't hesitate. They told Nick..."God! Yes! Hire him...he's perfect for us. He'll work his tail off here. He eats, sleeps and drinks radio! You GOTTA hire him!"

Seems my work ethic, combined with my past ratings performance in Dayton and what my former co-workers all thought about me is what got me the job.

I will forever be grateful to them for that. I WAS COMING HOME TO DAYTON TO STAY! But, not only that, I was going to work at the best damn broadcasting company in town...the one place I thought would NEVER hire me in a million years.

You see, Cox/Dayton was the home of so many local legends. Hell, Phil Donahue started his career there. The late local TV News anchor, Don Wayne ruled the roost for Newscenter 7 for decades. Late weathercaster Gil Whitney almost single handedly was credited for saving the lives of hundreds of people during the 1974 Xenia Tornado. Late morning show host Lou Emm spent 50 years on the air there!

And now, that list of people working there was going to include me. Little Kevin Fodor. And I was going to work for yet another legend.

All because our General Manager at the time, Donna Hall went along with Nick's idea of combining two part time jobs into a full time gig. Today, Donna is the publisher of the Atlanta Journal Constitution newspaper for Cox...I call her "Mama Bear" because I have never met a manager more protective of the staff than she. And I call her that every time I see her today. We ALL love her to death. And always will.

I drove back and forth from Columbus for 2 years, but decided I didn't want to commute anymore. And I didn't want to live in an apartment anymore. So, I looked around and found a house to rent about 15 minutes from the radio station. And despite the fact that I had to declare bankruptcy once about 2 years later, I emerged from it and was able to buy the house a few years later. Paid around $70,000 for this house that was actually built by my boyhood friend, Phil Layne's grandfather…and I have paid about $26,000 on it so far.

I worked several years in that venerable building on Wilmington Pike…and moved downtown in 2009 to the new building we currently occupy there with the Dayton Daily News. I am proud to be working aside some very fine journalists there… and they seem to respect me as a co-worker and fellow journalist.

We no longer own the newspaper, though. A judge in Pennsylvania decided in his infinite stupidity that the cross-ownership rules didn't allow for such a thing, so Apollo Cox sold the paper, back to Cox Enterprises which turned out to be a great fit for them. I still see my newspaper friends and still buy their product.

In 2019, we dealt with a lot in Dayton. 15 tornadoes in one night…in a three hour period. One of which went right over the top of my house, but didn't, fortunately, touch down.

That was one crazy night. My nephew was visiting his mother in West Virginia and I was by myself.

Channel 7 and its' Chief Meteorologist McCall Vrydaghs was on the air warning people of the storms. Suddenly, around 11 pm, she issued a warning for my area…our Doppler radar can go to street level and tell you where the storm is. McCall said, the funnel was coming up Spinning Road which is just yards from where my house is.

I stepped outside and hid behind a storage area which is

right next to my backdoor to give me some shielding. I wanted to see if I could hear the funnel coming. I did not. But, boy did I catch hell from McCall the next day. "You're not supposed to outside in a tornado!!!". But, the winds shortly began kicking up and I quickly went back in and locked the back door.

I texted my nephew and told him what was going on and said "If you don't hear from me in a few minutes, contact the Sheriff and have them come look for me."

Then, I thought, "My God! How am I going to get my cats to go into the one place they hate to go into the most...the bathtub?" I later spoke with an animal behaviorist who told me animals can sense fear in humans. If I went in the bathtub for safety and called to them, they would likely have followed me there.

Just seconds later...absolute quiet. The storm had passed, and we were all fine. Our power went out a few minutes later, but, no problem, that's what alarms on cell phones are for.

The next morning, I went outside to assess the situation. The tornado had obviously gone over the top of the house, because it dropped debris in both my front and back yards. But, there wasn't even one shingle blown off the house. We had been spared.

My nephew came home the next evening, bringing ice because our power was out...at least it had been a few hours earlier when I checked at home. Well, by the time he got here, the power was back on. And, our lives go on.

We had a mass shooting in the Oregon District downtown where a number of people were killed and others injured. 9 officers were brought to the White House by the President and commended for their valor and service. I was disappointed when all of his "haters" cropped a photo of he and the First Lady smiling and giving a "thumbs up" claiming that it had been a photo of he and the victims. When I tried to correct people online about this,

I, along with a reporter for another local TV station were "doxxed" by liberals online for daring to take the defense of the President.

Look...I don't give a crap what your politics are. But to take a picture out of context and claim it's something it's not is bullshit. Just because you don't like a politician.

I know the picture was NOT of President Trump with the victims. We had a reporter on scene who told us NO photos were taken, at the direction of the President. Why? He didn't want those photos used by his enemies to do just exactly what they tried to do with the one that was released.

God! I HATE politics. The divisiveness between the left and the right is going to ruin the country someday, unless both sides stop this crap.

Then, a veteran Dayton Detective was killed by an idiot as they tried to serve a warrant on a home. So sad, because he had a wife and kids who now will have to make it without a father, just because some jackass decided to unload a weapon on an officer. It is truly sad.

All that being the case, though, I can't believe I get to work in a place like this. And a good friend of mine from high school once called me a genius in an on-line conversation. Now, I don't believe I really AM a genius, but he explained it this way: "Kevin, you decided when you were a very young boy what you wanted to do for a living. And, by God, you did it. You made a career out of it. Do you realize how few people ever get to choose their profession and work in it a life time? That, to me, is the mark of a genius." I still won't call myself that, but I appreciated the sentiment. Me, the kid that was, in a few cases picked on and bullied a bit at school, ends up not only doing the job he has wanted to do all his life, but made a career of it...and today, enjoys the respect and, I guess, admiration of his classmates, his teachers, his co-workers and I think, my bosses, too.

You don't think I didn't feel blessed getting that job?

Chapter 17

Home At Last

My first day on the new job was February 1, 2004. Walking into that storied building at 1414 Wilmington Pike in Dayton, Ohio was humbling, to say the least. As I walked in the employee entrance, I remembered when I first walked those halls as a Cub Scout, and marveled at the fact that I was now employed at the place where everybody in broadcasting in town wanted to work.

I learned the building and its history from the folks that worked there. Learned the tale of a ghost citing in the building... of WHIO-AM's late morning man, Lou Emm. So the story goes, our present morning host, Larry Hansgen arrived at work early one morning to discover the "apparition" of Lou at the end of a hallway. Approaching him, Larry tells me the "ghost" of Lou appeared confused, telling him, "I can't find my office" before disappearing.

Years later when we moved to our new facility on West Main Street in Dayton, I couldn't resist getting on the "all page" in the old building and saying, "For crying out loud, people, don't forget to "pack Lou"!

It was in those early days I became "Assistant" Program Director for 80's formatted WDPT-FM (the Point) and 95.3, The Eagle. You might as well have considered me to be the PD as I performed all of the functions of a Program Director, but the company wanted to have only one PD "contact" to work with... and that was Nick. No big deal. Nick oversaw all programming. My cohorts Glenn Moore and Tommy Collins handled K-99.1 and WHIO AM-FM, respectively...and I had the other stations.

Same job...same issues. I remember one day we got a proposal from a "major" hamburger chain. Not a bad proposal...they wanted us to "throw a party" in a city park where they would provide lunch for 1,000 people of their "new" sandwich. The station would come up with a thousand dollar prize to give to a grand prize winner.

So far, so good...until I got to the bottom of the page of the proposal. There, I found one troubling line. It read, "The station agrees the grand prize ticket will not be in any of the first 500 lunch bags to be distributed."

That was a deal breaker. You see, it's illegal by FCC rules to determine the outcome of a radio contest. What the client wanted us to do was make it impossible for any of the first 500 people to arrive to win the big prize. That's "contest fixing".

Ask McDonald's how that worked with their Monopoly game one year. Cost them a lot of money to get out from underneath the court action.

Not to mention...we could have lost our FCC licenses over it.

I told the Sales Manager in no uncertain terms we would NOT do that contest. That angered him. He grabbed the proposal out of my hand and said, "We'll see about that", and stormed out of the programming office and went straight to the General Manager about it.

I followed Mr. Sales Manager down to the boss's office (aka "Mama Bear") and listened as the sales manager told her how "un-cooperative" I was being with the Sales Department and demanded I be ordered to do the promotion.

"Mama Bear" (Donna Hall), asked me for my side of the story. I explained the client wanted us to fix the contest and our station licenses would be endangered if we did it.

Donna asked to see the proposal. I gave it to her. She read the whole page...got down to the problematic statement...

looked up...handed it back to Mr. Sales Manager and said, "I don't think we'll be doing this promotion". The Sales Manager stormed out of the office.

Donna said to me, "You did exactly what I needed you to do. You protected our license and I'm proud of you."

In many stations, I would have lost that battle. But, Donna was one hell of a boss.

One day, I had just finished with my morning shift as a news anchor on WHIO Radio when, walking out of the anchor booth and into the newsroom where the police monitors were and heard an ambulance call for Wright Brother's Airport. This is not Dayton International Airport, which is north of town, but a general aviation field south of the Dayton Mall area. I knew the area well. That airport is where I have taken, so far, 32 hours of flight training, soloed and flew at least a couple of dual "cross country" flights. That day, though, the ambulance call included the words, "plane crash".

Now, I didn't know what type of plane it was, or the circumstances behind it. But I DID know whatever the circumstances were, they couldn't be good.

The newsroom was connected to the programming office where my desk was...I ran to the edge of the programming office and yelled, "Tommy, Glenn, Nick...I need help! There's been a plane crash at Wright Brothers Airport!" Help came running. Our News Director, my friend from Wilmington, Jim Barrett had already left for the day...I got him on the phone and he headed for the airport.

We were also fortunate because another station part time host had a full time job in the Lexis/Nexis building across the street from the airport. He said he'd walk on over. It wasn't long before he called back and said a plane, that appeared to be a small, general aviation plane had, indeed, gone down. That there was a fire department on site putting out the fire from the crash... and tarps were being placed over it. Not good news, because that generally meant someone was dead.

Someone was dead. Two people, in fact. We reported on it all afternoon. And then, I learned from my friend Jim that, when the identities of the victims were released, the people who died were members of his church. Sad, indeed.

Later that year, though, came word that Jim and I had been nominated for a state news award from the Associated Press for Best Spot News Coverage, and Jim asked me to go to the awards ceremony. We won there and also won the similar award from the Society of Professional Journalists. Both are on my walls at home now, and I am very proud of them.

Cox moved the radio and TV operations to a new station building in downtown Dayton with the staff of the Dayton Daily News. It was a building once occupied by the National Cash Register company. We became "corporatized" and frankly, not always for the better. I don't mind saying this, because several people, even at the corporate office in Atlanta would agree with me. Among them, Governor Cox's great-great grandson who had told us at the time of the move that it was his hope that the enthusiasm we shared in radio would rub off on the newspaper staff. Unfortunately, that never happened and we were, in effect "swallowed by the Borg".

Nonetheless, I found myself immensely proud to meet these folks at the newspaper. Most of them were very friendly to me. A few weren't...including a member or two of the editorial staff with whom I had clashed while we were over on Wilmington Pike. Basically, my beef was that those editorial staff's pieces were clearly leaned to one side of the political equation. WHIO radio aired programming which leaned to the other side. I had been asked by Nick Roberts to write some pieces for the station's website which told the other view. That I did. And what irked me was the fact that a rally the station had held downtown which had attracted, according to the Dayton Police, a crowd of 8,000 people...was characterized by the DDN as having been a rally at which only "a few" had attended.

I threw it in the Dayton Daily News editorial staff's face, and this one writer didn't like it one bit. Despite my attempts to be friendly to the man, he never, even once said hello, how are you, go to hell, nothing to me. I found that telling.

You see, the Dayton Daily News, at that time, was on the skids, on the way to failing...rapidly. But, it occurred to Cox that it had never really done a research study of the newspaper and its readers.

Really? You've been in business since the late 1800's and you have never, EVER, asked your readers for their opinion of the job you're doing? No successful business operates that way.

So, as I was told, a research study, similar to a radio station perceptual research study was placed into the field. I won't disclose what it reportedly said, but what happened over the next few weeks made it pretty obvious.

The editorial staff was totally disbanded...its' members allowed to "retire". And the paper publicly instituted a new policy... that only the publisher, or the editor could write editorials...and only...when an issue was of such serious import, that newspaper leaders felt compelled to speak out.

It also pledged that every day, the editorial pages would include columnists speaking on topics from the perspective of both conservative and liberal sides. And it continues to live by those rules today.

You see, the late Governor Cox, when he was alive was a well-known "progressive" Democrat. And, not surprisingly his paper aggressively promoted those views.

But, at that time, there was another daily newspaper in town, known as the Journal-Herald. It took the conservative side to the Dayton Daily News.

Throughout the decades, Dayton and its city government were leaned very Democrat and often very progressive, especially in the 1900's through at least the 1970's.

What began to cause rifts there...was the fact that, one by one, Dayton's manufacturing base was packing up and moving out. First NCR, then Frigidaire, then General Motors, then Delco... whose Moraine Assembly plant was shuttered. I reported on its final day. I couldn't help but think that my maternal grandfather, who was a master tool maker for GM would have, indeed been sickened seeing that plant close. Because it closed all of the local parts manufacturers who had been supplying NCR, Frigidaire, GM and Delco. Dayton was hurtling rapidly toward becoming a ghost town. A city that once home to a quarter-million people, was down to about 166-thousand and still declining.

In terms of radio markets, it went from #45 to #64 in the blink of an eye. It's actually gone up a notch recently to #63.

But, city fathers finally got their acts together. There has been talk of regional government, which has never gotten off the ground, but, nonetheless, Dayton is undergoing a spurt of revitalization now. We got a minor league baseball team, the Dayton Dragons who have a stadium and whose games have been sellouts forever.

Nearby, the Oregon District's collection of record stores, a movie theater, shops, restaurants and bars thrives. We have "Tech Town" east of downtown, where many technology oriented companies have located offices.

Then, one day, we started hearing rumors that something was about to happen in Moraine again. And, a few days later, the announcement was made. That the Chinese auto glass manufacturer, Fuyao, was buying a large section of the old Moraine Assembly Plant and would manufacture auto windshields and glass there.

What a stroke of luck! And despite some of the problems and lawsuits that company has encountered, it has, at least so far, stayed loyal to the area and has employed thousands of people again. And, not surprisingly, the tool shops around the area are beginning to boom again, both near the plant, and throughout the region.

I remember reporting on that story literally with tears in my eyes and a giant lump in my throat. I led one newscast by saying, "Go ahead, Moraine. Celebrate. You certainly deserve to."

Dayton has also worked to help its downtown area. A lot of people, at one time, stopped feeling safe walking around downtown. Teens waiting for buses after school were starting fights...and there were reports of people being shot and stabbed downtown. Many businesses said "the hell with this", and moved to the suburbs. Both the Dragons Stadium and the Oregon District helped. And now, came Riverscape.

The Miami River runs through downtown Dayton...and a plan was hatched to take out a "low dam" in the river to allow for canoeing and kayaking. The Cox organization gave the city of Dayton a million dollars as "seed money" for the project. It is now complete and in the summertime you can see those canoers and kayakers on the river and runners along the riverbank.

And, the once "jewel" of downtown Dayton, The Arcade, is being rebuilt now. Once a series of shops and businesses (kind of like a downtown shopping mall), The Arcade will have businesses, apartments, and students running around the place soon...as the University of Dayton stepped up to the plate and said it would help with the rebuilding. I remember being in the old Arcade as a child. It's been a boarded up eyesore for many years. At one point, it was literally falling apart and sidewalks near it were blocked so people wouldn't be hit by falling debris. But, soon, it will be open again.

We still have to figure out what to do with the Convention Center downtown…it's been losing money consistently. However, one good thing our Mayor has done lately was authorize and get money for the construction of an outdoor music amphitheater across the street from the Convention Center that does over 50 concerts a year, mostly local and regional acts, though, occasionally, a national act is brought in to act as a fundraiser for the facility. It's across the street from the Convention Center. So far, it's done amazingly well, and I was skeptical about it at one time.

The quality of life in Dayton, Ohio has definitely improved over recent decades and, frankly, I'm glad to see it. And, if you haven't figured it out yet, I love my hometown. And it's an honor to me, to be one small part of it all. Nick was moved out of the programming office and bumped up to the job of Vice President of Marketing. Oddly enough, just a couple of years later, the job of overseeing the radio stations and helping PD's Jeremy Ratliff and Nancy Wilson was given back to him. I thought it was a good decision. For us…and for Nick. And, the intention…is to re-create the "old programming office". And I can't be happier. Not long ago, Jeremy went back to Florida to our sister station and Brittany Otto too over as News Director and Nick took a more direct role now as VP of Marketing AND Radio.

You see, my friend, Nick is just like me. We're both radio geeks. It's in our blood. I see him almost daily and we almost always get into some discussion about radio programming. I don't run a station now for Cox. But, I am on the programming team for Eagle, the 80's station…and am frequently in discussions about it either in offices or in e-mails. And I know a good part of the senior leadership in the company.

I continue to be on-air at K-99.1 and am a News Anchor,

Reporter and Interviewer and talk host for WHIO. It's not a bad job...just...different.

I still love being on the air. I still love the listeners, even the News-Talk audience, despite the continuing complaints from Liberals that they are sure I'm a Conservative and Conservatives that I HAVE to be a liberal. (Sheesh!) I still love working with clients (even if occasionally, it's a love/hate relationship). I am actually neither. I vote for the person and not the party.

I go on stage to MC a concert, introduce myself and the vast majority of the time, the people in the crowd cheer me. You can't believe the thrill I get from that. It's obvious they know WHO I am, they love the station and I suppose I get the benefit from that love.

These listeners donate hundreds of thousands of dollars to charitable causes thanks to our stations every year.

I do a remote broadcast at a car dealership or store, and people want to shake my hand, talk with me and meet me. (Do I really deserve this?)

We're in double digit ratings and there aren't many stations that can say that. K-99.1 has been #1 in the market for over 4 dozen rating books. WHIO is steady #2. And if only Eagle had a full market signal, I guarantee you it would be #3.

Just recently, the majority shares of Cox Media Group were purchased by an arm of Apollo Global Management. Normally, that might have been a scary situation. Usually when the bankers and hedge fund managers take control, the bean counters start interfering with the operation and heads roll. These folks, though, seem to be different. They have stated their admiration for how Cox operates their radio, television and newspaper properties. And why not? They make money with them. And with very little of the blood letting you see at other companies. I think they want to learn from us. And if they want to ask a question of me, I'll gladly answer to the best of my abilities.

As I write this, that sale is now complete. Some of the Cox Senior Leadership are still there and, in the same jobs they had with the old company. And, despite people in the industry predicting that I would be the first to be thrown out on my ear, because, in their words, I "make too much money", I'm still standing.

Could more good things happen? Of course, they can. In fact, we may be able to work on that soon. You see, I want to right a few wrongs in the broadcasting community here. With God's help, and that of my employer, perhaps it can be so. We're already talking about it. And Nick and I know how to do it.

And some people think radio is dead? Nope. You'll never hear me say it. And, don't argue with me about it, either. You won't win.

I have now spent…and survived…over 16 years with this company. Most likely, I'll retire from it in a few years. I'll go home with retirement money, a small pension, most likely the ability to do contract work for the station as long as I want, and will still have the ability to voice track for pay and work part time in other pursuits on the side. Plus Social Security. I have life insurance and health insurance.

I think my Dad would be proud today…even if he still couldn't figure out how I pulled off around 50 years and managed to achieve this being a "disc jockey"…if only that describes part of the job today. Dad did always respect my desire to be a journalist, though I think he would have preferred I become a newspaper writer. At least they typically go to college for that sort of thing. Knowing him, he would have wanted me to get a job with the Washington Post or the New York Times. I've been to both cities… they're fine cities, and D.C.'s historic landmarks are something to see. But, I am not a big city type. I know people who work on radio in New York City. It's a great place to visit…I love the food in the taverns and the "city that never sleeps" vibe. But, I couldn't deal with Manhattan's traffic...or having to ride the subway every day to get to work. And the rents are absolutely ridiculous. The same goes for Chicago and Los Angeles.

I love acting. And, perhaps I could have gone to L.A. and been in movies or television. Or, gone to New York and been in the cast of "Saturday Night Live". But living in a city like Los Angeles and dealing with ten lane interstate highways and all of those taxes? Or Manhattan and their massive traffic jams? Or Chicago and an interstate highway that can be mortally clogged at 1 in the afternoon? Not this kid. Sometimes, it's bad enough in Dayton with the dumb dumb drivers on I-75. By themselves they can manage a 10 mile traffic jam.

Fortunately, some folks I know IN those big cities have defended me on Facebook from total jerks who think I am nobody because I've never worked in a "major market". The fact is: I did that by choice. If I really wanted to and had the break to get in it, I'm good enough to work in one. Maybe someday, somebody will let me come to visit one of those stations and do overnights for them once. I'd gladly accept the offer if it was given.

OK, so I'm not John "Records" Landecker, or Larry Lujack or Robert W. Morgan or the "Real" Don Steele. But, I do the same damn thing they did for years. I am one with them and they are one with me. We all survived a career in a business fraught with peril. And, we all came up smelling like roses.

And, I really wish my grandmother could see me today. She would be so proud. I am working for her favorite radio station and if she were here, would be my best listener and biggest fan.

I am...and have been...blessed.

Chapter 18
Lights...Camera...Me!

I mentioned in the last chapter that I always wondered what "might" have happened had I not gotten into radio, but instead, went to New York or California to try and make it as an actor. Oddly enough, I got the chance to get a major role in a motion picture a few years back.

It might interest you to know, if you don't that movies are now made all over the country, and not just in Hollywood. And film making is now taught in many colleges and universities. For a while, we were dabbling in it at the International College of Broadcasting. One of our instructors, a man named Joe Bargdill actually wrote, produced and released a couple of independent films. Some of those who appeared in these films were our students...graduates...and even instructors.

I had been kidding Joe for a while that he needed to write a movie that had a radio station as part of its plot. And if so, I wanted to be in it. So, one day, he comes to me and says, "Kevin you wanna be in a movie? I have a screen play idea to talk with you about."

Turns out that the movie was set in small town America. Like many such small towns, the town had a single radio station in it, and this one was not financially well off. In fact, it was near bankruptcy. (Where had I heard of THAT before? (insert smile emoji here)).

But, one day, the manager was driving to work when he saw an object whiz by his car and explode in a field nearby. Rushing over to see what it was, he discovers an alien looking piece of electronics. He grabbed it and took it back to his Chief Engineer and asks him to figure out what the box did. Upon turning it on, they discover that the box actually sent out a sort of backmasked signal that could make people want to turn to the frequency of any particular radio station. Of course, the not-so-scrupulous station manager, a guy named Frank, has the engineer set the box to the frequency of HIS radio station. Listening begins to pick up, and suddenly...he's selling advertising again, with the help of his electronic box.

Unfortunately for Frank, the box also attracts something else to Earth...a major swarm of "Killer Hornets"! (And what's the big scare of 2020 today, besides Covid-19? Yes! MURDER HORNETS!!!!)

Actually, killer hornets...insects capable of killing humans do exist, though typically are rare. And that's from where Joe got the idea for the movie. So, Joe needed a small town, and a small town radio station to do the basic movie filming. Turns out, I had the perfect idea for that.

My late friend, Lee Hendee had secured a construction permit for a low powered FM station in Wilmington, Ohio and had just gotten it on the air. The station, WALH-LP at 106.7 on the dial had a "storefront" office in a building in the downtown area there. And Wilmington had a small coffee shop (perfect for filming a scene or two in) that was once a local department store, and a city park that would be perfect for filming the final scene of the battle between the military and those dastardly bugs.

Oh, yeah. It was definitely a B-grade horror movie to be sure, but Joe wanted to make parts of it kinda campy...you know, a little along the lines of the old Batman TV show in the 1960's. It sounded fun to me, and, though I had taken acting classes and had a "head shot" made decades back, I had never made a movie before, so I told Joe I'd be happy to do it.

But, of course, I work full time for a living...so it was going to necessitate me taking some time off from work. So, I had vacation time coming and Joe told me he could arrange things so I could shoot all of my scenes in a week, so I made the time off request to the people at WHIO, and told them exactly why I wanted the vacation time.

Then WHIO Program Director, Jeremy Ratliff sent an e-mail that I have kept, because I loved the way he put it to the upper management. "I've never heard a better reason in all my years in broadcasting to take time off than THIS". Needless to say, the vacation time was immediately approved.

So the appointed week came and I found myself waking up in the morning around 6, putting a suit and tie in the car (what else does a Station Manager wear on the job?), and driving back down to Wilmington at around 7 AM to make the movie. We had a cast meeting every morning at 8 with coffee and pastries supplied, went into make up and headed either to the station or on to another nearby filming location to shoot scenes.

Now, the "campy" part of my character was that I was a nasty SOB...the kind of manager a lot of employees might have punched out. Yes, "Frank" was testy, ruled as a dictator and often screwed up because of it.

The first scene...the "morning guy" on the station was on the air doing a break...and in mid-break, I come flying into the station's front door, throw open the studio door and proceed to berate the morning guy using every 4 letter word in my adult vocabulary to make my point (including those you are not allowed to say on radio!) never realizing that the studio microphone was on and everything that I was saying was "supposedly" going out on the station's air. I get done, slam the studio door closed, and the morning guy looks at the camera and deadpans, "And, we'll be right back with more of your favorites in a moment!"

Because of Joe Bargdill, I learned another facet about movie making. Did you every try and memorize all of your lines from a movie script, especially when you work about 50 hours a week? I arrived on the set only basically familiar with what I was supposed to be saying not yet having everything totally committed to memory. Not a problem, Joe said. We'll put the pages of your scenes in "conveniently located spots" on the set so I could refer to them when I was not directly looking at the camera or having my face shown in the scene. Turns out that happens in Hollywood all the time. Actors write crib notes on their hands, their shirt sleeves, have cue cards next to the camera with the lines on them quite often.

And because proper lighting, shadow avoidance and camera angles are so important in moving making, be prepared to shoot a scene 5, 10, even 20 times. It can take 30 minutes or even an hour to shoot one minute of a film. So, I think I did that opening scene about 9 or ten times, sometimes I'd get lightheaded from screaming so much at the morning guy, or would almost lose my voice from doing it. It was hard work.

I also decided that I wanted to tone my character down in one scene to make myself seem more "human" and not just be the screaming lunatic all the time. It was my idea and Joe thought it was a good one. So, there is a scene in what was "supposed to be" my office where I am meeting with the morning guy. Though I remind him he is "only there primarily because you're my sister's husband", I also tell him, "I also happen to think you've got some talent for this business and that's why I'm so hard on you. I WANT you to succeed. So, I want you to listen to me and listen to me good. You will do everything I say and to the letter. Do it, or you're going to be the highest paid overnight talent this town has ever seen." The morning guy smiles at me, I return the smile and then say, "Okay, now get the hell out of my office and get back to work!" He stands up, stiffens, gives me a military salute and a "Yes, SIR!" and walks out. I laugh a little bit and the scene ends.

I say this because of a chance online encounter I had with the late PD from Z-93 I worked for. Jeff Ballentine was hell on wheels there. He was the raving lunatic that everyone was afraid of...especially me. I did NOT want to get on his bad side. And yet, Jeff never, EVER said a bad or unkind word to me, and I could never figure out why. So, one day, years later on Facebook, I asked him about it. He told me, "I always thought you were a different type of person. You were kind to everybody. You WANTED to do things right. You were a serious talent and I knew I couldn't rule over you like that. So, in your case, I knew I had to encourage you...I made a mistake trying to change your delivery. I let you do your thing and you immediately sounded GREAT. So much that I told the GM's secretary I was going to make you a star. And I meant every word of it."

The line in the movie, "Do what I say or you'll be the highest paid overnight talent this town has ever seen" was a direct Ballentine line. I heard him say it to the Z-93 morning show once. And I ad libbed it into the movie so that, if it ever gets seen, my old friends Dr Dave (Gross) and Alan Kaye will have a good laugh at it, because only THEY will know from whence the line came!

I asked Jeff about his career change and what he learned from it. Jeff, you see, got out of radio and went into emergency medicine. I found his answer telling, "Kevin, he said, I used to think radio was life or death. Then, I got into this business and discovered the real meaning of life and death." Not too long after that, Jeff's "Type A" personality got the best of him and he died of a massive heart attack. I might have been afraid of Jeff once, but he was a man who showed me he was a good judge of people. So, rest in peace, Jeff.

And, now...back to the movie!

Even harder was on site shooting. The scene where I "discover" the electronic box was shot in a field on the outskirts of Wilmington. I had a camera and operator behind me in the emptied "box" of my small van shooting to capture an over the shoulder shot looking out of my front windshield in which time the "meteor" of the electronic box's arrival would be added electronically by

CGI in the movie's post production phase. I had to "react" as though I was seeing it and, on cue, skid my car to the side of the road. So, I was having to, kind of, be a stunt driver, too.

The scene switches to an "outside of the car" shot. I have to, on cue, exit the car and run over to where the box is... sometimes completely missing it and having to start over again. Then, when I do find it, I have to pick it up and look at it. That required another "over the shoulder" shot. So that one (probably) 60 second sequence was a series of about 4 or 5 shots all from different angles. In a lot of respects, movie making is a lot like it's depicted in the movie, "Once Upon A Time In Hollywood", a movie with a GREAT radio soundtrack taken from actual complete recordings made from 93/KHJ in Los Angeles. A great movie to watch if you're a radio geek like I am.

By now, with 2 or 3 scenes (and about 3 minutes of actual movie in the can), it's time for lunch, which the producers provide from a local eatery. We waste about an hour eating and it's back to what we did all morning, till about 5 or 6 pm, when it's take off the makeup and head for home. Rinse, repeat, rinse for the next 5 or 6 days.

Oh, yes, I don't survive in the movie. I get stung to death by the Killer Hornets. Doing the death scene was funny. They do a close up of my face, as I am screaming bloody murder turning around and around until I'm dizzy and, every few seconds the camera stops. They add more fake "stings" to my face and pour red syrup on my head which drips down onto my face and my dress shirt. Back to screaming, flailing my arms and turning around and around. Stop...add more stings, more red syrup. Do it some more, over and over and over. Finally, I collapse in a heap on the ground and "expire". There's never a hornet on me as I'm filming the scene...they were all added by CGI in post production.

So, my week as a movie star is over and I go back to work, but I'm not done with the movie just yet. Now, I have to go back and do "overdubs". For 2 or three 3 evenings, I went back, looked at "rushes" of my scenes and re-record lines from the script which Joe then used in places where the sound was thin, or where a semi may have gone by the station and interfered with the sound of the movie being recorded inside it. That was about 3 hours of work.

Has the movie ever seen the light of day? Not yet. Joe was trying to make a distribution deal for the movie, and in the process, almost got it stolen out from under him by an unscrupulous distributor. (Yep...Hollywood is full of those types of people) and has, as of yet, been unable to release it. He is continuing work on it and may be soon able to release it to You Tube. I hope you do. If it shows up in your feed, give it a look.

I DID, however, get credit for doing the movie in the international movie database, www.imdb.com. They misspelled my last name, but that's happened before. Nonetheless, I can now say I am a "professional movie actor".

Recently, I joined an online casting group where agencies and movie directors look for commercial voice over talent and actor possibilities. So, who knows? Maybe someday I'll do another movie. Or TV ad, or radio spot. Hey, Tom Hanks...if you ever want to do "That Thing You Do 2", I know a great DJ for a part in your movie. And, "That Thing You Do" is a show that I would LOVE to direct at my old high school some day. And I would do it just like Tom Hanks did...find four people at the school...2 who can play 6 string guitar (rhythm and lead), a bass guitar player and a drummer. Now, let's make sure 3 of them can do harmony...and make them learn the 2 or 3 songs from the film. "That Thing You Do" is an easy song to play and MAKE them play and sing it on stage. Fiction THEN becomes real.

When I worked as a PD for Saga in Illinois, the PD's who were musically inclined decided to be the entertainment at the annual Manager's Meeting. A set list was put together, which we all picked songs that we wanted to learn (it was not necessary that we learn every song, but we decided which ones we wanted to do). We held ONE rehearsal in a hotel room the night before the show. The company paid for a rental P.A. system and amps. We brought our own instruments from home.

The managers were skeptical about the whole thing. They thought we were going to suck. We got on stage...did the first song and the house was rocking in no time. Saga-Turner Overdrive, as we called ourselves, was actually a pretty damn good cover band! We did a three hour show! Life imitates art which imitates life.

That was the magic behind the Monkees. They were actors in a TV show, but once they learned to play their assigned instruments, they "became" a real band. Or, as Micky Dolenz once said, that's when Leonard Nimoy "became" a real Vulcan. And, they managed to make some pretty good music...good enough, anyway, to have hits that have lasted over 50 years.

Hey, you never know. This business of the "world of make believe" is a strange one, and sometimes, a sordid one. The "casting couch" is, sadly, real. Ask Harvey Weinstein. There's lots of reports of rampant drug use in it, some of which are probably true. (Back when I went to acting school a long time ago, I was invited to a party on a Saturday night at a Dayton hotel which had a completely open bar, but in an adjoining room, there were a whole lot of drugs being consumed...cocaine, pot, for all I know, maybe heroin. I had one drink and left. The whole thing scared the hell out of me.) If it happens here, you can be damn sure you can find it in Hollywood. New York, too.

Just think of all the great actors, actresses and comedians whose lives have been snuffed out. John Belushi, John Candy, Chris Farley, River Phoenix, Marilyn Monroe, Lenny Bruce, Judy Garland, just to name a few. Not to mention the singers and musicians, like Jim Morrison, Prince, Elvis Presley, Whitney

Houston, and of course, Michael Jackson. His death hit me hard...I mean...I MET him once, when he was a teenager. No doubt. Michael was an absolutely incredible talent. Singer, dancer, performer. Get a copy of the movie, "This Is It" which was filmed just before his death and watch it. I would have paid $500 bucks for one ticket to see that show.

Donny Osmond is one of the survivors. He made hit records, did concerts and TV shows for decades and has lived to talk about it. One time when I was at Z-93 in Dayton, Donny did a show at a local nightclub to support the release of his song "Soldier Of Love". I'm backstage in a tiny office with Donny and I couldn't resist. "Donny, do you mind if I ask you something personal?" "Sure, he said". I asked him, point blank, "How in the hell have you managed to put up with all of the shit you've taken in the past 30 years?" He laughed...I laughed, he looked at me and said, "It hasn't always been easy, but somehow I've managed."

Yes, I drink. Yes, I've done some drugs in my life. (And there's a lot of them I wouldn't touch with a ten foot pole). But, I've seen enough of the downsides of it to know what to stay the heck away from, and so I do.

I guess people ARE living longer these days, and there are movie roles for older guys, maybe...it's something I could pursue in my retirement years.

"So you better get ready...I may coming to your town!"

Chapter 19

A Few Words About Journalism

Now, I know as I write this chapter I am going to outrage a few people, but frankly, I don't give a damn.

I was always taught that true journalism was neither left nor right, but down the middle. Which means, each side gets to express their views.

Sadly, our political system in the U.S. has broken down to the point where if you're not "spewing the party line", whatever it is, you should be censured, or not allowed to speak.

Recently, I got lambasted on Facebook from some liberal types asking, "How can we get rid of Fox News?"

Now, don't get me wrong, I don't necessarily think Fox is all that. They clearly lean right, especially during their prime time programming. Just as MSNBC leans left and CNN, which at one time was a great network, now tries to "straddle the middle between MSNBC and "the middle".

More than anything, I think some people hate the fact that Fox found a successful niche and has made a lot of money occupying it. You can't "take away their broadcasting license" because, as a cable network, there is no FCC license to take.

A book I once read, Reis and Trout's "22 Immutable Laws of Marketing" states, "If you can't be number one, create another "hill" and declare yourself number one at it." That's what MSNBC is doing. They lean far left, because Fox is right. CNN tried being in the middle, but another marketing law says "If you don't stand for something, you stand for nothing". So, it's trying to cut the middle between MSNBC and the middle. And, so far, they're not successful at it.

Friends, the only way you're going to "get rid of Fox" is to convince a lot of people to stop watching them. Do that, and it'll go away on its own. Until then, or unless it happens, you are S.O.L.

Politically, I consider myself Libertarian. I am right on fiscal policies…center to left on some social issues. But, as I've said, I vote for the person and not the party.

I admired John and Robert Kennedy as a child. I still think RFK would have been one of the greatest American Presidents who ever lived. But, some idiot made that impossible.

John Glenn was a news source and a friend of mine over the years. And I voted for him, even though I didn't always agree with his policies. But, learning about his background, I learned he wouldn't support ANY policy if he truly thought it wasn't morally right. I respected that. To me, it is just too sad, we don't have legislators on either side of the aisle with any of his moral backbone today. This "moral relevance" is harming our country. There's a few, but not many.

President Trump? He's not the devil incarnate. He's also not a professional politician and that is the reason he was elected. People have tired of people on both sides feeding them bullshit just to get a vote. Sure, some of his tweeting makes me want to go up to D.C. and steal his cellphone. But like him or not, he did a tremendous job pre-pandemic with the economy and my 401K thanks him for that. Sadly, though, his trade policies are making it hard for certain sectors of America. But, for a time black unemployment was down around 3.5 percent. Hispanic unemployment is close to that. Minorities are finding jobs for the first time in 20 years. .

No American Republican has EVER gotten more than 8 percent of the black vote.

So, now, we've had this "pandemic" called COVID-19. And

President Trump has had to spend money like water, money we don't have by the way, to keep the country from going into a depression. Frankly, I'm grateful for the cash. I have NEVER made enough money as a radio personality and have always had to do remotes and DJ weddings to make ends meet. And right now, the "gig" economy is dead. But, I do believe it will recover. Whether that will be enough to give Mr. Trump a second term, I offer no guesses.

And, Hillary Clinton...I respected your husband, though I didn't always agree with him. But there is NO WAY, you will EVER be elected President. Sit down. Give up this fantasy of yours. Be glad you were our First Lady and elected a Senator from New York State. I would respect you more if you did that.

I can vote for a woman. Tulsi Gabbard has my attention, but, as it turned out Joe Biden is the nominee.

At our station, being down the middle is not a request. It is demanded of us. And sometimes, that ain't easy. Radio network news and the AP shows either "sloppy journalism" or a flat out bias. I spend a lot of time editing your so called "reporting" because of this. And I am not the only one. We are cautioned by our bosses to watch out for such things.

To my way of thinking, Ronald Reagan was right. We are, but a generation away from losing our country.

And one of our biggest problems...our schoolchildren don't know ANYTHING about government anymore. They are "schooled" by the political views of their teachers, on both left and right.

Folks, it is no better that a child is taught that "Democrats are Good, while Republicans are EVIL" and more than the reverse is true.

And the radio talk shows don't help either. There ARE

journalists who are trying to be down the middle. I respect the success that Rush Limbaugh has had, but if I could sit down with him for 5 minutes, I would politely ask him to stop lumping local radio journalists in with everybody else. Same thing with Sean Hannity.

Please, schools…teach civics to middle and high school students again. Teach them about government and how it's supposed to work. Do that, and I'll back your requests for higher pay. I do think you're not paid enough. But, when students come into my college level classes and tell me "Fox News is racist", I shake my head. I ask them, "Who told you that"? They're reply? "All my friends think so."

Believing your friends without checking on what they're saying is dangerous. So, too is getting all your news from Facebook. Watch both right and left…and in the middle and decide for yourself. It won't kill you to watch a few reports. Watch the evening news and watch it from ALL sides. It's the ONLY way you can make an educated opinion about a candidate or an issue. Here's a thought: read a newspaper once in a while. Study issues yourselves. Don't let ANYBODY tell you how and what to think. Sadly, this goes on way too much in America today.

If you're a conservative, it won't hurt to watch CNN once in a while, or at least a Sunday show. If you're a liberal, you won't explode in a pile of dust to watch a news show on Fox once in a while, either.

The biggest problem to me: is the internet. Google, Facebook. I am all for Freedom of Speech, but Google and Facebook seem, at times, intent on telling people what THEY think they should think. Facebook ads can be manipulated. "Likes" and "Clicks" can be, and are with regularity, paid for. Now, they want to be the "fact checkers" and it is plainly obvious many of the fact checkers are tilted left.

This is why some advertisers and agencies are moving

AWAY from digital ads and going back to radio.

Now, I am NOT saying there isn't a place for digital. It is the future and, as I have said before we may all be "streaming stations" as opposed to AM/FM one day. But digital is one part of the whole.

And if Google and Facebook are going to act like news outlets, I would have no issue with the Federal Government coming in and requiring them to sell political ads to ALL politicians 90 days out from an election just as radio and television is required to do. It's called "Equal Time Laws" (not to be confused with the "Fairness Doctrine" which was eliminated in 1987). If they want to be considered news organizations, let them be regulated just as broadcast outlets are.

Why Facebook should "limit" or "suspend the accounts" of people who express a political view with which they don't agree is a travesty. Same for Google.

You are NOT a news organization when you only allow one point of view. And both of these organizations have become too powerful, IMHO. They can manipulate our elections at the drop of a hat because of the power they now have.

And, though some will take issue at me saying this: some level of scrutiny should also come of NPR and so called "Community Radio". These are both non-commercial operations. I find it amusing that I run one of those "community stations". Unfortunately, it is in a county in Ohio so deeply red that the local GOP Congressman is virtually immune from a challenge from an opponent. (He does, however represent his district well and that's why he keeps getting re-elected by a huge majority every time).

I have sent e-mails to the local GOP and Democratic organizations inviting them to share information they want to get out to the public, though my station will NEVER engage in "campaigning" for anyone from either side. I have heard from the

GOP...the Democrats have never returned an e-mail, nor do I ever hear from them. (I literally have had to go to one of our Ohio Senators about this.) But, I am amazed at the number of such stations who seem to feel they MUST offer far left programming as some "antidote" to commercial radio's talk programs.

Got news for you guys with 100 watts at 100 feet. You don't cover enough ground to do that. Even if you got 250 watts (which I favor), you still won't cover enough ground.

Entertain your audiences, don't preach to them. Politics is not a religion. If it's right to have separation of church and state, it's also right to have separation of politics, too.

I wonder how long it might be before a Congress might approve such a power increase, but then restrict such stations from airing purely political programming? Or airing it without airing an opposing viewpoint? (Almost a non-commercial station "Fairness Doctrine" of sorts). Now, that suggestion will leave some flipping their lids at me. And I am not, at all sure that it's a good idea, but, it's a thought.

Originally, these stations were to operate with 1,000 watts of power. And anywhere between 100 watts and there, I would be comfortable with. Many commercial broadcasters and their powerful lobbying group, the National Association of Broadcasters would disagree. And I do not think there isn't a place for these stations.

They were created as a response to the 1996 Telecom Act which brought about all the consolidation...all the job losses in the business...and the ridiculously high prices that go into owning radio stations these days. It has become a millionaire's game. No one such as myself, a humble radio station on air employee who makes, all told, about $60 to $70 thousand dollars a year, can, without literally "taking" an old man who offers to self-finance his station to get out from under it, can even think about broadcast ownership.

Typically, though MOST of these community stations are NOT purely "advocacy stations". And, to be fair, many LPFM supporters prefer and are urged to stay away from politics. This, to me is a good thing. I heard of a few stations clamoring to air the Presidential Impeachment hearings of President Trump, but then balk at airing the GOP's response at the trial.

Uh...you're not a news organization to do that. You've, again, become advocates. You air it all...or nothing. I hope the few people who were talking about doing this thought better of it.

And hey, you lefty LPFM-ers...YOU are keeping LP-250 from becoming a reality. Don't believe me...ask Michelle Bradley at RECNET about it. And she's a liberal.

My station will allow ANY candidate to come on our Saturday morning live show to talk about what they want to talk about. We WILL, however, offer Equal Time to their opponent 90 days out from an election. We will NOT, though, accept paid political advertising, because we are not allowed to do "Calls To Action" (which the words "Vote November 7th", or whenever, would be), or use comparative or qualitative language, which are all over political ads.

America is at a precipice. I pray we don't fall into the brink.

Chapter 20
How DOES Radio Programming Work?

Okay, since I am aiming this book at largely young people interested in the business (with maybe a nod toward listeners who enjoy it and may wonder about it), I thought I might give you an idea of "how it all works". I promise you won't have to look at the sausage, just how it's made.

When you first get a programmer's job, you probably are not going to have to do things such as "invent" the format. But, since I found myself in the position of being the first to program "All 80's" as a format, how should you do something like that?

First, understand, you are NOT going to be finding thousands and thousands of songs to play. There are many people out there who think radio SHOULD do this. It doesn't get ratings. Your job as Program Director is to find "the right music" (whether a library based format or a current and recent based format), and play those songs often enough that listeners keep listening. In most formats, once you get above a thousand song titles, you start losing listener's interest and they listen less to you. This is a statistic in the rating book called "Time Spent Listening". If your TSL stinks, you have likely done something wrong, because that low number means people are not hearing the songs they want to hear often enough.

Playlist size is debatable, to a degree. But, shorter is better. Is there room for a bigger list? Perhaps. Is there such a thing as being too tight? Yes, it can happen. We hear a lot of complaints from older radio people about the so-called "250 song playlists". Oh, yes, they are tight, particularly if this is a gold based station with no current music with which to freshen it up. And the "powers" (the best liked songs) will play about six times day or more. So, how do you keep that from happening?

Easy. You "test" more than 250 songs! Typically 800 to 1,500 depending on format. And you switch about 50 titles in and out about every 4 to 6 weeks. This reduces listener "burnout" and keeps listener interest.

So, how do you test music? The most expensive way is to do what is known as an "Auditorium Music Test". You get a company to recruit a panel of about 100 people (usually promising them a free meal and, maybe $50 to $100 bucks for their time). And for about 2 hours, the listeners are played "hooks" of songs. These are eight to ten second pieces of the most recognizable part of a song. They are typically "scored" on a scale of 1 to 5... with 5 being "like a lot" and 1 being "hate it". The number "0" is there, too. It's for "I don't recognize the song". When it's done, the company doing the test (No, you won't be in the room...you might watch it on a TV monitor, or from behind a one way mirror... but you're not supposed to be in there, and those taking the test are not told what station is paying for this information.)

When it's all done, the scores are tallied by the company and you get a rather large book of information on how the songs are scored. Since 5 was the highest number, you look for the songs with the highest "4+5" score. There's your power rotation. Some 3's and 4's may be high enough to be your "Medium" rotation, and lower 3's may be the "light rotation."

Now, scoring can be different with different companies. This is just the basics of it. But, traditionally, if a song can't score with at least a half or two thirds of your panel in your specific target gender and/or age group liking the song, why would you play it? You certainly don't want to drive half of your audience away playing the wrong song, right?

How much does this cost? To do it professionally, about $25 or $30 thousand dollars. Can you do it less expensively? Yep.

Most radio stations have websites and most stream their

signals on the internet or through apps, right?. You can do a "mini music test" on your website. Test 40 different titles at a time posting the hooks on your website and invite listeners within your target audience to register for your "listener advisory board". Have the ability, though to render some listeners as "inactive", without them knowing it. Some people love to try and "screw up" a competing station's test (or just one they don't like) by not voting honestly. Once you have a "sample" of 100 actives listeners, those 40 songs are tested. Then, test another 40 songs. You can typically test 40 songs about every 3 to 4 weeks. If you have the budget, tell the listeners that everyone who takes the test goes into a drawing for $100 (or $200 or whatever your budget can bear).

After you have tested about 300 titles, start looking for "trends" in your research. For me, when I did "Star 107.9" in Columbus, it was pretty obvious.

I had spoken over the phone with a consultant named Randy Kabrich. He was consulting stations early in the 80's format for companies like Cox and his research was showing that "the rock songs drive the bus". And that urban and dance songs, for the most part, didn't work. It was the only thing he told me in a phone conversation, obviously not wanting to give away trade secrets.

Son of a gun, that's what our test showed. What groups were at the top? John Mellencamp, Def Leppard, Bon Jovi, etc. Who was at the bottom? Klymaxx with "Meeting In The Ladies Room". Only Michael Jackson and Madonna and a few others tested reasonably well from that Urban/Dance category. Pop 80's such as Rick Springfield, Men At Work, Cyndi Lauper, etc did well, too.

Once you have tested enough titles, you "sort" the songs to come up with the strongest ones to play. That is your playlist. In a library based (gold) format, hopefully, you have a couple hundred or so which don't test "great", but are recognizable enough that they won't drive people away. Those songs can be your "stress relievers". More on that in a minute.

Now, consider the other portions of your programming. What type of "DJ presentation" does this format need? An uptempo "lively" jock approach, or a more laid back "album rock" style? If the first, consider using station I.D. jingles. My overall favorite company for this is Jam Creative Productions of Dallas, Texas. Yes, they're expensive. About $500 a cut at the time of writing this. "TM/Century" is another jingle supplier and there are cheaper options. Typically, though, you get what you pay for. If your station will be more "laid back", look for a good "station voice" to do your "image liners".

How often should you play these depends on the format. In Album Rock, Classic Rock or Country, I would say I.D. every other song. In CHR, Hot A/C, Classic Hits, Oldies and maybe Classic Country, I.D. between EVERY song with either a jingle or sweep or jock talk.

DJ's talk over record intros and into commercial sweeps. And the jocks need to learn to do talkovers correctly. Talk right up to the vocals, but without "stepping" on them, and talking over the singer. Even a jock doing Classic Rock CAN talk over the very beginning of a song. You typically NEVER stop the music unless going to commercials. And you do NOT talk over the end of one song and the beginning of another. The idea is to create "forward momentum"

Even if they are voice tracked (pre-recorded to "sound live"), make sure that your DJ's are up on what's happening in the local community and that they are talking about the local area. Is a High School Football or Basketball team playing in the State Championships? TALK ABOUT IT. And, at least have the final scores the next day. Big festival or concert coming up with a "core artist" in your area, TALK ABOUT IT. You can pre-record an interview with the artist if you can talk to their management or a record label ahead of time and use portions of the interview ahead of time to engage your listeners and get them excited about the show.

After the show, do a "concert after the concert". If that artist has a live album, play cuts for about 45 minutes or so after the show is over. It gives your audience the chance to "relive" what they just saw and they will lock their radios on to YOUR station to hear it as they're driving home.

Using voice-tracked talent from out of town, for God's sake, make sure they know how to pronounce the names of local towns and places of interest. Know the difference in pronouncing "LAN-CAST-er", Pennsylvania and "LANK-uh-ster", Ohio.

Got a station meteorologist? Run at least 2 and preferably more different weather forecasts a day. Run one 4 times an hour in morning drive time (listener turnover is about every 20 minutes then), once an hour after 9 am, and I would skip weather after 6 pm, with the sole exception of emergency weather information. All of that can be tracked just before airing, or with the right deal from your meteorologists, you can get them on live (even if you take a TV audio feed) and air that during the time of the emergency.

School closings are STILL important, despite the fact that schools have apps. Why? How many people die every day because they're on their phones in traffic? That's why radio still does school closings. People want them.

And if you are running a "cluster operation" of 3, 4 or 8 stations, find the money to have at the very least, ONE overnight part timer in the building 24/7/365 to keep watch over all of the stations. Satellite programming DOES screw up occasionally. The worst thing to hear at 2 AM is a satellite delivered program that is airing no programming. You are supposed to be airing at least a Station Identification at the top of the hour. If that ain't happening because the satellite feed is stuck on an empty channel, you are operating illegally.

Giveaways. You need 'em. During the pandemic, we did Zoom Concerts where we had all of the invitations to them, and listeners who won them also won the right to talk to the artist during the show. It's the "virtual" way of giving away backstage passes, and those are still very popular.

What do you give away at a remote broadcast? Sure, station T-shirts are always good. But avoid the "card table" remote. Nobody wants to come out if all they can get from you is a 29 cent plastic key chain. A register to win entry box for concert tickets (if for a good show), or tickets to an Amusement Park, Football Game, NASCAR Race, College Football Game, The Super Bowl, etc will ALWAYS have listener interest. But, you should have key chains, bottles of hand sanitizer and masks (with the station logo on them), even ice scrapers with your logo.

Cash is king. One thing your sales department could do is build into the cost of a remote broadcast an offer to allow the listener to pull from "The Cash Box". Take $500 and split it so that there is one $100 prize, and lots of $20, $10 and $5 prizes. You can say that the first 102 or 95 or whatever keyed to your station frequency of listeners who come out get to pull an envelope from the box for a chance to win up to $100 in cash. Free food is also a good thing. Burgers and Hot Dogs with sodas and potato chips, pizza, chicken sandwiches are also good incentives to drive listener interest.

Keep your remote breaks to within a reasonable amount of time. Yes, you can do them exact time 60 seconds, but that's hard to do...best to have a remote jingle made up that can be looped with an I.D. of some sort at the end to close the break out. Unless you're able to control your studio computer on site (and it can be done), you'll want a board op at the studio to do this. Send your talent with a stop watch and keep them to within, say, ten or fifteen seconds of the length of the break.

The so-called "collective" contests. They can be good

and bad. If there are so many stations in the collective that you only get a local winner once every 15 rating books, they are no good at all. The odds of winning are too low. But with a smaller number of stations in the prize pool, your chances of having local winners goes up dramatically. We have done giveaways with a small number of stations in the pool and have had 20 to 25 local winners of $1,000. THAT moves the ratings needle. Make sure you can record the voices of the winners for promos. Have your jocks congratulate and talk about your winners. Let people know "Fred" from Xenia won...and "Shirley" from Tipp City.

But, ALWAYS make sure at least one local person wins something. Even if you're doing an "annuity game" where the odds of winning the "big" prize are next to impossible, have at least one local winner getting $5,000. Or something substantial for your listening market.

Oh, yes, "stress relievers" in your music. Deploy those once an hour at a "drop position" on your format clock. And, maybe 2 or 3 times an hour on the weekends. This will allow the "illusion of depth" your station needs to keep from burning out your titles in an extremely tight listed station. Take, for example, the traditional "oldies" format. You can have 350-450 titles on a playlist. But, there's a total of about 1,500 "playable" titles. Use that "B" list to take the stress off your playlist. Do "theme weekends"...Class of 1969, Class of 1975, Class of 1983, New Wave Weekend, Beatles from A to Z, etc.

Remember, at the height of its success, the legendary WABC in New York had a playlist of 14 current songs (plus recent hits and "gold" titles). (Don't believe me? Ask "Cousin" Bruce Morrow), KHJ and the other Drake stations like KYA, KHJ and CKLW had the "Boss 30". And they all WON. Don't ever let anyone tell you that you need to play a 60 record current list. A record label would love it. The listener's, though, would not. THAT's who you're programming to. The only time Bill Drake ever lost a battle was in Cincinnati at WUBE-AM. And the only reason "Boss Radio 1-2-3, U-B-E" lost is because its signal was substandard to 1360/WSAI. What did he say that he learned about it? "Never take a shitty signal".

Signal is everything. If you don't have a good signal, how high the ratings can get is a crap shoot. But, can you still make money with a lesser signaled station? Yes, IF you program it carefully. In that case, aim younger, not older. Young people will seek out a station and will tolerate some signal reception issues IF the station is giving them something they want to hear.

Yes, you need, in most cases, some semblance of a "News Department" and you should have a "News Network" for long form emergency coverage. In a small town, 2 full time people is a minimum. Bigger market should have at least 4 or 5 people. A news-talker with an all news morning show needs more than that. Local News from local anchors at least 24 hours a day weekdays is possible.

A Program Director needs to be a "coach", a "Father Confessor", and a "shoulder to lean on" from your staff. Everybody has problems in life. You need to be there for your staff when they need you. NO daypart is unimportant. Get up and listen to the all night person at least once a month for a half hour. That person tends to get the least attention from the Program Director...and needs a little love and constructive criticism from you, too.

One last thing – you must always remember that a radio station...any radio station whether commercial or non commercial...is a business. Without advertisers or underwriters they will not last long. Part of a Program Director's job is to work WITH sales to achieve revenue goals. And it can be very tough to change advertiser "perceptions" about certain demographics. I learned that the hard way at WKIO-FM in Champaign, Illinois. And sometimes advertisers are averse to doing changing their perceptions, such as how they think about Baby Boomers. That's why the 25-54 demographic still rules the advertising business.

But, despite all of this, radio still thrives. Newspapers have been around for a long time. Longer than radio, that's for sure. But, most people will tell you days are numbered for actual "printed on paper" newspapers. They're extremely expensive to run. You need to be able to pay for all of those reporters and editors. Some papers are surviving by turning their reporters into photographers with i-Phones, thus cutting the need for those employees. But, newsprint is expensive...presses are expensive, especially the automated ones today. Many newspapers outsource their printing now because having an in-house press has become too expensive.

Television will likely survive, but it is under major pressure these days. Why? Everything television does comes with a cost. Paying the rights fees to air the Super Bowl, or the Academy Awards or College or Pro Football, or Major League Baseball are not cheap. Where once upon a time, a TV studio had 3 full time camera operators, directors, floor directors all running around behind cameras and the talent, the cameras are now robotic, operated by one person in a control room. You DO have a "studio operator", running the lighting and studio operations. But, where once were 7 or 8 people, there is now...one. Oh, and don't forget the cost of employing 2 or 3 shifts of anchors, reporters and photographers. (That's also why there are few "all news" radio stations. Very talent heavy, and very expensive.) Not to mention that many "Big Event" TV shows are moving to streaming and away from over the air television. People are "cutting the cord", too. Why? You want full tier A.T. & T. Uverse? Last I subscribed, it was nearly $400 a month. If you can have high speed internet and a good antenna, you can get local channels, plus Netflix, Hulu and maybe Disney and have most of what a family needs or wants from television for under $150 a month.

Television and radio survive because of one thing no one else offers. Outside of the cost of the receiver (and a streaming subscription or 2), it is FREE. Why has satellite radio not really caught on? Ask its CEO why the "churn rate" is so high? His quoted answer, "I don't want to PAY" Most of the subscribers to satellite radio are old radio guys who "think" everything on it has no commercials. Then they discover that Sirius/XM discovered a long time ago they needed a combination of commercial and free channels to survive.

"Oh, You Tube is free.", you say. It is, but You Tube TV is not...and it is pretty expensive. Ad supported You Tube online is nice, but when they're streaming something that gets a lot of hits, expect to sit through about 3 or 4 ads before you get to your programming...and maybe have it interrupted by 3 or 4 more 20 minutes later.

And what does radio require? A receiver. No subscription fees. You just have to tolerate a couple of commercial breaks, which I will agree today that some companies take to extremes. But, the ones who do are still paying now massive debt from the 1990's and early 2000's. Not all companies operate that way. And people of all ages still listen to radio. The one "legacy" media that may still be standing once streaming media eventually takes over. Radio has invested in streaming. It DOES pay music licensing for online streaming (ASCAP/BMI/SESAC, Sound Exchange and GMR). 100 years old...and still going strong.

And that is a short course in how great radio stations are made, and programmed.

Chapter 21

Name Droppers

It's the one question people seem to always want to ask you when you meet them for the first time…"How many famous people have you met?" More than likely, my answer is, "Too many to remember them all". I've told a few of the stories in this book. But, here, I'll try and at least talk more about my more memorable brushes with celebrity.

As a young child, I remember meeting the late Ohio Governor James Rhodes on a number of occasions. (It was easy to do…he was Governor for, like, 20 years or so!) But, as for my broadcasting career…

I have met many politicians…I met Senator Edward Kennedy in the Greater Cincinnati Airport at a press conference once. Getting to be able to speak with one of the "Kennedy brothers" is hard enough when you're in media, as the late "Lion of the Senate" attracts a big crowd…and it's mostly reporters.

So on the day I went, I found myself at the back of a large group of journalists and TV cameramen…which is a problem when you realize you only have a microphone that can pick up a maximum of two feet away. And there is no "desk" or "podium" to put it on. And on this day, I decided to try some physical gymnastics…snaking around a few in the crowd, and going underneath a few cameras. Eventually I got near the first row, but just couldn't penetrate it. So, I stuck my arm holding the microphone underneath a camera and held it as close as I could get it bent over almost in half. It was close enough.

I asked a question. The Senator heard me, looked down, grinned and quizzically asked, "Is someone really down there?".

My reply? "Yes, Senator and I'm getting cramped. Could

you please answer the question?" Senator Kennedy and all of the reporters laughed and he answered my question...I squirmed back out the crowd and unfolded myself!

John Kasich is another pol with whom I have met. Now, he's an interesting character. Was a Congressman from Columbus, whom I knew when I worked there, and frankly, got along with pretty well. When I came back to Dayton, he made an appearance in nearby Xenia...so I went to see him. Asked him a single question. Frankly, I thought it was a complete softball. But, Kasich took it personally and proceeded to castigate me about it. I was pretty put off by this. I wanted to say, "Hey, remember me? We used to talk all the time in Columbus! Why are you acting like this?"

Later some people who know him personally told me this is a character flaw of his. That he apparently has a "messianic" complex and really does think God put him on this planet to achieve high office.

Got news for you, John, my friend. You ain't God. And He's not going to put you in the White House...not without you making amends to a LOT of people you've ticked off because of that personality of yours. You, Sir, are your own worst enemy, though I do think you've got some good ideas.

I am also on decent terms with Jim Jordan...Ohio's present 4th district Congressman. He's a straight shooter and will answer questions whether you personally agree with him or not. I can generally get him on the phone...well, as long as he's not tied up all day with Sean Hannity.

Recording artists: Well, for starters, Garth Brooks. I met him in Columbus, Ohio the week BEFORE his famous free concert in Central Park that attracted a million fans.

I was doing a live show in the parking lot of the baseball stadium where he would play for the first of 5 nights of concerts when my buddy, John-Boy Crenshaw (our WCOL Music Director at the time) says to me, "Recognize that song that they're playing?" (they were doing soundcheck at the time).

I listened and said, "That's...Billy Joel's "New York State Of Mind", isn't it?" John smiled and said, "Yep". You see, Garth was promising a major "surprise guest" at the New York show. I said to JB, "Wait a minute...are you telling me...?"

His reply? "You didn't hear it from me...I just heard it from a record rep." Needless to say, I was not surprised when he brought Billy out on stage during the show which was televised live on HBO.

So, our Program Director arrived and said to me, "Hey, do you want to take our contest winners backstage to meet Garth? I've met him already and I know you haven't."

I said, "Hell, yes! And thank you." And I got the PD's backstage pass!

Our winners (2 young ladies) come up to our table, I collected them up and we all go backstage. I was told to head for Garth's bus and just go inside. So, up the bus steps I went with the winners in tow.

Got to the top of the steps, turned left and...there he was. Garth looked up and said, "Hi! I'm Garth. Want a beer?" I was like, "Sure!". He replied, "Budweiser, OK?" I said, "Absolutely". So, all got our beers and sat down for a chat with Garth.

Garth's meet and greets, you see, are not like your usual 5 seconds in and out, take a picture, maybe get a question or two from the artist, and out you go. When you do one with Garth, he literally blocks off 30 minutes to spend with you.

So, we chatted about his family, his kids, his career. He asked us about our lives (even me), and seemed genuinely interested in our answers. It was almost like he lives in such a "surreal" world of stardom and fame that he enjoys talking about what it's like to live a "normal" existence...one he hasn't had in decades.

During the course of the conversation, he saw both of our contest winners had their tour books with them, they asked if he would sign them, and Garth whipped out his Sharpie to sign. As he collected their tour books, he asked "Did you get these out front at the souvenir stands?"

The listener replied they had. So, Garth turns and holds up 2 fingers to an aide on his bus, who went back in the back and returned about a minute or two later. In his hands were two $20 bills. He gave them to Garth, who gave one of them to each of the winners.

"You ladies are guests of the radio station. You shouldn't have to pay for these."

I couldn't believe what I was hearing...nor could they. I also thought, "What a marketing genius this guy is."

Unless I miss my guess, I'm betting both of those ladies have those twenties at least in a scrapbook...or...in a frame hanging on a wall in their houses.

I have an autographed picture from Garth which came from his personal collection. It hangs on my wall at home, and usually attracts some big attention from guests when they come to my house for the first time.

I met some of the original lead singers of the Temptations. Otis Williams, Eddie Kendricks and Dennis Edwards while in Columbus, too. They were the headliners on the bill of an oldies concert we did that I emceed mentioned earlier in the book.

So, we're backstage during intermission ahead of their performance and I am chatting with them about their early days. Motown, you see, literally put their young performers through "school" of sorts. It included how to handle interviews, how to present themselves in public...they even went to dance classes to learn the moves they'd use on stage. I asked them about the dances they did.

They tried to teach them to me. I say "tried", because it was an unmitigated disaster!

I don't dance. Not without a LOT of practice. And 2 minutes backstage ain't enough. As I was back there trying my darnedest at doing a "leaping gazelle", I'm panting and puffing and saying, "Hey, guys...do you notice something? I'm WHITE! I can't do this!" All of us had the biggest of laughs at that. What wonderful people they are...and were. In fact, I reconnected with Otis Williams of the Temps (the sole surviving original member) just last year.

I've also met Rick Springfield (of "Jessie's Girl" fame)... introduced him in concert at least twice. Met, John Mellencamp, John Taylor (original bass player for Duran Duran), Peter Noone of Herman's Hermits, too...a couple of times.

I've also spoken by phone with actor Tom Hanks, who played astronaut Jim Lovell in "Apollo 13" and many other great roles.

It happened when he was producing "That Thing You Do" about the fictional one hit wonders, the Oneders. "One-ders", though a lot of people call them, the "Oh-NEED-ers" and it all happened very quickly.

I was on the air at WCOL when PD, Gary Moss stuck his head in the studio door. "Hey, Jason...would you like to interview Tom Hanks?"

"Sure", I said. "When?"

Gary said, "In 5 minutes. He's calling the hot line."

I gasped and said, "OK…why am I talking to him?"

Gary said, "He's making a movie and called to get permission to use our call letters in it. I told him, I'd grant permission IF he would do an interview with us."

Five minutes later, the hotline rang and, sure enough, I was on the phone with Tom Hanks talking with him about the film that became "That Thing You Do", also talked with him about "Apollo 13" and discovered he is every bit the "Space Geek" that I am. We seemed to hit it off pretty well.

And, if you have the DVD of "That Thing You Do", watch for a very quick 5 second scene of a DJ in the control of a radio station playing the song. Look on the wall behind him and you will see, "WCOL – Columbus, Ohio" behind the DJ character.

More Country stars: Aaron Tippin, Chris Janson, Jason Aldean, Florida Georgia Line, Reba McEntire, the late Marty Robbins, Grandpa Jones and Minnie Pearl, too.

And yes, I've met the late, great George Jones, too. He was playing a huge "Gilley's" style club in Springfield, Ohio once and was as sick as a dog that night when I met him on his bus. Not hung over, just terribly, terribly ill with bronchitis and a fever.

I asked him, "Possum…are you going to be OK to go out on stage and perform?"

His reply, I have never forgotten. "Son, the last time I was supposed to be here, I didn't show up. I've always felt sorry about that. I've got a packed house of people out there and I'll be damned if I'm going to not show up this time. I'll be alright. Don't you worry."

He went out on stage and did 60 minutes of his biggest hits. His voice showed a little strain and was a little "nasal", but he belted 'em out to a standing ovation from the crowd.

He got back on his tour bus and went straight to a local hospital that filled him up with antibiotics and fluids before sending him on his way.

He was one of the best. No. He WAS the best. Period. And I cried a little bit when he died. He may not have always followed the straight and narrow in life, but at its end, he found peace.

I remember meeting Jerry Lee Lewis in the very same bar. Backstage, on a couch surrounded by the most glamorous ladies I have ever seen. He was "The Killer" for sure.

One of my favorite newer artists is a guy by the name of Chris Janson. He's part of the "New Country" crowd, but his music has a traditional sound…if produced toward the newer sound a bit.

At the Champaign County Fair in Urbana, Ohio, I introduced him by saying, "People talk a lot these days about the new rock and roll influences in today's country music. George Jones once asked, "Whose Gonna Fill Their Shoes", speaking of the great artists of country".

"Well, me? I don't worry about the future of country. It'll be just fine…as long as it has singers in it like the guy you're about to meet. Ladies and Gentleman, please welcome, Chris Janson!"

The crowd cheered. I walked down the steps of the stage. Chris met me at the bottom, on his knees, doing the Wayne and Garth. "I'm not worthy! I'm not worthy!" thing. He got up and said, "I've never had an introduction like that."

I said, "I meant every word of it, Chris. Now, get up there and get 'em".

Songwriters. I know many. The first was a local guy by the name of Frank Meyers. He was a player in a house band in Dayton that I did some appearances at. One day, he told me he was moving to Nashville to pursue his dream of being a songwriter and artist. I gave him my phone number and told him to keep me posted.

I didn't hear from him for a while. But, one Saturday morning, I was awakened by the sound of my telephone in the living room. I stumbled out to the phone and answered it. It was Frank.

"Hey, sorry about the early call. But, I just got out of the studio last night. Eddie Rabbitt and Crystal Gayle have just recorded one of my songs. I got it on a cassette here from the session and wanted to play it for you and see what you think about it." "Sure, go ahead", I said.

If you haven't figured it out yet. The song was "You And I". And I was the first disc jockey in the world to hear it.

When it was over, Frank said, "Well, what do you think?"

I said, "Frank, I heard you just bought a house down there in Nashville." He said, "I did".

I said, "I think that song is gonna make your house payments for a long time."

He said, "Really?" I replied, "Really."

By the grace of God, I was right. "You and I" became a monster #1 hit at both Country and Pop. Multi-platinum…a Country Music Award winner…and a Grammy winner. In fact, I learned later his first "monthly" royalty check for that song was $40,000. (I think they had to pick him up off the floor at the BMI office when he saw the check!)

Years later, he co-wrote a song called "I Swear"…which was a major chart topping country hit for John Michael Montgomery and for the Pop/Soul group All-4-One.

I couldn't be more proud of him.

Another dear songwriting friend is another local guy... raised at Indian Lake, Ohio about 70 miles from Dayton. Even Stevens is a child of the 60's, as am I. A little older than I am, though. He was a teenager in a teen night club in 1965 when a group named "Rick and The Raiders" appeared on stage to play their "new" record for the crowd.

It was called, "Hang On Sloopy". And everyone my age knows Rick Derringer and the McCoys.

Even followed his passion to Nashville, too. Started writing songs. And has had massive numbers of hits. And his songs have sold millions and millions of records and CD's. I am honored to be his friend, and am humbled that he considers me a friend.

Remember, "Driving My Life Away"? "I Love A Rainy Night"? "Step By Step"? "When You're In Love With A Beautiful Woman"?That's just a FEW of his hits. And, there are hundreds more.

He is a two time "Songwriter Of The Century". It has been estimated that "I Love A Rainy Night" has been played on the radio around 10 million times.

We became friends because he decided to stage an annual benefit show at the Lake (where the LPFM operation I run is located), called "Nashville Hitmakers". He and his friends come up and do a "songwriter in the round" show talking about and playing their hits. The proceeds go to the Indian Lake Watershed Project (which keeps the lake one of the cleanest in Ohio), as well as provides money to the music programs at Indian Lake schools.

The LPFM and K-99.1 both promote his charitable shows and they are virtual sellouts every year. And because it IS a charity, the LPFM can now...legally...promote the show.

I have met many, many of his songwriting friends (way too

numerous to list here) in this manner, and I cherish meeting them and being friends. A few of them? The late Mac Davis, Beth Nielsen Chapman, the late Lari White, Scotty Emerick. I know and knew them, their husbands and wives, I even played with their dogs.

They are all incredibly talented people and I am humbled to be in their presence.

I would love to meet Phil Donahue. I would loved to have met the late Ruth Lyons.

Who's Ruth Lyons?

Only the biggest daytime TV talk host of the 1950's and 1960's…seen here in Ohio, Kentucky and Indiana…and syndicated in other stations and states, over the old Avco TV Network.

Women in broadcasting talk about having to fight a "glass ceiling" and that is truly a shame that it happens and needs to go. But, Ruth didn't just get past it…she shattered it into a million pieces…becoming an executive with Avco Broadcasting so powerful she could veto ANYTHING the bosses decided.

Why? She connected with the viewers (and the people listening to her over WLW Radio). She refused to "endorse" a product on her show unless she had tried it and knew it worked. And when she endorsed a product, it flew off shelves like gangbusters.

She brought color television to Cincinnati all the way back in the 1950's. But a series of strokes created health issues which became too severe for her to overcome. And so, she retired in 1967. Her program was taken over by her co-host, Bob Braun who continued to do the show into the 1980's. I knew his cousin, Bucks Braun very well.

Sometimes I have said I wish I could have been born ten

years earlier so I could have been a part of that "broadcasting business"...to have worked for a KHJ, a CKLW, a WLW in their heyday. These were all fantastic radio stations with tremendously talented people.

Don't get me wrong. I think I've had a great career. It just seemed though like it was more fun back then.

What we really need to do is put the fun back into the business. If we can't be live all the time, fine. But DJ's are not meant to "read liner cards" all day long. Let them grow and develop into personalities. Make all radio local...let your personalities shine in your cities and towns and don't inhibit their growth by not allowing them to relate to the local audience.

I love it that a certain company talks a big deal about being "Live and Local". But, few of their stations actually are, and many of them are firing people right and left and are just going with computerized formats which are liner, song, liner, song, liner, song and a 8 to 10 minute commercial set because they, too have bought too many stations and are having to manage debt.

That's not radio. That's garbage programming. And no one believes your "Live and Local" crap...because the audience knows you're not. Disagree with me all you will, I don't care.

Bill Drake wouldn't allow it. Ron Jacobs wouldn't allow it. Gordon McLendon wouldn't allow it. Neither would Todd Storz. And I'll be damned if I will allow it. Ever.

Chapter 22

A Few Words About Journalism

Now, I know as I write this chapter I am going to outrage a few people, but frankly, I don't give a damn.

I was always taught that true journalism was neither left nor right, but down the middle. Which means, each side gets to express their views.

Sadly, our political system in the U.S. has broken down to the point where if you're not "spewing the party line", whatever it is, you should be censured, or not allowed to speak.

Recently, I got lambasted on Facebook from some liberal types asking, "How can we get rid of Fox News?"

Now, don't get me wrong, I don't necessarily think Fox is all that. They clearly lean right, especially during their prime time programming. Just as MSNBC leans left and CNN, which at one time was a great network, now tries to "straddle the middle between MSNBC and "the middle". And now, you have OAN (One America News) which is trying to "out right" Fox.

More than anything, I think some people hate the fact that Fox found a successful niche and has made a lot of money occupying it. You can't "take away their broadcasting license" because, as a cable network, there is no FCC license to take.

A book I once read, Reis and Trout's "22 Immutable Laws of Marketing" states, "If you can't be number one, create another "hill" and declare yourself number one at it." That's what MSNBC is doing. They lean far left, because Fox is right. CNN tried being in the middle, but another marketing law says "If you don't stand for something, you stand for nothing". So, it's trying to cut the middle between MSNBC and the middle. And, so far, they're not successful at it.

Friends, the only way you're going to "get rid of Fox" is to convince a lot of people to stop watching them. Do that, and it'll go away on its own. Until then, or unless it happens, you are S.O.L.

Politically, I consider myself Libertarian. I am right on fiscal policies…center to left on some social issues.

I admired John and Robert Kennedy as a child. I still think RFK would have been one of the greatest American Presidents who ever lived. But, some idiot (or idiots) made that impossible.

John Glenn was a news source and a friend of mine over the years. And I voted for him, even though I didn't always agree with his policies. But, learning about his background, I learned he wouldn't support ANY policy if he truly thought it wasn't morally right. I respected that. And we need more of that political courage today. To me, it is just too sad, we don't have legislators on either side of the aisle with any of his moral backbone today. This "moral relevance" is harming our country. There's a few, but not many.

President Trump? He's not the devil incarnate. He's also not a professional politician and that is the reason he was elected. People have tired of people on both sides feeding them bullshit just to get a vote. Sure, some of his tweeting made me want to go up to D.C. and steal his cellphone. But like him or not, he did a tremendous job with the economy early on and my 401K thanks him for that. Sadly, though, his trade policies are making it hard for certain sectors of America. But, right now, as I write this, black unemployment was down around 5.5 percent. Hispanic unemployment is close to that. Minorities were finding jobs for the first time in 20 years. If you don't think that was remembered in November 2020, you're out of your mind. But, then came Covid-19 and it all fell to crap. So, I do agree with those who say that he was "defeated by the virus". Still, my 401K is doing well. I only hope this will be impressed upon all future Presidents that

Americans have the right to save money for retirement, because politicians raided our Social Security program and I know of NO ONE who "lives comfortably" on Social Security.

So, now, we've had this "pandemic" called COVID-19. And President Trump has had to spend money like water, money we don't have by the way, to keep the country from going into a depression. Frankly, I'm grateful for the cash. I have NEVER made enough money as a radio personality and have always had to do remotes and DJ weddings to make ends meet. And right now, the "gig" economy is dead. But, I do believe it will recover.

And, Hillary Clinton…I respected your husband, though I didn't always agree with him. But there is NO WAY, you will EVER be elected President. Sit down. Give up this fantasy of yours. Be glad you were our First Lady and elected a Senator from New York State. I would respect you more if you did that.

I can vote for a woman. And, I can and have voted for Democrats. Tulsi Gabbard has my attention, but, as it turned out Joe Biden became the nominee. I am surprised, though Hillary didn't swoop in and try to grab the nomination from Mr. Biden. Perhaps the party (or someone in it) prevented that and, if so, they were smart to do it.

I recently read an old book…it's called "Conscience Of A Conservative Democrat". It was written by the late Commerce Secretary Charles Sawyer. Why him? Because it was Charles Sawyer whose interest in broadcasting was given to him after doing some legal work for Powel Crosley helping him keep his radio company and station WLW when someone wanted to buy it. Later, he purchased station WSMK in Dayton and renamed it, "WING"…and I would work for them in the 1980's. What I notice in reading that book (and I would agree with the author), is that the definitions of "Conservative" and "Liberal" and "Progressive" apparently meant MUCH different things in the past.

The late TV Hostess Ruth Lyons grew up a Republican, and

was convinced by her her husband, Herman Newman to switch parties. Ruth was every bit a champion for civil rights and the right of all people to live as they wished to live. And no one can, or should be against any of that. I certainly am not. I just don't believe that government should constantly be on the throat of the American people. We ALL have the right to be ourselves and make it in this world. If we ever lose that, we'll be lost for good.

At our station, being down the middle is not a request. It is demanded of us. And sometimes, that ain't easy. Radio network news and the AP shows either "sloppy journalism" or a flat out bias. I spend a lot of time editing your so called "reporting" because of this. And, I am not the only person in the news business who thinks this.

Hey, I'll interview anyone. I interviewed Bernie Sanders. I gave him time to express his views and did not interrupt. I also asked some tough questions of him. And, sorry, but I don't believe he answered some of those questions well. It was obvious that he had never thought of one I asked him about education. He sidestepped it quickly.

To my way of thinking, Ronald Reagan was right. We are, but a generation away from losing our country.

And one of our biggest problems…our schoolchildren don't know ANYTHING about government anymore. They are "schooled" by the political views of their teachers, on both left and right.

Folks, it is no better that a child is taught that "Democrats are Good, while Republicans are EVIL" and more than the reverse is true.

Please, schools…teach civics to middle and high school students again. Teach them about government and how it's supposed to work. Do that, and I'll back your requests for higher pay. I do think you're not paid enough. But, when students come into my college level classes and tell me "Fox News is racist", I shake my head. I ask them, "Who told you that"? They're reply? "All my friends think so."

Believing your friends without checking on what they're saying is dangerous. So, too is getting all your news from Facebook. Watch both right and left…and in the middle and decide for yourself. It won't kill you to watch a few reports. Watch the evening news and watch it from ALL sides. It's the ONLY way you can make an educated opinion about a candidate or an issue. Here's a thought: read a newspaper once in a while. Study issues yourselves. Don't let ANYBODY tell you how and what to think. Sadly, this goes on way too much in America today.

If you're a conservative, it won't hurt to watch CNN once in a while, or at least a Sunday show. If you're a liberal, you won't explode in a pile of dust to watch a news show on Fox once in a while, either.

The biggest problem to me: is the internet. Google, Facebook. I am all for Freedom of Speech, but Google and Facebook seem, at times, intent on telling people what THEY think they should think. Facebook ads can be manipulated. "Likes" and "Clicks" can be, and are with regularity, paid for. And make no mistake, they admit to censoring speech which they do not like. Free Speech means EVERYONE has it. Not just one side. Does that make me dangerous? I don't think so. I think it makes me a patriot.

This is why some advertisers and agencies are moving AWAY from digital ads and going back to radio.

Now, I am NOT saying there isn't a place for digital. It is the future and, as I have said before we may all be "streaming stations" as opposed to AM/FM one day. But digital is one part of the whole.

And if Google and Facebook are going to act like news

outlets, I would have no issue with the Federal Government coming in and requiring them to sell political ads to ALL politicians 90 days out from an election just as radio and television is required to do. It's called "Equal Time Laws" (not to be confused with the "Fairness Doctrine" which was eliminated in 1987). If they want to be considered news organizations, let them be regulated just as broadcast outlets are.

Why Facebook should "limit" or "suspend the accounts" of people who express a political view with which they don't agree is a travesty. Same for Google. Same for Twitter.

You are NOT a news organization when you only allow one point of view. And both of these organizations have become too powerful, IMHO. They can manipulate our elections at the drop of a hat because of the power they now have.

And, though some will take issue at me saying this: some level of scrutiny should also come of NPR and so called "Community Radio". These are both non-commercial operations. I find it amusing that I run one of those "community stations". Unfortunately, it is in a county in Ohio so deeply red that the local GOP Congressman is virtually immune from a challenge from an opponent. (He does, however represent his district well and that's why he keeps getting re-elected by a huge majority every time).

I have sent e-mails to the local GOP and Democratic organizations inviting them to share information they want to get out to the public, though my station will NEVER engage in "campaigning" for anyone from either side. I have heard from the GOP…the Democrats have never returned an e-mail, nor do I ever hear from them. (I literally have had to go to one of our Ohio Senators about this.) But, I am amazed at the number of such stations who seem to feel they MUST offer far left programming as some "antidote" to commercial radio's talk programs.

Got news for you guys with 100 watts at 100 feet. You don't cover enough ground to do that. Even if you got 250 watts (which

I favor), you still won't cover enough ground.

Entertain your audiences, don't preach to them. Politics is not a religion. If it's right to have separation of church and state, it's also right to have separation of politics, too.

I wonder how long it might be before a Congress might approve such a power increase, but then restrict such stations from airing purely political programming? Or airing it without airing an opposing viewpoint? (Almost a non-commercial station "Fairness Doctrine" of sorts).Now, that suggestion will leave some flipping their lids at me. And I am not, at all sure that it's a good idea, but, it's a thought.

Originally, these stations were to operate with 1,000 watts of power. And anywhere between 100 watts and there, I would be comfortable with. Many commercial broadcasters and their powerful lobbying group, the National Association of Broadcasters would disagree. And I do not think there isn't a place for these stations.

They were created as a response to the 1996 Telecom Act which brought about all the consolidation…all the job losses in the business…and the ridiculously high prices that go into owning radio stations these days. It has become a millionaire's game. No one such as myself, a humble radio station on air employee who makes, all told, about $60 to $70 thousand dollars a year, can, without literally "taking" an old man who offers to self-finance his station to get out from under it, can even think about broadcast ownership.

Typically, though MOST of these community stations are NOT purely "advocacy stations". And, to be fair, many LPFM supporters prefer and are urged to stay away from politics. This, to me is a good thing. I heard of a few stations clamoring to air the Presidential Impeachment hearings of President Trump, but then balk at airing the GOP's response at the trial. That is NOT being an objective journalist.

Uh...you're not a news organization to do that. You've, again, become advocates. You air it all...or nothing. I hope the few people who were talking about doing this thought better of it.

And hey, you lefty LPFM-ers...YOU are keeping LP-250 from becoming a reality. Don't believe me...ask Michelle Bradley at RECNET about it. And she's a liberal.

My station will allow ANY candidate to come on our Saturday morning live show to talk about what they want to talk about. We WILL, however, offer Equal Time to their opponent 90 days out from an election. We will NOT, though, accept paid political advertising, because we are not allowed to do "Calls To Action" (which the words "Vote November 7th", or whenever, would be), or use comparative or qualitative language, which are all over political ads.

And of this, "socialism" idea? Social programs that help people (such as Medicare, Medicaid, Social Security) are and can be good ideas (even if Congress ruined Social Security by stealing from the trust fund). Socialism, though? Well, if they were around, I would say ask my Grandparents about it. Sadly, not enough colleges teach the downsides of it.

The environment? I want clean air...and water...beautiful parks and majestic mountains and monuments. I was around at the first Earth Day in 1970. What was I hearing then as a young student? That America was only ten years away from the brink of an ecological disaster. Some people are still saying those same words today. It's not that I don't believe it...but that ten years has taken a long time to get here.

I have hope for alternative fuels and even electric vehicles. The technology is improving. My concern, though, is the cost. The average person can barely afford a new car these days. (In fact, my $21,000 car I own today is $6,000 more than the bigger house I grew up in than the one me and the bank own today!) The technology needs to get in line with the fuel efficiency of a modern gas powered automobile...and at a similar cost. Otherwise, average people won't buy into it. You want to go "solar", I'm fine with that. But it's not inexpensive. It should not just be for people of great means. It's just not that hard to understand.

America is at a precipice. I pray we don't fall into the brink.

Chapter 23

A Few Words About The Radio Business And It's Future

So, why do I get angry when someone tells me "radio is dead" or "radio is dying"?

Simple. There is no reasonable indication that it's true.

A couple of facts: AM/FM Radio listening...on air and online reaches 92 percent of the American public every week. 92 percent. Let that sink in for a minute.

It's true that, for a little while, "digital advertising" was all the rage and advertisers were moving money out of so-called "legacy media" and into it. That's why radio moved into selling digital ads. We could, did and do offer advertising online. But, then, advertisers and agencies figured out that advertising on Facebook and where ever wasn't what it was cracked up to be. That "clicks and likes" were being bought and sold...that the "metrics" could be skewed. The digital ad salesman will answer, "Sure. But, so can the radio ratings".

Well, sure. Radio ratings can be bought with a good cash promotion. But that doesn't mean the listening isn't there. Having a company "buy" likes and clicks is selling an audience that isn't really there. That's the difference.

You do know radio revenues were up in 2019? And as I write this in early 2020, the Presidential Election is just getting started. Radio's listening is totally stable (though time spent listening has declined slightly, due to people having busier lives these days).

We must have had a really good year here last year. How do I know this? My annual bonus was paid at a rate of 160 percent!

We've been dealing with this pandemic, and guess what? People are actually buying radios again! We've seen it. WalMart, right now, can't keep radios on their shelves. Amazon is selling them like hotcakes. People want radios again!

What medium's audience is declining…rapidly? Television. Stations are being eaten alive by rights fees for carrying network programming and the number of eyeballs to local stations are declining. Cable TV? About the same thing. Why be watching channel 2003 on your cable for $150 or more a month, when you can stream a movie on You Tube anywhere from free to $10 bucks a showing?

Like your cable news shows, but don't want cable? An hour after they're over, they're posted on the network's You Tube Channel with ads, of course, but they're there and they're free. I understand, though, You Tube is not finding it easy to get people to subscribe to their paid service. Why? People can't pay for EVERY service out there.

By comparison, only 9 percent of Americans listen to XM/Sirius. And only 4 percent listen to "Internet Radio"…that's the "pure plays" such as Spotify and Pandora as well as so-called "internet only radio stations".

I believe in the potential for internet radio. But, I contend it will never reach critical mass until those doing it learn a lesson or two from commercial radio about how we obtain and maintain audience loyalty and listening. Go on an "internet radio station" Facebook page. About every other day, you'll see a post from someone in the U.S. saying, "I want to start an internet oldies station. How do I do that"? Here's how I would answer the question:

"You do know, don't you that the success of any radio station depends on that station having a "unique selling proposition" to the audience and to advertisers? Now, there are about 20,000 internet only "oldies" stations. What will make yours so unique that people will seek out your station to listen to over the others? A giant playlist (unlike those dirty 300 song lists played by those "corporate bastards" on AM/FM radio)? Most of those 20,000 stations are already doing that.Live talent? (Nope...a few are, but most are jukeboxes set up as "tribute" stations to KHJ, CKLW, WLS, name your favorite legacy Top 40 station). There's even one about my "80's Station". Just visit Star1079-dot-com. I don't run it. Friends and former employees do.

There are already over 15,000 AM and FM stations...not all of them are financially successful. 20,000 internet oldies stations cannot be successful, either. And few have a unique proposition that would drive listeners to them.

So the first rule of marketing is being broken by internet radio. Will they learn? Some may eventually, but I'm willing to bet most won't. And they are also hampered by the high cost of music licensing. I agree that, because of the low listening levels of most of those stations, they should get a break on licensing costs. But, many of those operators want to know how to do it without paying licensing costs. Sorry, ain't happening.

Most people don't listen to streaming radio in cars, though a few do. I do on occasion. But, when I'm driving to work, I don't want to take the time to set up streaming. I just punch in a station and listen to it.

Oh, that'll change, they say. When you can replace every old car on the road with a new one, perhaps. That is YEARS down the road.

But, the biggest threat to radio today are the damn commercial loads. We're talking about it. A few stations are trying to do something about it. But not nearly enough. Too many overly cautious managers are afraid to upset the advertisers and agencies by cutting the load and demanding more money per spot.

With a 92 percent reach, this shouldn't be a problem. But, it is…unless you have a good manager who wants to deal with the issue.

There is no reason radio cannot go back to 8 units an hour. Two sets…4 units a set. That differs from 2 sets of up to 10 units each today, depending on the company and station. John Sebastian's station in Phoenix only does 3 minute long commercial sets.

Radio, stop talking and start acting. And do a better job of training your salespeople. Just recently, I did an appearance for a business whose out of town owner wanted to do the spot with me? OK, that's not a problem. We can do that on the phone. The PROBLEM was…the copy he sent. He wanted me to say "I'm sitting on a beautiful couch with (Name), the President and CEO of (business) and this is a beauty of a sofa…"

What's wrong with that? He is OBVIOUSLY on the phone with me and is NOT sitting on the couch next to me. He is breaking the premise of his commercial and smart listeners can figure that out.

If you're an advertiser who doesn't care about that, you NEED to.

It's something easily fixable. Ever make a call on Skype? Full quality sound. That would have fixed the promise and made the spot sound as though the CEO WAS sitting next to me. But, some advertisers just don't care and that's sad.

Yeah…we pulled it off. But, I had listeners come in that day who asked for Mr. CEO and I had to tell them he wasn't there…and they knew it. They could tell it was a phone call. They did look around the store…but I'm not sure whether or not they bought anything.

But, the salesperson was not the slightest bit concerned about a broken premise when it means commission in the pocket. It's this lack of caring and lack of respect for the listener which is a BIG problem in broadcasting these days. OK, so you can sell a lot of commercials. Good for us...but listeners are smart enough to know when you're trying to put one over on them. And that used to be a concern in radio. Not so much today.

Old radio guys. My, I could go on and on and on about them. In fairness to them, since, after all I AM an "old radio guy", I understand their feelings. But, as a programmer, if there is anything I learned from my experiences programming WKIO-FM in Champaign, its that radio is a business driven by advertisers and audience demographics.

The original "oldies" format is now pretty much relegated to small town AM stations, though iHeart has its "BIG" stations, a pretty tight list of the big 60's and 70's hits on in quite a few cities. The company I work has a similar list on KONO-AM in San Antonio. It's their sister FM, KONO-FM which is the "Classic Hits" station, which plays music pretty much as my old "Star 107.9" did.

The complaint today, though is about "Classic Rock" stations. And it's the same complaint..."Van Halen" had a lot of hits, but on my Classic Rock station, they only had one..."Jump" (from 1984). And where's my Jimi Hendrix...and Zeppelin?"

Sadly, the answer is: You don't play "All Along The Watchtower" and necessarily get 25 to 54 year old listeners with it anymore. Some of the early Van Halen songs are now considered "Classic Hits". Rock songs tend to "mellow" with listeners as they get older. You can now play a song at 10 AM... that stations in the 70's only played at night (because back then, they were considered "too hard rock" to be played in the daytime).

I read people gasping in horror at the thought that Hip Hop and Rap will eventually make its way into radio "Classic Hits" lists. It will...eventually. It's already started.

Today's Pop music will be the Classic Hits in about 25 years. So, around 2045 or so, expect to hear 24KGoldn, BTS, Ava Max, Justin Bieber and Kanye West coming to a gold based station near you. And whatever is on a Pop Chart then will be complained about by those above 55, "Whatever happened to the good music? You know, songs by Bruno Mars?"

I am also concerned about schools and colleges who have taken the attitude that broadcasting is "not a career field young people should think about because of the expected loss of jobs in that field". Hey, professors…a lot of older radio people are nearing or reaching retirement age. You don't think they'll have to be replaced?

"But, but"…"there's no "farm team" in radio, anymore. Where will the new people get their start?"Answer: the same places they used to get them from. Small market radio stations. While some are, of course, satellite operations, others are pretty vibrant local stations with live and voice tracked local staff, a news reporter or two, play by play sports people and more.

Don't live in a small town? Start as a part time board op and keep working your way up to an on air position. It IS possible, and some of the students from my broadcasting classes have already done it. We are starting an internship program in our shop with the Broadcasting College to help us develop a farm team.

"But the pay is crap." Always was and always will be. Get used to it. Once you're full time, expect to need a side gig or a part time job. Or, both.

Is automation helping to lose jobs? Yes. Of course it is. And it will continue to do so. But that's not just true in broadcasting. Go into any factory in America and look at the robots that are there. Every one of those robots used to be a live person. And there were more people than the robots. Why? Before robots they needed more people to get the job done. Problem is, the robots can do the job faster and more efficiently.

What people will be needed? The people to run these robotic machines, who are also trained to fix them when they break.

Say, professor...how will that "Bachelor's Degree" in Liberal Arts get someone a $100,000 a year job in a real profession? And why should someone pay your school six figures and have them spend 5 years or more of their lives getting that degree only to find there are no jobs in their profession...and even if you can find one, you're not going to make as much as you think you should make. That's what you're doing to the typical college graduate today. And that's why student debt is out of control. These former students don't need "debt forgiveness". They need JOBS.

You can go to a media college...and get an Associate's Degree in 15 months to 2 years and be working in that period of time. At a cost far less than a 4 year school.

Whether you work in a radio or television station or a factory, make sure you are computer literate. Even if you've been off the air for a number of years. If you can't run a computer, there's no way you'll find work. It's been 15 or 20 years since I've seen a cart machine, a reel to reel tape machine or a turntable in a radio station. A few stations that do "mix shows" do have turntables, or can bring them in and hook them up, but they are no longer "standard equipment" in a broadcast booth.

Whatever you decide to do with your life, love doing it. If you love your job or your profession, it's a heck of a lot easier to get out of bed in the morning. Especially on those mornings when you have to get up at 3:30 AM to go do it...and work till 3 in the afternoon.

You know one of the reasons I like working in radio? People recognize you. Now, I know this is anathema to those who think nobody is listening to radio anymore, but I get recognized in grocery stores, in the barbershop, the liquor store, restaurants, on remote broadcasts, and yes...not long ago, I was recognized by the nurses prepping me for a colonoscopy.

Okay, make all the jokes you'd like about me "talking out of my butt", but it's true. One nurse recognized my voice and then told all her nurse friends about who was in prep bed #4. They were all smiling and pointing at me! I waved back.

Well, it sure passed the time before I was taken into the procedure room and put to sleep. (By the way, you're no longer put into "twilight sleep" during these types of things.) You know what they use? Propofol...the stuff that killed Michael Jackson! And let me tell you, now that I've had it done twice, I know why he liked it so much. You're out in 3 seconds flat. And you don't wake up until you're back in the recovery area.

Ah! The joys of working in this business!

It disgusts me when I read a veteran broadcaster say, "I'd never let my son or daughter do this work". Why? It ain't your life. If your kid really wants to be in this business, they'll work for it...and will pay their dues and find their way into a career. Sure, it's not easy to do today. Was it really that easy for you? It sure wasn't for me. Go back and re-read this book. I was 25 years in the business before I cracked $25,000 a year. That's the reality of the business.

"But, there's no money in the major markets anymore." I'm on the fence on that one. If you make it to New York City, dammit, you SHOULD be making enough money to live there. If that takes $100,000 a year, so be it. Maybe the morning person doesn't need a limo...maybe they do. Want to make more money? Get better sales people and get your damn rates up. Stop dropping dimes to pick up pennies!

Don Imus comes to my mind. Now, the controversies of his final years not withstanding, Don was very successful. Yes, he was very brash, some would say a pain in the ass. (I know...one of my high school buddies was his producer for a few years in New

York so I know first hand what working with him was like.) But, he was loyal to his staff, ran a charity and taught more than a few people survival skills needed for a business like broadcasting.

Does that make what he said about that women's basketball team right? Absolutely not. And he paid a stiff price for what he said. But, that doesn't completely de-value his career, either.

There are so many radio "Halls Of Fame" now, including a national one. It saddens me to think that Bill Drake and The Real Don Steele are not in it. And why? There's just no sense in it.

Again...the radio business is NOT DYING. What it IS doing is "evolving". 50 years from now, there will still be a business called "broadcasting" and the audio side of it will be called "radio". We're already seeing evidence of that today. We call it "podcasting". The listeners call it, "radio". Whether it is AM and FM, or streaming only remains to be seen. We may all be "streaming stations" someday. Why? Do you know what it costs to keep and maintain a transmitter site these days, assuming you actually own the land the tower is on? Many stations no longer own their towers.

What to do about AM? Well, you better do something, because it will be gone in about 10 to 15 years if you don't. This new digital proposal (MA3) is interesting, but the jury is still out on it. And today, a lot of once BIG AM operations are literally at death's door. WSB-AM 750 in Atlanta, for example. Fewer than 10 percent of the station's audience listens to the AM today. That's why it is only identified on air at the top hour legal identification. Why extend the length of an identifier 15 times an hour just to salve the feelings of 7 or 8 percent of the audience?

So, there you have it, warts and all. Would I have done it any differently if I could have? Maybe. Perhaps I could have been an actor. Maybe I could have gone to a major market and been on the air. But, I don't believe in second guessing what I've done. I have done something few in my profession have been able to do. Make a career in your hometown. And a few years away, I will be able to finally sit down and maybe realize just what I accomplished.

I'll still be in broadcasting even after I retire. But, when I do, I'll have more time to engage in activities that'll keep me alive and breathing.

I can't wait. My exploits at the gym have made me stronger and more confident. And I am no longer afraid if someone comes at me on the street. But, I am a lover and not a fighter. I just won't take crap anymore. My former wrestling coach from high school is finally impressed with me. Okay…I only started 50 years late. Call me a late bloomer.

But, the exercise keeps me healthy…and perhaps I can make it another 25 or 30 years. I sure hope so. Like the late George Burns once said, "I can't die now. I'm booked!"

Chapter 24

The Career Of A Lifetime

This is the hardest part of writing this book. I'm sure I am going to forget to thank someone…(and if I do…you're all in my thoughts), but here goes:

First…my thanks to Mom and Dad. Grandma wanted one of her grand kids to be in "show business"…guess it fell upon me to pick up that mantle. Thank you for not discouraging me and allowing me to pursue my dream. And Grandma…can you even believe where I ended up? At YOUR favorite radio station! I've even been on the air filling in on the "Lou Emm" time of the day. First day that happened, I thought of you right before I turned the microphone on for the first time.

A special note to my Father: Dad, you weren't wrong to bring your concerns to me about my career in our final phone call. Every point you were making was valid and was not lost on me. The only point you were not right about is the assertion that it would never get better. Because it did. It took me a while, and I went through all kinds of hassles to get there, including serious debt, bankruptcy and recovery from it, I got through it all. Today, let me assure you I HAVE health insurance, I HAVE retirement money saved and I'm still saving it, I HAVE life, accident, A.D. & D and disability coverage.I own a house and a two year old car. It's not a big house, but it's comfortable for my nephew and I. Over a third of the mortgage is now paid. My car will be paid off in the next couple of years, and my credit score is outstanding. By the time I retire, I should be able to make it ok. I may downsize my living arrangements, but that's not a major issue. I never married. But, I HAVE raised 4 teenagers…all boys. So, I know what a handful I must have been to you and Mom. I only wish I had known how ill you were. I would have been there for you as you were there for Mom. I miss you both dearly. And Mom…thanks for telling the old man he needed to get out of the house and go on the gig with me to "see what I was all about" while you were in the hospital recovering from surgery. The concert in Indiana was a blast. You would have loved it and we played well that night. (Oh, yeah...Dad got a "contact high" from the pot smoking crowd...and decided it wasn't so bad. Today, he'd probably be on it medicinally which is now legal here in Ohio. It might just have settled him down a bit.) I have very good, close friends now who are constantly looking after me. And, even though my nephew will eventually move out to start a family of his own, he has promised I will never be out of his life. He'll look after me in my old age...as will my "brothers" from my extended family.

Thank you, Miamisburg High School and all of my teachers. And for the same reason. Thank you, to my Journalism teacher and Drama coach, Dick Arrowood. Without you, I would never have achieved all of this. You brought a shy kid out of his shell and, in the process, created a monster...and let me find my dream. I couldn't thank you, Marv Dalton, Bob Pinkus, Cindy Vogt, Sally Wargo, Tom Robinson, John Waddell, and everyone there enough. And to "Mrs. Chief", Lela – thanks for keeping your old man well grounded. He helped to create a monster. Who knows what might have happened had I gone to L.A. to be an actor...

Thank you, International College of Broadcasting in Dayton. From you, I got legitimacy in the business. And now, I get to work for you and give back to young people who want what I've achieved. And that...is the greatest feeling in the world. I am so glad that CMG/Dayton is working with you to create for us a "farm team" of young broadcasters...and don't think for a moment we're not going to need them.

Thanks to my first Program Director, Ed Hater and my first boss, Ed Shaper. Thank you for believing in a young teen with a squeaky voice who dreamed of being an air personality. To Ed Shaper: You didn't do badly with WDHK. And it was a damn shame what Gannett did to you and your business. That they weren't smart enough to see FM coming on as it did and that they apparently aren't smart enough to see the current demise of the publishing business and its need to move to digital platforms explains why they are now losing their shirts. You won in the end, Ed...good for you!And to Dick Jones and his family: thank you for being a taskmaster and teaching me programming discipline. You might have been wrong that 60's pop hits would never make a comeback...but you weren't the only one who ever made that mistake. Some pretty big companies didn't believe in "oldies" or the idea of "classic hits". They were all wrong. My thanks!

Thank you to my late friend and one of the best damn engineers in the business, Kurt Farmer. You were unconventional, to be sure...but that's not always a bad thing. I learned a lot from you and had a lot of fun in the process. We kicked ass in Cincinnati, Dayton, Xenia...and all the while, I never lost respect for you, even with some of your crazier programming ideas. You left me too soon, damn it. But, maybe we can do even more astounding things someday..."out there".

To nationally known broadcast programming consultant, Jaye Albright. I don't know what you saw in that 13 year old kid that showed up at your remote at the Dayton Mall in late summer of 1970 who talked your ear off about wanting to be a DJ. But, I'm glad you did. I have always respected your knowledge and advice. I was proud then, and still today...to call you my friend. That time you went to the restroom and left ME in control of the remote, well...starting that next song was a bug biting moment for sure.

To my former boss, the late Dave "Rock and Roll" Robbins. Dave - you taught me programming and, armed with the knowledge, got in on the ground floor of helping to "create" the Classic Hits radio format. You did it. I did it. Several other consultants and programmers did it. CBS did it. I don't care who gets the credit, but we proved every generation has its' "oldies"...

and that the "format" (no matter what it's called) will never die with the audience. I miss you, Dave...and will thank you the rest of my life. Now, MY boss is telling me I taught HIM how to program oldies. Imagine that!

To Saga Communications and its' founder, Ed Christian. Ed, you were a great boss and you have one of the best broadcasting companies in the business. I still believe that. It wasn't really your fault that you didn't see the coming classic hits radio format. But, then, no one thought that the oldies format was going to go the way it did, either. Either way, I am proud to have worked for the company. It was so much fun to have entertained you and your managers as a proud member of the PD's band, "Saga Turner Overdrive" at the manager's meeting. And, I really had a blast working for your company.

To my Saga boss, Steve Goldstein. Steve, you really were a great boss and now you're leading the business into the digital revolution with your new company and its emphasis on podcasting. I have podcasts which I listen to...so does my nephew. So does just about everybody these days. I have always been grateful to have known someone who worked for 77/WABC in its musicradio days. I only wish I had been old enough to see that studio and have known people like Dan Ingram and Ron Lundy. What a staff...what a station!

Oh yes, to a new friend...former and current Musicradio 77/WABC DJ "Cousin" Bruce Morrow. Cousin, I listened to you as a child. We both have the "passion" for this business. A little while back, you and I got to talk about this business we're both in that means so much to both of us. You left Sirius/XM and went right back to your radio home. I KNOW New York City listeners appreciate hearing you back on that radio channel. I know I do. Hearing oldies music coming out of WABC brought tears to my eyes...and you were sounding right on top of your game. I sure hope to come to NYC some day and shake your hand. I'll be glad to talk up an intro for you or run your board. By the way, Tell

Tony Orlando who follows you on the air I said "hi". I still have the yellow ribbon that draped one of his CBS cameras here...I gave it to my mother when she was in her final cancer battle and she loved it. It's now a memento to me from my Mom.

To the late 93/KHJ program consultant, Bill Drake. Sir, I never met you, or spoke with you in life. But, you knew how radio stations, then and now, should be run. And you created some of the best stations that ever graced American airwaves. You figured it all out...so completely that it took Ron Jacobs ten pages of typewritten copy to explain the basics of it to me. By the way, to RJ: I was never more proud to make your acquaintance even if was just by e-mail and Facebook. I have to assume you're Program Director of some radio station upstairs today. When I get there, my air check will be on your desk, and I will pray to be able to be part of a staff that, no doubt today includes Robert W. Morgan and the "Real" Don Steele. A weekend shift will be fine... and I do a great overnight shift. You may not have played him on the air, but you were, in so many ways, "The Big Kahuna"! Aloha!

To Steve Kirk: A lot of people just don't know the "real" Steve Kirk. But, I sensed your goodness from the first day we met...I was 10 and visited the WING studios at 128 West First Street. You saw me sitting in the lobby and came out with a box in your hand, looked at me and said, "Here, kid...have a doughnut!" Joining the WING staff in 1987 was the biggest thrill of my life... and still is. Before I go, I hope to right the wrongs of its current owners. WING deserves better. And your kindness in helping me move down the hall to Z-93 allowed me to go to Columbus, where, finally, my career took off. And YOU made it happen. I am glad we are colleagues...and I will be eternally grateful we crossed paths and became friends. You are STILL a blast to be around.

To a man I've never met, but hope to someday...the comic genius of all in this business, Gary Burbank. Gary, you've made me laugh, cry, and almost wet myself listening to your comedy bits. Our common friend, Bob Moody once showed me the picture of his wedding with you as best man. I remarked, "That had to be a funny wedding". His reply, "Well, with Gary as your best man, you sure don't have time to be worried about the ceremony!" I heard you do a bit one time on WLW, talking about "Charterites In Space". The one character said, "Gosh, look at all these levers and buttons and switches. You know, with just a little work, I'll bet we could even pick up WCIN on this thing!" You have no idea how true that statement was…I know, you "must be off"! Thanks!

To the man who gave me my country radio name…"Rowdy J"…the late broadcast consultant, Rusty Walker. You said that the name would "test well" in perceptual studies. You weren't kidding. Every time I've used the name, it generally tests right beneath the morning show. I so enjoyed playing rock and roll trivia with you. All of us died a little inside when we heard of your passing. God bless, my friend. See you on the other side someday.

To a guy I met on radio on my 10th birthday, "Big" Jim Quinn: You taught me how to cue a record…and I was hooked. I wanted to have fun like you sounded like you were having. And look what happened – you turned me into a disc-jockey! Thanks. You're my leee-dah for life!

To "Tall Tom Campbell": Thank you for putting up with my endless weekly calls to your car phone when I was about 11 years old. I can't believe you endured the publishing of your home phone, your car phone and your business phone numbers back then. But, then again, that's was a great way to endear yourself with your listeners.

To my late friend and colleague, Gene "By Golly" Barry: You were the first person to put me in a real radio studio and teach me how to use the equipment in it. I wish I still had the tape. And when we got you back on the air at WING in 1989, we felt so blessed to be able to give our listeners one last ride on the "Barry-Go-Round". I wanted to come out on Saturday night to see you at the Radisson Hotel...and you graciously insisted I come up to the DJ booth with you and stand in your spotlight. You didn't have to do that, but that's the kind of guy you were. I was heartbroken on the night I heard of your passing and I think I cried for a couple hours at home. It was the deepest honor of my life to search for the verifiable public service credentials that got you inducted into the Dayton Area Broadcaster's Hall of Fame. It was fun meeting your daughters and they inducted you well. I miss you, Gene...bye, Clyde!

To Nick Roberts, VP of Marketing and former Operations Manager of Cox Media Group/Dayton: The Cox stations were the last group I EVER thought would ever hire me. And now, I still shake my head that you guys have put up with me for 17 plus years and I KNOW it hasn't always been easy. You always said, you knew something important had happened when I came running into your office with smoke coming out of my ears! Glad you had a fire extinguisher for that. Yeah...I miss the old programming office. That's the only bad thing that happened when we moved...we just couldn't de-corporatize the place. And soon, we'll be even bigger. Nonetheless, know how grateful I am that you and I were finally able to seal a deal.Waking up that Sunday morning, opening my eyes and realizing I was home... for good...was the best feeling in the world. And still is. And when that day actually comes for me to take my leave and finally sit down for once...I still can't fathom what it'll feel like. I think you know I'll never be able to totally walk away from this. I'm still having too much fun.

To all of the people at the new Cox Media Group: Thank you for letting me continue to help you make money in Dayton. There's plenty more money to be made, too. I can't wait to help you make it. Radio is alive...despite all of its detractors and it has a place in the future. We can do keep making it happen. Thank you for believing in local radio. Still...and in the years ahead.

To my late best friend, Dean Eggenschwiller: I didn't ever

explain why our friendship ended here, so a quick word about that. Deano, you see went into the hospital for routine back surgery in June of 2003. He came through it fine…even called me after the surgery and told me, he'd come over to Champaign to see me soon. It would never happen. The next morning around 7, the phone rang and it was Dean's dad. Dean had apparently asked for a sleeping pill around 2 am to help him get to sleep from some understandable post-operative discomfort, went to sleep, rolled over…and suffocated. On Wednesday morning, I get a call from Don telling me they were going to have to pull the plug on Dean before nightfall and if I wanted to see my best friend still alive, I needed to get back to Columbus immediately. I told the boss I had to go and was on my way to Ohio a half hour later. The second I got off the elevator, I was spotted by my nephew, Dean. He hugged me, and asked how I was doing. I told him, "That's not relevant, how are YOU?" We went in to see Dean, I spoke with him, though he clearly was in a coma and couldn't answer me. I told Dean, I hadn't forgotten the promise I had made to him as his son's Godfather…and told him I would look after the boy the rest of my life. We buried Dean three days later in the cemetery just south of New Carlisle. So, Dean…I kept my promise. I'm not sure how it came out, but your boy turned out to be a good, hard working young man who will likely someday, find himself making some pretty good money. But, he still tells me I can come live in his basement, and has told me he'll never leave me. I just hope you think I did well helping him grow and that I did my best. I'm very, very proud of your son.

To my staff at Star 107.9: What an experience we had. I still shake my head about it. We got in on the ground floor of inventing a radio format…and that format is still on radio stations in about every market in the country 20 some years later. Nobody believed it would work except a handful of people in the country… and us. I wish I could have kept it from ending the way it did. I would have been happy just watching that format grow. There's no shame in having been ahead of our time. We got the last laugh. We revolutionized the radio business and taught 'em all how gold based formats are run! Kelly Quinn told me recently on Facebook one night when I was being a little wishful about wanting to change the past, "You know darned good and well the product wasn't the problem. The ownership was. You did just fine with the station". I'm proud that she would say that.

To Bill Cusack: You were one of the best General Managers with whom I have ever had the opportunity to work. We killed WBNS with oldies...Star 107.9 now, we know, contributed a solid radio format to the business. You were right about making it a "different kind of oldies radio". I admit I'm not the Marine type, but you and I shared a radio "foxhole" to be sure...and it was an honor doing radio battle commanded by you. Thank you, General. And, Semper Fi!

To Radio: You're my muse...and my mistress. And it's been one hell of a love affair. I do have to leave some thoughts. I got in trouble once for speaking out about advertising agencies. I'll be kind here, but to a point. Stop letting these people lead you around by the nose so badly. They are not perfect, nor are they infallible. That you let them get away with blaming you for their mistakes is ridiculous. They're dropping dimes to pick up pennies for the short shrift they give the Baby Boom generation. And, if they really were being honest, every PD in America would agree to that statement. Oh yeah, do something about the damn commercial loads today. If anything is going to kill this business, that will be its' undoing, and it'll be YOUR fault. 20 unit stop sets are STUPID. You still have the medium with the biggest reach... and it is inexcusable that your salespeople can't get this point over to an agency buyer. GET YOUR ACT TOGETHER, my dear. Love, me.

To anyone who has ever listened, laughed (to me, at me or with me) on the air: You cannot believe how much I have enjoyed informing and entertaining you. Meeting you at remotes or on station tours has always been a thrill. When I am introduced on stage to bring on an act and you cheer me as I walk to the microphone, well, I simply cannot believe how blessed I am that you care enough about me to do that. Doing that now for what will ultimately be around 50 years or more has been an absolute honor. And as long as God gives me breath, I will continue to do so as long as someone will give me a microphone. Thank you and God bless you and your families. The pleasure has been all mine.

And, now...as the old saying says...the hits...just keep on coming! Excuse me. In the words of my buddy Gene...I gotta go now. Got to see a man...about a record. It's been a hell of a ride.

WHAT PEOPLE ARE SAYING...

About "Turn It Up! Confessions Of A Radio Junkie!

I first met Kevin Fodor 50 years ago when, as a high school student, he came out to nightly remote broadcasts I was hosting for WAVI Radio. He has gone from voluntarily helping set up and tear down broadcast equipment back then to over-achieving almost every goal he would have had back then. Kevin has done it all, while leading, mentoring and inspiring many, many others. His wisdom and creative brilliance are all on display in these pages. I know you'll love getting to know my friend, Kevin Fodor thanks to this enlightening and inspiring book. - Jaye Albright, Retired Broadcasting Consultant for Albright, O'Malley and Brenner Broadcasting Consultants.

Kevin is one of the best friends a radio transmitter ever had... and one of the best weapons a radio programmer can have in his arsenal. He not only KNOWS but LOVES the business of radio and always shows up with 100% to give (no matter what the task) to get the job done. I don't believe there's a job inside a radio station that Kevin hasn't tackled in his long radio career – whether or not he actually held a particular job title. That alone should make this an interesting read. He's dedicated to a fault because he is passionate about the business. I'm positive that somewhere there's a marriage certificate that proves he's been married to radio all these years. - Former "in the trenches" co-worker and occasional boss – Rob Ellis, Vice President/Owner AQ Productions.

Rowdy (Kevin Fodor) is part of a rare species of broadcasters. He grew up enchanted by legendary Top 40 stations like CKLW, then went on to build a successful radio career for himself and has survived by being versatile enough to handle diverse formats on multiple stations. Can't wait to read this book! - Bob Moody, former Country Programming Format Leader for Nationwide Communications and former on air talent at CKLW/Detroit-Windsor (known as "The Big 8").

Working "in the radio biz" for 43 plus years, I've had the pleasure to cross paths and work with Kevin many times. The one word that comes to mind is "versatility". He truly is a "jack of all trades" when it comes to radio. Even in his role as a broadcast instructor, Kevin brings a depth of experience and perspective that is priceless.
-Tommy Collins, Radio Department Head, International College of Broadcasting; Dayton, Ohio.

Kevin's long career in Broadcasting created some great stories that anyone who has ever worked in radio can relate to. Kevin has been part of broadcasting dynasties in Ohio and has a unique perspective unlike any other. -Nick Roberts, Radio Vice President and Marketing Director for Cox Media Group, Dayton, Ohio.

Author's Gallery

Enthusiasm Fills 'Voice' of 'Burg

www.ingramcontent.com/pod-product-compliance
Lightning Source LLC
Chambersburg PA
CBHW042111120526
44592CB00042B/2693